Performance Analysis

This revolutionary coursebook brings together classic texts in critical theory and shows how these texts can be used in the analysis of performance.

The editors put their texts to work in examining such key topics as:

- decoding the sign
- the politics of performance
- the politics of gender and sexual identity
- performing ethnicity
- the performing body
- the space of performance
- audience and spectatorship
- the borders of performance.

Each reading is clearly introduced, making often complex critical texts accessible for students at an introductory level and immediately applicable to the field of performance. The ideas explored within these readings are further clarified through innovative, carefully tested exercises and activities.

Colin Counsell is Senior Lecturer in Theatre Studies and Performing Arts at the University of North London and is the author of *Signs of Performance* (Routledge, 1996). **Laurie Wolf** is Assistant Professor for Theatre at The College of William and Mary, Virginia, USA.

LONDON AND NEW YORK

Performance Analysis

An introductory coursebook

- Edited by
Colin Counsell and Laurie Wolf

First published 2001
by Routledge
11 New Fetter Lane, London EC4P 4EE

Simultaneously published in the USA
and Canada
by Routledge
29 West 35th Street, New York,
NY 10001

*Routledge is an imprint of the Taylor &
Francis Group*

Editorial and introductory material,
selection and exercises
© 2001 Colin Counsell and Laurie Wolf

Typeset in Sabon and Futura
by Florence Production Ltd, Stoodleigh,
Devon

Printed and bound in Great Britain
by TJ International Ltd, Padstow,
Cornwall

*British Library Cataloguing in
Publication Data*
A catalogue record for this book is
available from the British Library

*Library of Congress Cataloging in
Publication Data*
Performance analysis: an introductory
coursebook / edited by Colin Counsell and
Laurie Wolf.
    p. cm.
    Includes bibliographical references and
index.
    1. Performing arts—Political aspects.   2.
Performing arts—Semiotics.   3. Gender
identity—Political aspects.   4. Body,
Human—Political aspects.   5. Semiotics.
I. Counsell, Colin, 1956–   II. Wolf, Laurie.
PN 1590.P4 P47 2001
791′.01′4—dc21   00–045789

ISBN 0–415–22406–3 (hbk)
ISBN 0–415–22407–1 (pbk)

Contents

Preface

The aim of this book is to introduce readers to the theorized analysis of performance. To this end, the texts we have selected offer a range of different theoretical perspectives, each addressing a key dimension of the performed event or else illustrating an analytical principle which can be applied to it. While the texts offer a variety of approaches, they can nevertheless be brought into useful dialogue with one another, for they all focus on the meanings which performance generates and the means by which it does so.

In choosing our texts, we sought not to impose formulas or given interpretations but to enable readers themselves to explore drama, dance, mime, etc. Thus our criterion for selection was usability, with each fragment judged for its potential to illuminate the meaning-making processes of the stage. A number of pieces are drawn from outside the field of Performance Studies proper. This is in part because we have, whenever possible, included the original theories which performance analysts most often employ – the works of Saussure and Bakhtin themselves, for example – rather than those later writings which merely use them. But it is also because, in addressing certain key issues, we have turned to those disciplines in which their study is most advanced, using sociological

writing to address the question of cultural frames, work in Film Studies to explore the 'gaze', and so on.

Each of the pieces is preceded by a brief introduction and followed by one or more practical exercises. The introductions will not serve as substitutes for the excerpts themselves, they seek merely to place the piece in its context and/or flag some key terms or issues. The exercises are designed to help you put the theories to use. Even if you decide to design your own practical exercises, those provided here will aid you in doing so, illustrating the logic of each piece's potential application.

The chosen excerpts are organized developmentally on two levels. On the micro-level, each of the book's sections is arranged as a progression, texts drawing upon and expanding the perspectives of the pieces preceding them. Thus Part one, 'Decoding the artefact', begins by introducing the basic Saussurean and Peircean models of the 'sign'; it then expands this 'semiotic' view, examining the ways such signs are deployed in systems of meaning; it goes on to explore their mobilization within the wider structures of culture; finally, it examines how those meanings are framed as 'readable' in the individual object or action. Part two, 'The politics of performance', follows on from this, first giving a theoretical account of the domain of ideology with which such meanings inevitably engage; then describing a form of theatre designed to oppose ideology; finally considering an aesthetic mode which presumes to undermine the very ground on which ideological representation rests.

Building on this, the book is also structured on the macro-level, for Parts one and two not only provide the conceptual tools to analyse cultural objects and practices in general, they also prepare the ground for Parts three to eight, which are more narrowly focused on specific, performance-related issues. Part nine, 'Analysing performance', comprises only one piece, a questionnaire compiled by French semiotician Patrice Pavis which is widely used in performance analysis. Do not wait until the end of your course of reading before trying it but do so throughout, using it to interrogate all the performances you see, bringing into play those theories you have studied so far.

Acknowledgements

For permission to quote from copyright material the editors would like to thank the following: Peter Owen Ltd, London, for extracts from *Course in General Linguistics* (1974) by Ferdinand de Saussure, translated by Wade Baskin; Vintage, Random House, and Hill & Wang for extracts from *Mythologies* (1993 edition) by Roland Barthes, translated by Annette Lavers, Jonathan Cape Ltd, reprinted by permission of Hill & Wang, a division of Farrar, Straus & Giroux, L.L.C.; Penguin Books Ltd for extracts from *Frame Analysis: An Essay on the Organization of Experience* (1974) by Erving Goffman; Penguin Books Ltd and Basic Books, a member of Perseus Books, L.L.C., for permission to reprint the section on 'The Structural Study of Myth' from *Structural Anthropology* (vol. 1) (1963) by Claude Lévi-Strauss, translated by Claire Jacobson and Brooke Grundfest Schoepf, and to Penguin Books Ltd and Georges Borchardt, Inc. for *Discipline and Punish: The Birth of the Prison* by Michel Foucault (1977), trans. Alan Sheridan, publisher Pantheon, originally published in French as *Surveiller et Punir; Naissance de la Prison* (1975), Editions Gallimard for extracts from *Discipline and Punish: The Birth of the Prison* (1977) by Michel Foucault; Methuen UK and Hill & Wang, a division of

Farrar, Straus & Giroux, L.L.C., for extracts from *Brecht on Theatre* (1990 edition), edited and translated by John Willett; Ihab Hasan, Editor, *Innovation/Renovation: New Perspectives on the Humanities*, the University of Wisconsin Press, and Manchester University Press for extracts from Jean-François Lyotard's *The Postmodern Condition* (copyright 1983); I. B. Tauris & Co. for extracts from *The Newly Born Woman* (1996) by Hélène Cixous and Catherine Clément, translated by Betsy Wing (original, French language edition copyright by Union Générale d'Éditions, Paris: English Translation copyright 1986 by University of Minnesota); Cornell University Press for extracts from 'Women on the Market' from *This Sex Which Is Not One* (1985) by Luce Irigaray, translated by Catherine Porter and Carolyn Burke, and *Places of Performance: The Semiotics of Theatre Architecture* (1989) by Marvin Carlson; Routledge for extracts from 'Brechtian Theory/Feminist Theory: Towards a Gestic Feminist Criticism' by Elin Diamond, published in *A Sourcebook of Feminist Theatre and Performance* (1996) edited by Carol Martin, *The Politics and Poetics of Camp* (1994) by Moe Meyer, *Gender Trouble* (1990) by Judith Butler, the section on 'De-scribing Orality: Performance and the Recuperation of Voice' by Helen Gilbert, published in *De-scribing Empire: Post-colonialism and Textuality* (1994), edited by Chris Tiffin and Alan Lawson, 'The Body of Signification' by Elizabeth Grosz, published in *Abjection, Melancholia and Love* (1990), edited by John Fletcher and Andrew Benjamin, and *Carnival and Theatre: Plebeian Culture and the Structure of Authority in Renaissance England* (1985) by Michael Bristol; Abdul R. JanMohamed and the University of Chicago Press for extracts from 'The Economy of Manichean Allegory: The Function of Racial Difference in Colonialist Literature', originally published in *Critical Inquiry* 12 (1985); Oxford University Press for extracts from *Love and Theft: Blackface Minstrelsy and the American Working Class* (1995) by Eric Lott, and *Marxism and Literature* (1977) by Raymond Williams; Performing Arts Journal Publications (PAJ) for extracts from *Language of the Stage: Essays in the Semiology of Theatre* (1982) by Patrice Pavis, and *From Ritual to Theatre: The Human Seriousness of Play* (1982) by Victor Turner; Elizabeth Wilson for extracts from *Adorned in Dreams: Fashion and Modernity* (1985), published by Little, Brown & Co.; Cambridge University Press and the Wenner-Gren Foundation for Anthropological Research Inc. for extracts from Yi-Fu Tuan's 'Space and Context', reprinted in *By Means of Performance: Intercultural Studies of Theatre and Ritual* (1990) edited by Richard Schechner and Willa Appel; Princeton University Press for extracts from 'Interaction Between Text and Reader' by Wolfgang Iser, published in *The Reader in the Text: Essays on Audience and Interpretation* (1980), edited by Susan R. Suleiman and Inge Crosman; Laura Mulvey and *Screen* for extracts from 'Visual Pleasure and Narrative Cinema' (1975); the MIT Press for extracts from *Rabelais and His World* (*c.* 1984) by Mikhail Bakhtin, translated by Hélène Iswolsky; HarperCollins Publishers for extracts from *The Interpretation of Cultures* (1993 edition) by Clifford Geertz; Patrice Pavis, Cambridge University Press and the editors of *New Theatre Quarterly* for Patrice Pavis's questionnaire from the article 'Theatre of Analysis: Some Questions and a Questionnaire' (1985); Johns Hopkins University Press for extracts from *Shakespeare and the Popular Tradition* by Robert Weimann (1978) (permission conveyed through Copyright Clearance Center, Inc.); David Higham Associates for extracts from *Killing Rage: Ending Racism* by bell hooks (1996), publishers Henry Holt.

Every effort has been made to trace all copyright holders. If any copyright holders have been overlooked the publishers will be pleased to make the necessary changes at the first opportunity.

Part one

Decoding the artefact

If there is any common ground to the theories which dominated twentieth-century thought, it is their collective recognition of the distance separating the material world from our perceptions of it. Sigmund Freud (1856–1939) highlighted the role of the unconscious and of psychic experiences in shaping actions and perceptions, while Marxism stressed the capacity of ideology to determine our view of the real. For **Ferdinand de Saussure** (1857–1913) the individual never encountered the real world, only a version of it already mediated by sign systems, whereas Friedrich Nietzsche (1844–1900) saw reality as an unknowable void, all attempts to know it being merely projections. Albert Einstein (1879–1955) demonstrated that views of macro-physical phenomena are determined by our position relative to them, just as Werner Heisenberg (1901–76) showed how, on the scale of micro-physics, the act of perceiving inevitably alters the perceived. Phenomenology and various strands of existentialism focused on consciousness's construction of reality, while the theorists on whose work modern sociological thought was to be founded – Émile Durkheim (1858–1917), Max Weber (1864–1920) and Karl Marx (1818–83) – all stressed the social origins of conceptions of the real. Albeit that they are very different, all these theories and theorists acknowledge that our

1

perceptions of the world and its objects, the meanings we ascribe to them, are *made*, produced in the gaze of the perceiver. This general recognition developed in the second half of the century into a focus on the cultural processes involved in the manufacture of meaning, with structuralism and post-structuralism, semiotics, writings in psychoanalysis and feminism, and theories of ideology and postmodernism, exploring how 'reality' is constructed. Across the range of these later perspectives two key assumptions are shared. The first is that meaning does not exist in some abstract realm of thought but always involves the concrete. It is not simply that physical images, actions or words are necessary to communicate meaning; rather, meaning itself is born in the marriage of material object or action and immaterial concept – in the *sign*. The second is that meaning is always social in origin. The word 'cat' has no innate quality of cat-ness, its significance is conventional, the product of an implicit agreement between members of a given interpretative community.

The excerpts in this section introduce concepts which are fundamental to the reading of cultural artefacts in general, and which may be used alongside most of the writings reproduced in the rest of the volume. The pieces are organized developmentally, each establishing foundations that are built upon in the next. Saussure and Charles S. Peirce (1839–1914) outline their own, very different theories of the sign. Roland Barthes (1915–80) elaborates on the vantage offered by Saussure, showing how individual signs draw upon or are implicated in wider sign systems, the text reaching beyond its own confines in its generation of meaning. Claude Lévi-Strauss (b. 1908) broadens the perspective further, situating elements of narrative within the systematic organization of culture as a whole. Erving Goffman (1922–88) examines the mechanism by which the acts and objects of this culture are isolated as meaningful.

Further reading: Belsey 1980, Culler 1981 and Eagleton 1983 provide good, accessible introductions to the kinds of theoretical positions examined in this part of the reader; Carlson 1990, Fortier 1997 and Whitmore 1994 survey theories particularly useful in the analysis of performance, while Counsell 1996, Pavis 1982 and Reinelt and Roach (eds) 1992 offer working analyses of actual productions or practices; Barthes 1977, Berger 1972, Bignell 1997 and Williamson 1978 are comparable approaches to other disciplines and, as well as being interesting in themselves, provide ideas and insights relevant to performance analysis.

1.1 The sign

Ferdinand de Saussure, from *Course in General Linguistics*, trans. Wade Baskin, London: Fontana, 1974 [originally published 1916], and Charles S. Peirce, first published in *Collected Papers of Charles Sanders Peirce*, eds Charles Hartshorne and Paul Weiss, Cambridge, Mass.: Belknap Press, 1964

[Semiotics or semiology, the terms used by Peirce and Saussure respectively, involves addressing physical objects in terms of their ability to convey meaning: as signs. For Saussure, the sign is more than a means of communication, it comprises the basic fabric of culture. Saussurean signs do not merely express existing meanings, they are the mechanisms by which meaning is created, for in fixing abstract concepts (signifieds) to material objects (signifiers), sign systems provide the structures in which thought occurs, shaping our perceptions and experiences. Born out of the US philosophical tradition of pragmatism, with its focus on the practical function of ideas, Peirce's theory is less concerned with the constructive power of signs than with how they work. In distinguishing between the various forms, his three-part scheme of icon, index and symbol reflects the different kinds of connection that can exist between signs and their referents, the means by which one is able to signify the other. The influence of Saussurean semiology is vast, underpinning the broad movement of structuralism and, as an antagonist, post-structuralism (see **Barthes, Lévi-Strauss, Foucault**), and evident in work in a range of areas from psychoanalysis and feminism to theories of ideology. Peircean semiotics is less pervasive, and is most often encountered today in writing on performance.]

Ferdinand de Saussure, from *Course in General Linguistics*

Sign, signifier, signified

Some people regard language, when reduced to its elements, as a naming-process only – a list of words, each corresponding to the thing that it names.

This conception is open to criticism at several points. It assumes that ready-made ideas exist before words; it does not tell us whether a name is vocal or psychological in nature (*arbor*, for instance, can be considered from either viewpoint); finally, it lets us assume that the linking of a name and a thing is a very simple operation – an assumption that is anything but true. But this rather naive approach can bring us near the truth by showing us that the linguistic unit is a double entity, one formed by the association of two terms.

We have seen in considering the speech-circuit that both terms involved in the linguistic sign are psychological and are united in the brain by an associative bond. This point must be emphasized.

The linguistic sign unites, not a thing and a name, but a concept and a sound-image. The latter is not the material sound, a purely physical thing, but the psychological imprint of the sound, the impression that it makes on our senses. The sound-image is sensory, and if I happen to call it 'material', it is only in that sense, and by way of opposing it to the other term of the association, the concept, which is generally more abstract. [. . .]

The linguistic sign is then a two-sided psychological entity that can be represented in Figure 1. The two elements are intimately united, and each recalls the other. Whether we try to find the meaning of the Latin word *arbor* or the word that Latin uses to designate the concept 'tree', it is clear that only the associations sanctioned by that language appear to us to conform to reality, and we disregard whatever others might be imagined.

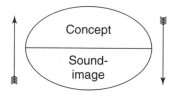

Figure 1

Our definition of the linguistic sign poses an important question of terminology. I call the combination of a concept and a sound-image a *sign*, but in current usage the term generally designates only a sound-image, a word, for example (*arbor*, etc.). One tends to forget that *arbor* is called a sign only because it carries the concept 'tree', with the result that the idea of the sensory part implies the idea of the whole (Figure 2). Ambiguity would disappear if the three notions involved here were designated by three names, each suggesting and opposing the others. I propose to retain the word *sign* (*signe*) to designate the whole and to replace *concept* and *sound-image* respectively by *signified* (*signifié*) and *signifier* (*signifiant*); the last two terms have the advantage of indicating the opposition that separates them from each other and from the whole of which they are parts. [...]

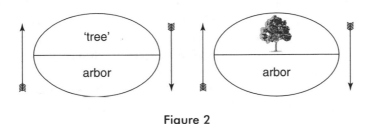

Figure 2

The arbitrary nature of the sign

The bond between the signifier and the signified is arbitrary. Since I mean by sign the whole that results from the associating of the signifier with the signified, I can simply say: *the linguistic sign is arbitrary.*

The idea of 'sister' is not linked by any inner relationship to the succession of sounds *s-ö-r* which serves as its signifier in French; that it could be represented equally by just any other sequence is proved by differences among languages and by the very existence of different languages: the signified 'ox' has as its signifier *b-ö-f* on one side of the border and *o-k-s* (*Ochs*) on the other. [...]

The word *arbitrary* also calls for comment. The term should not imply that the choice of the signifier is left entirely to the speaker (we shall see below that the individual does not have the power to change a sign in any way once it has become established in the linguistic community); I mean that it is unmotivated, i.e. arbitrary in that it actually has no natural connection with the signified. [...]

Language as organized thought coupled with sound

To prove that language is only a system of pure values, it is enough to consider the two elements involved in its functioning: ideas and sounds.

Psychologically our thought – apart from its expression in words – is only a shapeless and indistinct mass. Philosophers and linguists have always agreed in recognizing that without the help of signs we would be unable to make a clear-cut, consistent distinction between two ideas. Without language, thought is a vague, uncharted nebula. There are no pre-existing ideas, and nothing is distinct before the appearance of language.

Against the floating realm of thought, would sounds by themselves yield predelimited entries? No more so than ideas. Phonic substance is neither more fixed nor more rigid than thought; it is not a mold into which thought must of necessity fit but a plastic substance divided in turn into distinct parts to furnish the signifiers needed by thought. The linguistic fact can therefore be pictured in its totality – i.e. language – as a series of contiguous subdivisions marked off on both the indefinite plane of jumbled ideas (A) and the equally vague plane of sounds (B). Figure 3 gives a rough idea of it. The characteristic role of language with respect to thought is not to create a material phonic means for expressing ideas but to serve as a link between thought and sound, under conditions that of necessity bring about the reciprocal delimitations of units. Thought, chaotic by nature, has to become ordered in the process of its decomposition. Neither are thoughts given material form nor are sounds transformed into mental entities; the somewhat mysterious fact is rather that 'thought-sound' implies division, and that language works out its units while taking shape between two shapeless masses. Visualize the air in contact with a sheet of water; if the atmospheric pressure changes, the surface of the water will be broken up into a series of divisions, waves; the waves resemble the union or coupling of thought with phonic substance.

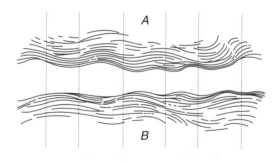

Figure 3

Language might be called the domain of articulations, using the word as it was defined earlier. Each linguistic term is a member, an *articulus* in which an idea is fixed in a sound and a sound becomes the sign of an idea.

Language can also be compared with a sheet of paper: thought is the front and the sound the back; one cannot cut the front without cutting the back at the same time; likewise in language, one can neither divide sound from thought nor thought from sound; the division could be accomplished only abstractedly, and the result would be either pure psychology or pure phonology.

Linguistics then works in the borderland where the elements of sound and thought combine; *their combination produces a form, not a substance.*

These views give a better understanding of what was said before about the arbitrariness of signs. Not only are the two domains that are linked by the linguistic fact shapeless and confused, but the choice of a given slice of sound to name a given idea is completely arbitrary. If this were not true, the notion of value would be compromised, for it would include an externally imposed element. But actually values remain entirely relative, and that is why the bond between the sound and the idea is radically arbitrary.

The arbitrary nature of the sign explains in turn why the social fact alone can create a linguistic system. The community is necessary if values that owe their existence solely to usage and general acceptance are to be set up; by himself the individual is incapable of fixing a single value.

In addition, the idea of value, as defined, shows that to consider a term as simply the union of a certain sound with a certain concept is grossly misleading. To define it in this way would isolate the term from its system; it would mean assuming that one can start from the terms and construct the system by adding them together when, on the contrary, it is from the interdependent whole that one must start and through analysis obtain its elements. [. . .]

Linguistic value from a conceptual viewpoint

When we speak of the value of a word, we generally think first of its property of standing for an idea, and this is in fact one side of linguistic value. But if this is true, how does value differ from *signification*? Might the two words be synonyms? I think not, although it is easy to confuse them, since the confusion results not so much from their similarity as from the subtlety of the distinction that they mark.

From a conceptual viewpoint, value is doubtless one element in signification, and it is difficult to see how signification can be dependent upon value and still be distinct from it. But we must clear up the issue or risk reducing language to a simple naming-process.

Let us first take signification as it is generally understood and as it was pictured in Figure 2. As the arrows in the drawing show, it is only the counterpart of the sound-image. Everything that occurs concerns only the sound-image and the concept when we look upon the word as independent and self-contained (Figure 4). But here is the paradox: on the one hand the concept seems to be the counterpart of the sound-image, and on the other hand the sign itself is in turn the counterpart of the other signs of language.

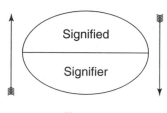

Figure 4

Language is a system of interdependent terms in which the value of each term results solely from the simultaneous presence of the others, as in Figure 5. How, then, can value be confused with signification, i.e. the counterpart of the sound-image? It seems impossible to liken the relations represented here by horizontal arrows to those represented above by vertical arrows. Putting it another way – and again taking up the example of the sheet of paper that is cut in two – it is clear that the observable relation between the different pieces A, B, C, D, etc., is distinct from the relation between the front and back of the same piece as in A/A′, B/B′, etc.

Figure 5

To resolve the issue, let us observe from the outset that even outside language all values are apparently governed by the same paradoxical principle. They are always composed:

1   of a *dissimilar* thing that can be *exchanged* for the thing of which the value is to be determined; and

2   of *similar* things that can be *compared* with the thing of which the
value is to be determined.

Both factors are necessary for the existence of a value. To determine what
a five-franc piece is worth one must therefore know: (1) that it can be
exchanged for a fixed quantity of a different thing, e.g. bread; and (2)
that it can be compared with a similar value of the same system, e.g. a
one-franc piece, or with coins of another system (a dollar, etc.). In the
same way a word can be exchanged for something dissimilar, an idea;
besides, it can be compared with something of the same nature, another
word. Its value is therefore not fixed so long as one simply states that it
can be 'exchanged' for a given concept, i.e. that it has this or that signification: one must also compare it with similar values, with other words
that stand in opposition to it. Its content is really fixed only by the concur-
rence of everything that exists outside it. Being part of a system, it is
endowed not only with a signification but also and especially with a value,
and this is something quite different. [. . .]

The sign considered in its totality

Everything that has been said up to this point boils down to this: in
language there are only differences. Even more important: a difference
generally implies positive terms between which the difference is set up;
but in language there are only differences *without positive terms*. Whether
we take the signified or the signifier, language has neither ideas nor sounds
that existed before the linguistic system, but only conceptual and phonic
differences that have issued from the system. The idea or phonic substance
that a sign contains is of less importance than the other signs that surround
it. Proof of this is that the value of a term may be modified without either
its meaning or its sound being affected, solely because a neighboring term
has been modified.

But the statement that everything in language is negative is true only
if the signified and the signifier are considered separately; when we consider
the sign in its totality, we have something that is positive in its own class.
A linguistic system is a series of differences of sound combined with a
series of differences of ideas; but the pairing of a certain number of
acoustical signs with as many cuts made from the mass of thought engenders a system of values; and this system serves as the effective link between
the phonic and psychological elements within each sign. Although both
the signified and the signifier are purely differential and negative when

9

considered separately, their combination is a positive fact; it is even the sole type of fact that language has, for maintaining the parallelism between the two classes of differences is the distinctive function of the linguistic institution.

Charles S. Peirce, from *Collected Papers*

A sign stands *for* something *to* the idea which it produces or modifies. Or, it is a vehicle conveying into the mind something from without. That for which it stands is called its *object*; that which its conveys, its *meaning*; and the idea to which it gives rise, its *interpretant*. [...][1]

There are three kinds of signs which are all indispensable in all reasoning: the first is the diagrammatic sign or *icon*, which exhibits a similarity or analogy to the subject of discourse; the second is the *index*, which, like a pronoun demonstrative or relative, forces the attention to the particular object intended without describing it; the third [the *symbol*] is the general name or description which signifies its object by means of an association of ideas or habitual connection between the name and the character signified. [...][2]

Turning now to the rhetorical evidence, it is a familiar fact that there are such representations as icons. Every picture (however conventional its method) is essentially a representation of that kind. So is every diagram, even although there be no sensuous resemblance between it and its object, but only an analogy between the relations of the parts of each. [...][3]

Let us examine some examples of indices. I see a man with a rolling gait. This is a probable indication that he is a sailor. I see a bowlegged man in corduroys, gaiters and a jacket. These are probable indications that he is a jockey or something of that sort. A sundial or a clock *indicates* the time of day. [...] A rap on the door is an index. Anything which focuses the attention is an index. Anything which startles us is an index, in so far as it marks the junctions between two portions of experience. Thus a tremendous thunderbolt indicates that *something* considerable happened, though we may not know precisely what the event was. But it may be expected to connect itself with some other experience. [...][4]

All words, sentences, books and other conventional signs are Symbols. We speak of writing or pronouncing the word 'man'; but it is only a *replica*, or embodiment of the word that is pronounced or written. The word itself has no existence although it has real being, *consisting in* the fact that all existents *will* conform to it. It is a general mode of succession of three sounds or representamens of sounds, which becomes a sign only in the fact that a habit, or acquired law, will cause replicas of it to be interpreted as meaning a man or men.[5]

Notes

1   From unidentified fragment, date unknown, in *Collected Papers*, vol. I, p. 171.
2   From 'One, Two, Three: Fundamental Categories of Thought and of Nature', *c.* 1885, in *ibid.*, vol. I, p. 194.
3   From 'That Categorical and Hypothetical Propositions are one in essence, with some connected matters', *c.* 1895, in *ibid.*, vol. II, p. 158.
4   From chapter two of 'The Art of Reasoning', *c.* 1895, in *ibid.*, vol. II, p. 160.
5   From 'Syllabus', *c.* 1902, in *ibid.*, vol. II, p. 165.

EXERCISE: Choose a performance you have seen. First, divide its various components into 'icons', 'indices' and 'symbols'. Try to address all areas of the production, the dynamic as well as the static – objects, words and images, but also movements, lighting changes, etc. Are there elements which signify in different ways, as different kinds of Peircean sign, simultaneously? If the piece seems to function primarily with, say, iconic signs, can you compare it with another in which the index or the symbol dominates? Do certain theatrical forms or genres inherently tend towards one of the three modes of signification?

Now consider the same piece from a Saussurean perspective. This will entail viewing it in a radically different way; as composed of material things, 'signifiers', to which are fixed conceptual 'signifieds'. Choosing five signs, each of a different kind – e.g. a costume, a gesture, a lighting arrangement, etc. – consider what *ideas* (rather than things) they evoke. Are certain qualities attributed to a location by colour or lighting or style of set design? Does a character's mode of movement tell us something *about* him or her? Do different kinds of sign in the production suggest the same general order of meaning, or meanings which are related (complementary, parallel or opposed); that is, do they work together as a sign *system*?

1.2 Myth

Roland Barthes, from *Mythologies*, trans. Annette Lavers, London: Granada, 1972 [originally published 1957]

[Much of Barthes's early work bears the trace of two major influences: Saussurean semiology, which explores how material objects function as meaningful signs, and Marxist cultural criticism (particularly the work of **Bertolt Brecht** (1898–1956) and Walter Benjamin (1892–1940)), which interrogates artefacts for their ideological weighting. The two positions come together in *Mythologies*, a collection of essays on aspects of popular culture which looks beyond the apparent neutrality of everyday products and events – wrestling matches, Hollywood films, soap powders – to uncover their covert meanings. The last essay, excerpted here, provides a theoretical overview in terms of what Barthes calls 'myth'. Whereas pure semiology examines the mechanics of signification, with myth he instead addresses the way existing signs are remobilized as tokens of socially and politically charged networks of meaning, while still managing to retain an appearance of 'naturalness', of 'what-goes-without-saying'. He thus shifts the focus of analysis from the study of signification in the abstract to its use in specific cultural and political formations. In doing so, he also anticipates the principle of 'intertextuality' which would prove central to subsequent post-structuralist writings (including his own; see Barthes 1974), showing how texts draw on existing cultural meanings – ultimately, that is, on *other texts* – in generating meaning.]

What is myth, today? I shall give at the outset a first, very simple answer, which is perfectly consistent with etymology: *myth is a type of speech.*

Myth is a type of speech

Of course, it is not *any* type: language needs special conditions in order to become myth: we shall see them in a minute. But what must be firmly established at the start is that myth is a system of communication, that it is a message. This allows one to perceive that myth cannot possibly be an object, a concept or an idea; it is a mode of signification, a form. Later, we shall have to assign to this form historical limits, conditions of use, and reintroduce society into it: we must nevertheless first describe it as a form.

It can be seen that to purport to discriminate among mythical objects according to their substance would be entirely illusory: since myth is a type of speech, everything can be a myth provided it is conveyed by a discourse. Myth is not defined by the object of its message, but by the way in which it utters this message: there are formal limits to myth, there are no 'substantial' ones. Everything, then, can be a myth? Yes, I believe this, for the universe is infinitely fertile in suggestions. Every object in the world can pass from a closed, silent existence to an oral state, open to appropriation by society, for there is no law, whether natural or not, which forbids talking about things. A tree is a tree. Yes, of course. But a tree as expressed by Minou Drouet is no longer quite a tree, it is a tree which is decorated, adapted to a certain type of consumption, laden with literary self-indulgence, revolt, images, in short with a type of social *usage* which is added to pure matter. [. . .]

Speech of this kind is a message. It is therefore by no means confined to oral speech. It can consist of modes of writing or of representations; not only written discourse, but also photography, cinema, reporting, sport, shows, publicity, all these can serve as a support to mythical speech. Myth can be defined neither by its object nor by its material, for any material can arbitrarily be endowed with meaning: the arrow which is brought in order to signify a challenge is also a kind of speech. True, as far as perception is concerned, writing and pictures, for instance, do not call upon the same type of consciousness; and even, with pictures, one can use many kinds of reading: a diagram lends itself to signification more than a drawing, a copy more than an original, and a caricature more than a portrait. But this is the point: we are no longer dealing here with a theoretical mode of representation: we are dealing with *this* particular image, which is given for *this* particular signification. Mythical speech is made of a material which has *already* been worked on so as to make it suitable for communication: it is because all the materials of myth (whether pictorial or written) presuppose a signifying consciousness, that one can reason about them while discounting their substance. This substance is not unimportant: pictures, to be sure, are more imperative than writing, they impose meaning at one stroke, without analysing or diluting it. But this is no longer a constitutive difference. Pictures become a kind of writing as soon as they are meaningful: like writing, they call for a *lexis*.

We shall therefore take *language*, *discourse*, *speech*, etc., to mean any significant unit or synthesis, whether verbal or visual: a photograph will be a kind of speech for us in the same way as a newspaper article; even objects will become speech, if they mean something. This generic way of conceiving language is in fact justified by the very history of writing: long before the invention of our alphabet, objects like the Inca *quipu*, or drawings, as in pictographs, have been accepted as speech. This does not mean that one must treat mythical speech like language; myth in fact belongs to the province of a general science, coextensive with linguistics, which is *semiology*.

Myth as a semiological system

[. . .] Let me therefore restate that any semiology postulates a relation between two terms, a signifier and a signified. This relation concerns objects which belong to different categories, and this is why it is not one of equality but one of equivalence. We must here be on our guard for, despite common parlance which simply says that the signifier *expresses* the signified, we are dealing, in any semiological system, not with two, but with three different terms. For what we grasp is not at all one term after the other, but the correlation which unites them: there are, therefore, the signifier, the signified and the sign, which is the associative total of the first two terms. Take a bunch of roses: I use it to *signify* my passion. Do we have here, then, only a signifier and a signified, the roses and my passion? Not even that: to put it accurately, there are here only 'passion-ified' roses. But on the plane of analysis, we do have three terms; for these roses weighted with passion perfectly and correctly allow themselves to be decomposed into roses and passion: the former and the latter existed before uniting and forming this third object, which is the sign. It is as true to say that on the plane of experience I cannot dissociate the roses from the message they carry, as to say that on the plane of analysis I cannot confuse the roses as signifier and the roses as sign: the signifier is empty, the sign is full, it is a meaning. Or take a black pebble: I can make it signify in several ways, it is a mere signifier; but if I weigh it with a definite signified (a death sentence, for instance, in an anonymous vote), it will become a sign. [. . .]

Naturally these three terms are purely formal, and different contents can be given to them. Here are a few examples: for Saussure, who worked on a particular but methodologically exemplary semiological system – the language or *langue* – the signified is the concept, the signifier is the acoustic image (which is mental) and the relation between concept and image is the sign (the word, for instance), which is a concrete entity. [. . .]

In myth, we find again the tridimensional pattern which I have just described: the signifier, the signified and the sign. But myth is a peculiar system, in that it is constructed from a semiological chain which existed before it: it *is a second-order semiological system.* That which is a sign (namely the associative total of a concept and an image) in the first system, becomes a mere signifier in the second. We must here recall that the materials of mythical speech (the language itself, photography, painting, posters, rituals, objects, etc.), however different at the start, are reduced to a pure signifying function as soon as they are caught by myth. Myth sees in them only the same raw material; their unity is that they all come down to the status of a mere language. Whether it deals with alphabetical or pictorial writing, myth wants to see in them only a sum of signs, a global sign, the final term of a first semiological chain. And it is precisely this final term which will become the first term of the greater system which it builds and of which it is only a part. Everything happens as if myth shifted the formal system of the first significations sideways. As this lateral shift is essential for the analysis of myth, I shall represent it as in Figure 6, it being understood, of course, that the spatialization of the pattern is here only a metaphor. It can be seen that in myth there are two semiological systems, one of which is staggered in relation to the other: a linguistic system, the language (or the modes of representation which are assimilated to it), which I shall call the *language-object,* because it is the language which myth gets hold of in order to build its own system; and myth itself, which I shall call *metalanguage,* because it is a second language, *in which* one speaks about the first. When he reflects on a metalanguage, the semiologist no longer needs to ask himself questions about the composition of the language-object, he no longer has to take into account the details of the linguistic schema; he will only need to know its total term, or global sign, and only inasmuch as this term lends itself to myth. This is why the semiologist is entitled to treat in the same way writing and pictures: what he retains from them is the fact that they are both *signs,* that they both reach the threshold of myth endowed with the same signifying function, that they constitute, one just as much as the other, a language-object.

Figure 6

It is now time to give one or two examples of mythical speech. [...] I am at the barber's, and a copy of *Paris-Match* is offered to me. On the cover, a young Negro in a French uniform is saluting, with his eyes uplifted, probably fixed on a fold of the tricolour. All this is the *meaning* of the picture. But, whether naively or not, I see very well what it signifies to me: that France is a great Empire, that all her sons, without any colour discrimination, faithfully serve under her flag, and that there is no better answer to the detractors of an alleged colonialism than the zeal shown by this Negro in serving his so-called oppressors. I am therefore again faced with a greater semiological system: there is a signifier, itself already formed with a previous system (*a black soldier is giving the French salute*); there is a signified (it is here a purposeful mixture of Frenchness and militariness); finally, there is a presence of the signified through the signifier.

EXERCISE: Take three contrasting examples of magazine advertisements for a single type of product (perfume ads, for instance). Examine each, analysing all its elements – pictures, words, graphics, colours, the overall organization of components – and consider what Barthesian myth(s) it mobilizes to make the product distinct and desirable. Does it employ an iconography of 'sophistication' or 'naturalness' or 'the exotic'? If the ad includes natural objects, with what mythic meanings have they been endowed?

Now analyse three contrasting stage sets (using pictures), choosing examples that are at least partly abstract, not purely mimetic. Consider their various elements, the shapes, materials and colours, scale and proportion, use of space and light. Do the shapes suggest the organic or the industrial, masculine or feminine, primitive or high-tech? Do the proportions suggest the public or private? Is there a recognizable 'mythology' of meaning to which all or most elements defer? If so, where else in your culture is this found – on what 'texts' does the set design draw? Once you have completed your reading, pick two plays you know and consider what the effect would be of staging them in those sets. Do not ask which set is most appropriate but consider instead how each would shape the play, inflect the meanings an audience would take from its performance.

1.3 Structure

**Claude Lévi-Strauss, from 'The Structural Study of Myth', in
Structural Anthropology (vol.1), trans. Claire Jacobson and
Brooke Grundfest Schoepf, Harmondsworth: Penguin, 1963
[originally published 1958]**

[Lévi-Strauss's 'Structural Anthropology' provided many of the conceptual
principles informing the broad movement of modern structuralism. Starting
from Saussure's premise that languages operate as systems, he argued that
cultures as a whole function in a similar way, the meaning of their individual parts being determined by their systematic relations with all others.
Such relations are of two kinds: *diachronic* relations govern the combination of elements in sequence, over time, as in the historical development of
a language or the word order of a specific utterance (or *parole*); *synchronic*
relations are those which structure the system in its entirety (the *langue*) at
a given instant in time. It is the latter which are central to the following
essay. Synchronic relations typically organize meaning in the form of
dichotomies – of male/female, raw/cooked, etc. – so that, to understand
the symbolic significance a culture grants an object or image, the analyst
must relate it to those dichotomies which structure that culture. In interpreting
the Oedipus myth, Lévi-Strauss consequently focuses less on the (diachronic)
sequence of events than on their repetition, the (synchronic) pattern of
connections and oppositions they establish *outside* sequential, narrative time.
By viewing the tale according to the logic of the orchestral score, his method
highlights those relations which organize that culture's meanings *per se*,
underwriting those of its individual artefacts.]

Mythology confronts the student with a situation which at first sight
appears contradictory. On the one hand it would seem that in the course
of a myth anything is likely to happen. There is no logic, no continuity.
Any characteristic can be attributed to any subject; every conceivable relation can be found. With myth, everything becomes possible. But on the
other hand, this apparent arbitrariness is belied by the astounding similarity between myths collected in widely different regions. Therefore the
problem: If the content of a myth is contingent, how are we going to
explain the fact that myths throughout the world are so similar?

It is precisely this awareness of a basic antinomy pertaining to the
nature of myth that may lead us toward its solution. For the contradiction which we face is very similar to that which in earlier times brought

considerable worry to the first philosophers concerned with linguistic problems. [. . .] On the one hand, they did notice that in a given language certain sequences of sounds were associated with definite meanings, and they earnestly aimed at discovering a reason for the linkage between those *sounds* and that *meaning*. Their attempt, however, was thwarted from the very beginning by the fact that the same sounds were equally present in other languages although the meaning they conveyed was entirely different. The contradiction was surmounted only by the discovery that it is the combination of sounds, not the sounds themselves, which provides the significant data.

It is easy to see, moreover, that some of the more recent interpretations of mythological thought originated from the same kind of misconception under which those early linguists were laboring. Let us consider, for instance, Jung's idea that a given mythological pattern – the so-called archetype – possesses a certain meaning. This is comparable to the long-supported error that a sound may possess a certain affinity with a meaning: for instance, the 'liquid' semi-vowels with water, the open vowels with things that are big, large, loud, or heavy, etc., a theory which still has its supporters. Whatever emendations the original formulation may now call for, everybody will agree that the Saussurean principle of the *arbitrary character of linguistic signs* was a prerequisite for the accession of linguistics to the scientific level.

To invite the mythologist to compare his precarious situation with that of the linguist in the prescientific stage is not enough. As a matter of fact we may thus be led only from one difficulty to another. There is a very good reason why myth cannot simply be treated as language if its specific problems are to be solved; myth *is* language: to be known, myth has to be told; it is a part of human speech. In order to preserve its specificity we must be able to show that it is both the same thing as language, and also something different from it. Here, too, the past experience of linguists may help us. For language itself can be analysed into things which are at the same time similar and yet different. This is precisely what is expressed in Saussure's distinction between *langue* and *parole*, one being the structural side of language, the other the statistical aspect of it, *langue* belonging to a reversible time, *parole* being non-reversible. If those two levels already exist in language, then a third one can conceivably be isolated.

We have distinguished *langue* and *parole* by the different time referents which they use. Keeping this in mind, we may notice that myth uses a third referent which combines the properties of the first two. On the one hand, a myth always refers to events alleged to have taken place long ago. But what gives the myth an operational value is that the specific pattern described is timeless; it explains the present and the past as well as the future. This can be made clear through a comparison between myth and what appears to have largely replaced it in modern societies, namely, politics. When the historian refers to the French Revolution, it is always as a sequence of past happenings, a non-reversible series of events the remote consequences of which may still be felt at present. But to the French politician, as well as to his followers, the French Revolution is both a sequence belonging to the past – as to the historian – and a time-less pattern which can be detected in the contemporary French social structure and which provides a clue for its interpretation, a lead from which to infer future developments. [...] It is that double structure, altogether historical and ahistorical, which explains how myth, while pertaining to the realm of *parole* and calling for an explanation as such, as well as to that of *langue* in which it is expressed, can also be an absolute entity on a third level which, though it remains linguistic by nature, is nevertheless distinct from the other two. [...]

To sum up the discussion at this point, we have so far made the following claims: (1) If there is a meaning to be found in mythology, it cannot reside in the isolated elements which enter into the composition of a myth, but only in the way those elements are combined. (2) Although myth belongs to the same category as language, being, as a matter of fact, only part of it, language in myth exhibits specific properties. (3) Those properties are only to be found *above* the ordinary linguistic level, that is, they exhibit more complex features than those which are to be found in any other kind of linguistic expression.

If the above three points are granted, at least as a working hypothesis, two consequences will follow: (1) Myth, like the rest of language, is made up of constituent units. (2) These constituent units presuppose the constituent units present in language when analysed on other levels – namely, phonemes, morphemes and sememes – but they, nevertheless, differ from the latter in the same way as the latter differ among themselves; they belong to a higher and more complex order. For this reason, we shall call them *gross constituent units*. [...]

The technique which has been applied so far by this writer consists in analysing each myth individually, breaking down its story into the shortest possible sentences, and writing each sentence on an index card bearing a number corresponding to the unfolding of the story.

Practically each card will thus show that a certain function is, at a given time, linked to a given subject. Or, to put it otherwise, each gross constituent unit will consist of a *relation*.

However, the above definition remains highly unsatisfactory for two different reasons. First, it is well known to structural linguists that constituent units on all levels are made up of relations, and the true difference between our *gross* units and the others remains unexplained; second, we still find ourselves in the realm of a non-reversible time, since the numbers of the cards correspond to the unfolding of the narrative. Thus the specific character of mythological time, which as we have seen is both reversible and non-reversible, synchronic and diachronic, remains unaccounted for. From this springs a new hypothesis, which constitutes the very core of our argument. The true constituent units of a myth are not the isolated relations but *bundles of such relations*, and it is only as bundles that these relations can be put to use and combined so as to produce a meaning. Relations pertaining to the same bundle may appear diachronically at remote intervals, but when we have succeeded in grouping them together we have reorganized our myth according to a time referent of a new nature, corresponding to the prerequisite of the initial hypothesis, namely a two-dimensional time referent which is simultaneously diachronic and synchronic, and which accordingly integrates the characteristics of *langue* on the one hand, and those of *parole* on the other. To put it in even more linguistic terms, it is as though a phoneme were always made up of all its variants.

Two comparisons may help to explain what we have in mind.

Let us first suppose that archaeologists of the future coming from another planet would one day, when all human life had disappeared from the Earth, excavate one of our libraries. Even if they were at first ignorant of our writing, they might succeed in deciphering it – an undertaking which would require, at some early stage, the discovery that the alphabet, as we are in the habit of printing it, should be read from left to right and from top to bottom. However, they would soon discover that a whole category of books did not fit the usual pattern – these would be the orchestra scores on the shelves of the music division. But after trying, without success, to decipher staffs one after the other, from the upper down to the lower, they would probably notice that the same patterns of notes recurred at intervals, either in full or in part, or that some patterns were strongly reminiscent of earlier ones. Hence the hypothesis: What if patterns showing affinity, instead of being considered in succession, were to be treated as one complex pattern and read as a whole? By getting at what we call *harmony*, they would then see that an orchestra score, to be meaningful, must be read diachronically along one axis – that is, page after page, and from left to right – and synchronically along the other axis, all the notes written vertically making up one gross constituent unit, that is, one bundle of relations. [...]

Now for a concrete example of the method we propose. We shall use the Oedipus myth, which is well known to everyone. I am well aware that the Oedipus myth has only reached us under late forms and through literary transmutations concerned more with esthetic and moral preoccupations than with religious or ritual ones, whatever these may have been. But we shall not interpret the Oedipus myth in literal terms, much less offer an explanation acceptable to the specialist. We simply wish to illustrate – and without reaching any conclusions with respect to it – a certain technique, whose use is probably not legitimate in this particular instance, owing to the problematic elements indicated above. The 'demonstration' should therefore be conceived not in terms of what the scientist means by this term, but at best in terms of what is meant by the street peddler, whose aim is not to achieve a concrete result, but to explain, as succinctly as possible, the functioning of the mechanical toy which he is trying to sell to the onlookers.

The myth will be treated as an orchestra score would be if it were unwittingly considered as a unilinear series; our task is to re-establish the correct arrangement. Say, for instance, we were confronted with a sequence of the type: 1, 2, 4, 7, 8, 2, 3, 4, 6, 8, 1, 4, 5, 7, 8, 1, 2, 5, 7, 3, 4, 5, 6, 8 . . . the assignment being to put all the 1's together, all the 2's, the 3's, etc.; the result is a chart:

1	2		4			7	8
	2	3	4		6		8
1			4	5		7	8
1	2			5		7	
		3	4	5	6		8

We shall attempt to perform the same kind of operation on the Oedipus myth, trying out several arrangements of the mythemes until we find one which is in harmony with the principles enumerated above. Let us suppose, for the sake of argument, that the best arrangement is the following (although it might certainly be improved with the help of a specialist in Greek mythology):

Cadmos seeks his sister Europa, ravished by Zeus			
		Cadmos kills the dragon	
	The Spartoi kill one another		
			Labdacos (Laios' father) = *lame* (?)
	Oedipus kills his father, Laios		Laios (Oedipus' father) = left-sided (?)
		Oedipus kills the Sphinx	
			Oedipus = *swollen foot* (?)
Oedipus marries his mother, Jocasta			
	Eteocles kills his brother, Polynices		
Antigone buries her brother, Polynices, despite prohibition			

We thus find ourselves confronted with four vertical columns, each of which includes several relations belonging to the same bundle. Were we to *tell* the myth, we would disregard the columns and read the rows from left to right and from top to bottom. But if we want to *understand* the myth, then we will have to disregard one half of the diachronic dimension (top to bottom) and read from left to right, column after column, each one being considered as a unit.

All the relations belonging to the same column exhibit one common feature which it is our task to discover. For instance, all the events grouped in the first column on the left have something to do with blood relations which are overemphasized, that is, are more intimate than they should be. Let us say, then, that the first column has as its common feature the *over-rating of blood relations*. It is obvious that the second column expresses the same thing, but inverted: *underrating of blood relations*. The third column refers to monsters being slain. As to the fourth, a few words of clarification are needed. The remarkable connotation of the surnames in Oedipus' father-line has often been noticed. However, linguists usually disregard it, since to them the only way to define the meaning of a term is to investigate all the contexts in which it appears, and personal names, precisely because they are used as such, are not accompanied by any context. With the method we propose to follow the objection disappears, since the myth itself provides its own context. The significance is no longer to be sought in the eventual meaning of each name, but in the fact that all the names have a common feature: All the hypothetical meanings (which may well remain hypothetical) refer to *difficulties in walking straight and standing upright*.

What then is the relationship between the two columns on the right? Column three refers to monsters. The dragon is a chthonian being which has to be killed in order that mankind be born from the Earth; the Sphinx is a monster unwilling to permit men to live. The last unit reproduces the first one, which has to do with the *autochthonous origin* of mankind. Since the monsters are overcome by men, we may thus say that the common feature of the third column is *denial of the autochthonous origin of man*.

This immediately helps us to understand the meaning of the fourth column. In mythology it is a universal characteristic of men born from the Earth that at the moment they emerge from the depth they either cannot walk or they walk clumsily. [. . .] Thus the common feature of the fourth column is *the persistence of the autochthonous origin of man*. It follows that column four is to column three as column one is to column two. The inability to connect two kinds of relationships is overcome (or rather replaced) by the assertion that contradictory relationships are identical inasmuch as they are both self-contradictory in a similar way. Although this is still a provisional formulation of the structure of mythical thought, it is sufficient at this stage.

Turning back to the Oedipus myth, we may now see what it means. The myth has to do with the inability, for a culture which holds the belief that mankind is autochthonous [. . .], to find a satisfactory transition between this theory and the knowledge that human beings are actually born from the union of man and woman. Although the problem obviously cannot be solved, the Oedipus myth provides a kind of logical tool which relates the original problem – born from one or born from two? – to the derivative problem: born from different or born from same? By a correlation of this type, the overrating of blood relations is to the underrating of blood relations as the attempt to escape autochthony is to the impossibility to succeed in it. Although experience contradicts theory, social life validates cosmology by its similarity of structure. Hence cosmology is true.

EXERCISE: Choose a fairy tale or folktale with which everyone is familiar and have one member of your group tell it in as complete a form as they can; this is your text. First, compare and contrast the elements of the story to find those which have some shared quality. Collate them to form a small number of general categories and give each a descriptive title. Take your time deciding on the titles; each must be wide enough to incorporate all the elements in the category but precise enough to pinpoint what it is they share. Now consider what ideas these 'bundles of relations' evoke for you as members of your culture. Everyone in your group should be consulted, as the group is a more complete and objective repository of cultural meanings than the individual. When you have discussed each category separately, consider them as a collection. Do they gather about an issue or theme, perhaps forming oppositional pairs? What symbolic relations are thereby revealed as underpinning the tale? Bear in mind that this process will only illuminate the symbolic significance of the story for *your* culture.

Now select a play you have studied and undertake the same analytical process. Do not pre-empt any of the stages: compare the elements, assemble categories, name them, consider them first singly, then in relation to each other. If you have chosen a performance of a play, you may include the elements of the production, the stage imagery, and so on, in your analysis; the performance too is a 'text', employing available cultural components.

1.4 The frame

Erving Goffman, from *Frame Analysis: An Essay on the Organization of Experience*, Harmondsworth: Penguin, 1974.

[Much of Goffman's work can be seen as a sociological elaboration of the principles of 'Role Theory', a school of thought in social psychology which analyses human activity in terms of its enactment of socially determined roles. In dealing with such topics as self-presentation and social interaction, Goffman focuses on the performative dimension of ordinary behaviour, the way individuals adopt and enact given personae as a means of negotiating established interpersonal situations (see Goffman 1969 and 1972). His principle of the 'frame' complements this, for it describes the perceptual mechanism by which actions are recognized as other than functional or literal; as 'play'. An understanding shared by s/he who acts and s/he who views the act, the frame indicates the nature and purpose of a behaviour, and hence how it is to be interpreted. It thereby offers a tool for understanding the implicit agreement of performer and audience on the symbolic, fictional status of performance.]

1. During visits to the Fleishacker Zoo beginning in 1952, Gregory Bateson observed that otters not only fight with each other but also play at fighting.[1] Interest in animal play has a clear source in Karl Groos's still useful book, *The Play of Animals*,[2] but Bateson pointedly raised the questions that gave the issue its wider current relevance.

Bateson noted that on some signal or other, the otters would begin playfully to stalk, chase and attack each other, and on some other signal would stop the play. An obvious point about this play behavior is that the actions of the animals are not ones that are, as it were, meaningful in themselves; the framework of these actions does not make meaningless events meaningful, there being a contrast here to primary understandings, which do. Rather, this play activity is closely patterned after something that already has meaning in its own terms – in this case, fighting, a well-known type of guided doing. Real fighting here serves as a model, a detailed pattern to follow, a foundation for form. Just as obviously, the pattern for fighting is not followed fully, but rather is systematically altered in certain respects. Bitinglike behavior occurs, but no one is seriously bitten. In brief, there is a transcription or transposition – a *transformation* in the geometrical, not Chomskyan, sense – of a strip of fighting behavior into a strip of play. Another point about play is that all those involved in it seem to have a clear appreciation that it is play that is going on. Barring a few troublesome cases, it can be taken that both professional observers and the lay public have no trouble in seeing that a strip of animal behavior is play and, furthermore, that it is play in a sense similar to what one thinks of as play among humans. Indeed, play is possible *between* humans and many species, a fact not to be dwelt upon when we sustain our usual congratulatory versions of the difference between us and them.

Since Bateson's discussions of animals at play, considerable work has been done on the subject, allowing one to attempt to state in some detail the rules to follow and the premises to sustain in order to transform serious, real action into something playful.

a.   The playful act is so performed that its ordinary function is not realized. The stronger and more competent participant restrains himself sufficiently to be a match for the weaker and less competent.

b.   There is an exaggeration of the expansiveness of some acts.

c.   The sequence of activity that serves as a pattern is neither followed faithfully nor completed fully, but is subject to starting and stopping, to redoing, to discontinuation for a brief period of time, and to mixing with sequences from other routines.

d.   A great deal of repetitiveness occurs.

e.   When more than one participant is to be involved, all must be freely willing to play or (if he is a participant) to terminate the play once it has begun.

f.   Frequent role switching occurs during play, resulting in a mixing up of the dominance order found among the players during occasions of literal activity.

g.   The play seems to be independent of any external needs of the participants, often continuing longer than would the actual behavior it is patterned after.

h.   Although playfulness can certainly be sustained by a solitary individual toward a surrogate of some kind, solitary playfulness will give way to sociable playfulness when a usable other appears, which, in many cases, can be a member of another species.

i.   Signs presumably are available to mark the beginning and termination of playfulness.

The transformational power of play is nicely seen in the way certain objects are prone to be selected for play or prone to evoke play. These often will be ones that, like balls and balloons, tend to sustain initial impact through movement, thus producing the appearance of current guidedness. Thorpe provides a statement: Play is often related to an object, a 'play-thing', which is not one of the normal objects of serious behavior. These objects may include the body as a whole, or its parts.[3]

A plaything while in play provides some sort of ideal evidence of the manner in which a playful definition of the situation can utterly suppress the ordinary meaning of the word.

2. By keeping in mind these comments on animal play, one can easily turn to a central concept in frame analysis: the key. I refer here to the set of conventions by which a given activity, one already meaningful in terms of some primary framework, is transformed into something patterned on this activity but seen by the participants to be something quite else. The process of transcription can be called keying. A rough musical analogy is intended.

Now if one is restricted to a look at otters or monkeys one won't find many things like play, even though play seems to be the sort of thing that leads one to think of things like it. Bateson suggests threat, deceit and ritual. In all three cases, presumably, what appears to be something isn't quite that, being merely modeled on it. When attention is turned to man, however, many different kinds of monkey business can be found. Keys abound. In addition to what an otter can do, we can *stage* a fight in accordance with a script, or *fantasize* one, or describe one *retrospectively*, or *analyze* one, and so forth.

A full definition of keying can now be suggested:

a. A systematic transformation is involved across materials already meaningful in accordance with a schema of interpretation, and without which the keying would be meaningless.

b. Participants in the activity are meant to know and to openly acknowledge that a systematic alteration is involved, one that will radically reconstitute what it is for them that is going on.

c. Cues will be available for establishing when the transformation is to begin and when it is to end, namely, brackets in time, within which and to which the transformation is to be restricted. Similarly, spatial brackets will commonly indicate everywhere within which and nowhere outside of which the keying applies, on that occasion.

d. Keying is not restricted to events perceived within any particular class of perspectives. Just as it is possible to play at quite instrumentally oriented activities, such as carpentry, so it is also possible to play at rituals such as marriage ceremonies, or even, in the snow, to play at being a falling tree, although admittedly events perceived within a natural schema seem less susceptible to keying than do those perceived within a social one.

e. For participants, playing, say, at fighting and playing around at checkers feels to be much the same sort of thing – radically more so than when these two activities are performed in earnest, that is, seriously. Thus, the systematic transformation that a particular keying introduces may alter only slightly the activity thus transformed, but it utterly changes what it is a participant would say was going on. In this case, fighting and checker playing would appear to be going on, but really, all along, the participants might say, the only thing really going on is play. A keying, then, when there is one, performs a crucial role in determining what it is we think is really going on.

3. Because our individual can now answer the question 'What is it that's going on here?' with 'They're only playing', one has a means of distinguishing types of answers to that question that was not available before. More is involved than merely a matter of variation in focus.

One answer speaks to the fact that the individual may be confronted by 'engrossables', a set of materials whose concatenations and interactions he can become caught up in or carried away by, as might warrant the answer: 'King Arthur has just unsheathed his sword and is about to defend Guenevere', or 'The little otter is about to attack his mother' or 'His bishop is about to threaten my knight', this last answer being the one he could give a sympathetic kibitzer or – with the pronouns changed – a forgetful opponent. These answers have an inward-looking experiential finality. They go as far as participants might feel it possible into the meaningful universe sustained by the activity – into what one might call a *realm*. (Only some realms ought to be thought of as *worlds*, since only some can be thought of as 'real' or 'actual'.)

The other possibility is to provide a commonsense version of what is here being attempted, namely frame analysis: 'In the Scott novel, the writer has the character Ivanhoe do all kinds of strange things', 'The otters are not really fighting', 'The men seem to be playing some kind of board game'.

When no keying is involved, when, that is, only primary perspectives apply, response in frame terms is not likely unless doubt needs combating, as in the reply: 'No, they're not merely playing; it's a real fight'. Indeed, when activity that is untransformed is occurring, definitions in terms of frame suggest alienation, irony and distance. When the key in question is that of play, we tend to refer to the less transformed counterpart as 'serious' activity; as will be seen however, not all serious activity is unkeyed, and not all untransformed activity can be called serious.

[. . .] For there are strips of doing which patently involve a keying but which are not much seen in these terms. Thus, as often remarked, our interpersonal greeting rituals involve questions about health which are not put or taken as literal requests for information. On these occasions kissing can also occur, the gesture following a form that is manifest in the more sexualized version, but here considerably disembodied. And between males, blows can be exchanged, but obviously ones not given or received as serious attacks. Yet upon observing any of these ceremonies we could say that a real greeting was occurring. A literal act can then have figurative components within it not actively seen as such. And for a keying of a greeting one would presumably have to look to the stage or, say, a training school for the polite arts. In order to be careful, then, perhaps the terms 'real', 'actual', and 'literal' ought merely to be taken to imply that the activity under consideration is no more transformed than is felt to be usual and typical for such doings.

Notes

1   See G. Bateson (1955) 'The Message "This Is Play"', in Bertram Schaffner (ed.), *Group Processes* (New York: Josiah Macy, Jr Foundation Proceedings).
2   K. Groos (1896) *The Play of Animals*, trans. Elizabeth L. Baldwin (New York: Appleton & Co.).
3   W. H. Thorpe (1966) 'Ritualization in Ontogeny: I. Animal Play', in *Philosophical Transactions of the Royal Society of London* (London: Royal Society), p. 313.

EXERCISE: Choose a performance you have seen and list (1) the various kinds of framing that occurred before you attended the event, and (2) those occurring at the venue, including any that were part of the performance itself. Consider how these guided or inflected your experience. How would a different kind of venue, or a different author, more or less famous, have altered your expectations or reading? If the piece had been staged in an unconventional space, with none of the usual keys to indicate the nature of the event, how would you have responded?

Now place before the class three objects: one which is not usually considered to have an aesthetic dimension (an ordinary classroom chair, for example), one which is (a painting, perhaps, or a vase), and one which was a prop in the performance you saw; you will of course have to imagine the presence of the last of these. Using your own responses as a starting point, discuss how the different types of frames, or lack of them, determine the way you see the objects. Would you read the painting or vase differently if it were on a stage? How would your perception of the chair change if it were recognizably antique, or known to be the work of an esteemed craftsman? If it were placed on a plinth in a museum, would you look for different qualities in it; indeed, would you *find* them, and if so, why?

Part two

The politics of
performance

Performance is a cultural practice, a practice of representation, and so inevitably enters the arena of ideology.
Although the explicit theorization of ideology began in the
nineteenth century, it was not at that time a central concern
of political thought – not least because social control was
still achieved largely by direct, coercive means. The first
half of the twentieth century, however, saw key changes in
the makeup of developed societies. The new Fordist mass-
production techniques were more complex, and hence
vulnerable to disruption, requiring that a consensus of beliefs
and values geared to maintaining social harmony be
created. These techniques also established an economy
driven not by production but by consumption, with a
resulting need to promote the purchase of goods. New
media developed – radio, cinema, television, advances in
printing leading to increased opportunities for advertising
– which together created a world in which individuals were
bombarded with 'messages' as never before. Modernist
experiment in the arts called into question traditional modes
of representation, while states like those of Nazi Germany
and Stalin's Soviet Union set about the explicit manipulation of images and ideas for political ends. Collectively,
such changes drew the issue of representation and its political consequences into the centre of critical debate. Perhaps

31

the first major development came from Italian theorist Antonio Gramsci (1891–1937), whose concept of 'hegemony' shifted the analysis of ideology away from organized systems of thought towards a study of those 'common-sense' world views which shape mundane social action (see Gramsci 1971). Examining high and popular culture for their political content in the 1930s, the social scientists of the Institute of Social Research or 'Frankfurt School' (Theodor Adorno (1903–69), Walter Benjamin (1892–1940), Max Horkheimer (1895–1973), Herbert Marcuse (1898–1979): see Held 1980, Jameson (ed.) 1977) similarly highlighted the ideological dimension to 'artistic' and everyday acts and objects. Such theorists reoriented critical analysis towards the kind of political interrogation of cultural objects characteristic of academic study today.

Pieces in other sections of this reader address specific areas of the politics of representation in performance; those in this section deal with broad, fundamental issues and positions. Louis Althusser (1918–89), continuing and redirecting the tradition begun by Gramsci, offers a modern theory of ideology. Bertolt Brecht (1898–1956) outlines a mode of performance which opposes ideology in two ways, both offering an alternative explanation of the social world and redrawing the stage's relationship with its audience. Jean-François Lyotard (1924–98) proposes an aesthetic strategy which counters the very structure of thought on which ideology rests.

(In this volume, see also **Part three** and **Part four**; and **Barthes, Foucault, Bristol, Bakhtin.**)

Further reading: excellent introductions to the concept of ideology can be found in Hawkes 1996, Slaughter 1980 and, especially, Eagleton 1991; Arvon 1973, Macherey 1978, Williams 1977 and Williamson 1978 offer very good explorations of the question of ideology and art/culture generally; for the politics of performance specifically see Blau 1992, Goodman and de Gay (eds) 2000 and Kershaw 1992.

2.1 Ideology

Louis Althusser, from 'Ideology and the Ideological State Apparatuses', in *Essays on Ideology*, London: Verso, 1971 [originally published 1970]

[Adapting more traditional Marxist models using principles drawn from the work of psychoanalyst Jacques Lacan (1901–81), in the following essay

Althusser proposed what is perhaps the most influential theory of ideology to emerge in the second half of the twentieth century. The piece comprises two complementary parts. In the first he asserts that, far from existing in some abstract realm of ideas, ideology is reproduced in familiar, apparently benign institutions that are part of everyday social life. In the second part he argues that its goal is the formation of individuals as 'social subjects'. Ideology's function is to maintain and reproduce the social, productive relations of the prevailing order, to this end imposing on individuals a conception of themselves which fosters their acquiescence in that order. This act of 'interpellation' is a psychic event; in being 'hailed' by ideology, the individual assumes the identity it offers him or her, a self-conception as someone who *wants* to behave in the required way. It is this insistence on a psychoanalytic dimension to ideology which had the greatest impact on cultural theory. Whereas previous theorists typically saw it as proposing a false picture of the world – a 'false consciousness' – for Althusser ideology first provides a distorted view of ourselves and our place in that world: 'Ideology represents the imaginary relationship of individuals to their real conditions of existence.']

How is the reproduction of labour power ensured?

It is ensured by giving labour power the material means with which to reproduce itself: by wages. Wages feature in the accounting of each enterprise, but as 'wage capital', not at all as a condition of the material reproduction of labour power.

However, that is in fact how it 'works', since wages represents only that part of the value produced by the expenditure of labour power which is indispensable for its reproduction: indispensable to the reconstitution of the labour power of the wage-earner (the wherewithal to pay for housing, food and clothing, in short to enable the wage-earner to present himself again at the factory gate the next day – and every further day God grants him); and we should add: indispensable for raising and educating the children in whom the proletarian reproduces himself (in n models where n = 0, 1, 2, etc. . . . .) as labour power. [. . .]

However, it is not enough to ensure for labour power the material conditions of its reproduction if it is to be reproduced as labour power. I have said that the available labour power must be 'competent', i.e. suitable to be set to work in the complex system of the process of production. The development of the productive forces and the type of unity historically constitutive of the productive forces at a given moment produce the result that the labour power has to be (diversely) skilled and therefore reproduced as such. Diversely: according to the requirements of the socio-technical division of labour, its different 'jobs' and 'posts'.

How is this reproduction of the (diversified) skills of labour power provided for in a capitalist regime? Here, unlike social formations characterized by slavery or serfdom, this reproduction of the skills of labour power tends (this is a tendential law) decreasingly to be provided for 'on the spot' (apprenticeship within production itself), but is achieved more and more outside production: by the capitalist education system, and by other instances and institutions.

What do children learn at school? They go varying distances in their studies, but at any rate they learn to read, to write and to add – i.e. a number of techniques, and a number of other things as well, including elements (which may be rudimentary or on the contrary thoroughgoing) of 'scientific' or 'literary' culture, which are directly useful in the different jobs in production (one instruction for manual workers, another for technicians, a third for engineers, a final one for higher management, etc.). Thus they learn 'know-how'.

But besides these techniques and knowledges, and in learning them, children at school also learn the 'rules' of good behaviour, i.e. the attitude that should be observed by every agent in the division of labour, according to the job he is 'destined' for: rules of morality, civic and professional conscience, which actually means rules of respect for the socio-technical division of labour and ultimately the rules of the order established by class domination. They also learn to 'speak proper French', to 'handle' the workers correctly, i.e. actually (for the future capitalists and their servants) to 'order them about' properly, i.e. (ideally) to 'speak to them' in the right way, etc.

To put this more scientifically, I shall say that the reproduction of labour power requires not only a reproduction of its skills but also, at the same time, a reproduction of its submission to the rules of the established order, i.e. a reproduction of submission to the ruling ideology for the workers, and a reproduction of the ability to manipulate the ruling ideology correctly for the agents of exploitation and repression, so that they, too, will provide for the domination of the ruling class 'in words'.

In other words, the school (but also other State institutions like the Church, or other apparatuses like the Army) teaches 'know-how', but in forms which ensure *subjection to the ruling ideology* or the mastery of its 'practice'. All the agents of production, exploitation and repression, not to speak of the 'professionals of ideology' (Marx), must in one way or another be 'steeped' in this ideology in order to perform their tasks 'conscientiously' – the tasks of the exploited (the proletarians), of the exploiters (the capitalists), of the exploiters' auxiliaries (the managers), or of the high priests of the ruling ideology (its 'functionaries'), etc.

The reproduction of labour power thus reveals as its *sine qua non* not only the reproduction of its 'skills' but also the reproduction of its subjection to the ruling ideology or of the 'practice' of that ideology, with the proviso that it is not enough to say 'not only but also', for it is clear that *it is in the forms and under the forms of ideological subjection that provision is made for the reproduction of the skills of labour power.*

But this is to recognize the effective presence of a new reality: *ideology.* [. . .]

The Ideological State Apparatus

What are the ideological State apparatuses (ISAs)?

They must not be confused with the (repressive) State apparatus. Remember that in Marxist theory, the State Apparatus (SA) contains: the Government, the Administration, the Army, the Police, the Courts, the Prisons, etc., which constitute what I shall in future call the Repressive State Apparatus. Repressive suggests that the State Apparatus in question 'functions by violence' – at least ultimately (since repression, e.g. administrative repression, may take non-physical forms).

I shall call Ideological State Apparatuses a certain number of realities which present themselves to the immediate observer in the form of distinct and specialized institutions. I propose an empirical list of these which will obviously have to be examined in detail, tested, corrected and reorganized. With all the reservations implied by this requirement, we can for the moment regard the following institutions as Ideological State Apparatuses (the order in which I have listed them has no particular significance):

- the religious ISA (the system of the different Churches)
- the educational ISA (the system of the different public and private 'Schools')
- the family ISA
- the legal ISA
- the political ISA (the political system, including the different Parties)
- the trade-union ISA
- the communications ISA (press, radio and television, etc.)
- the cultural ISA (Literature, the Arts, sports, etc.).

I have said that the ISAs must not be confused with the (Repressive) State Apparatus. What constitutes the difference?

As a first moment, it is clear that while there is *one* (Repressive) State Apparatus, there is a *plurality* of Ideological State Apparatuses. Even presupposing that it exists, the unity that constitutes this plurality of ISAs as a body is not immediately visible.

As a second moment, it is clear that whereas the – unified – (Repressive) State Apparatus belongs entirely to the *public* domain, much the larger part of the Ideological State Apparatuses (in their apparent dispersion) are part, on the contrary, of the *private* domain. Churches, Parties, Trade Unions, families, some schools, most newspapers, cultural ventures, etc., etc., are private.

We can ignore the first observation for the moment. But someone is bound to question the second, asking me by what right I regard as Ideological *State* Apparatuses, institutions which for the most part do not possess public status, but are quite simply *private* institutions. As a conscious Marxist, Gramsci already forestalled this objection in one sentence. The distinction between the public and the private is a distinction internal to bourgeois law, and valid in the (subordinate) domains in which bourgeois law exercises its 'authority'. The domain of the State escapes it because the latter is 'above the law': the state, which is the State *of* the ruling class, is neither public nor private; on the contrary, it is the precondition for any distinction between public and private. The same thing can be said from the starting-point of our State Ideological Apparatuses. It is unimportant whether the institutions in which they are realized are 'public' or 'private'. What matters is how they function. Private institutions can perfectly well 'function' as Ideological State Apparatuses. A reasonably thorough analysis of any one of the ISAs proves it.

But now for what is essential. What distinguishes the ISAs from the (Repressive) State Apparatus is the following basic difference: the Repressive State Apparatus functions 'by violence', whereas the Ideological State Apparatuses *function 'by ideology'*. [. . .]

Ideology is a 'representation' of the imaginary relationship of individuals to their real conditions of existence

In order to approach my central thesis on the structure and functioning of ideology, I shall first present two theses, one negative, the other positive. The first concerns the object which is 'represented' in the imaginary form of ideology, the second concerns the materiality of ideology.

THESIS I: Ideology represents the imaginary relationship of individuals to their real conditions of existence.

We commonly call religious ideology, ethical ideology, legal ideology, political ideology, etc., so many 'world outlooks'. Of course, assuming that we do not live one of these ideologies as the truth (e.g. 'believe' in God, Duty, Justice, etc. . . .), we admit that the ideology we are discussing from a critical point of view, examining it as the ethnologist examines the myths of a 'primitive society', that these 'world outlooks' are largely imaginary, i.e. do not 'correspond to reality'.

However, while admitting that they do not correspond to reality, i.e. that they constitute an illusion, we admit that they do make allusion to reality, and that they need only be 'interpreted' to discover the reality of the world behind their imaginary representation of that world (ideology = *illusion/allusion*). [. . .]

Now I can return to a thesis which I have already advanced: it is not their real conditions of existence, their real world, that 'men' 'represent to themselves' in ideology, but above all it is their relation to those conditions of existence which is represented to them there. It is this relation which is at the centre of every ideological, i.e. imaginary, representation of the real world. It is this relation that contains the 'cause' which has to explain the imaginary distortion of the ideological representation of the real world. Or rather, to leave aside the language of causality it is necessary to advance the thesis that it is the *imaginary nature of this relation* which underlies all the imaginary distortion that we can observe (if we do not live in its truth) in all ideology.

To speak in a Marxist language, if it is true that the representation of the real conditions of existence of the individuals occupying the posts of agents of production, exploitation, repression, ideologization and scientific practice, does in the last analysis arise from the relations of production, and from relations deriving from the relations of production, we can say the following: all ideology represents in its necessarily imaginary distortion not the existing relations of production (and the other relations that derive from them), but above all the (imaginary) relationship of individuals to the relations of production and the relations that derive from them. What is represented in ideology is therefore not the system of the real relations which govern the existence of individuals, but the imaginary relation of those individuals to the real relations in which they live. [. . .]

THESIS II: Ideology has a material existence.

I have already touched on this thesis by saying that the 'ideas' or 'representations', etc., which seem to make up ideology do not have an ideal (*idéale* or *idéelle*) or spiritual existence, but a material existence.

I even suggested that the *ideal* (*idéale, idéelle*) and spiritual existence of 'ideas' arises exclusively in an ideology of the 'idea' and of ideology, and let me add, in an ideology of what seems to have 'founded' this conception since the emergence of the sciences, i.e. what the practicians of the sciences represent to themselves in their spontaneous ideology as 'ideas', true or false. Of course, presented in affirmative form, this thesis is unproven. I simply ask that the reader be favourably disposed towards it, say, in the name of materialism. A long series of arguments would be necessary to prove it.

This hypothetical thesis of the not spiritual but material existence of 'ideas' or other 'representations' is indeed necessary if we are to advance in our analysis of the nature of ideology. Or rather, it is merely useful to us in order the better to reveal what every at all serious analysis of any ideology will immediately and empirically show to every observer, however critical.

While discussing the ideological State apparatuses and their practices, I said that each of them was the realization of an ideology (the unity of these different regional ideologies – religious, ethical, legal, political, aesthetic, etc. – being assured by their subjection to the ruling ideology). I now return to this thesis: an ideology always exists in an apparatus, and its practice, or practices. This existence is material. [. . .]

An individual believes in God, or Duty, or Justice, etc. This belief derives (for everyone, i.e. for all those who live in an ideological representation of ideology, which reduces ideology to ideas endowed by definition with a spiritual existence) from the ideas of the individual concerned, i.e. from him as a subject with a consciousness which contains the ideas of his belief. In this way, i.e. by means of the absolutely ideological 'conceptual' device (*dispositif*) thus set up (a subject endowed with a consciousness in which he freely forms or freely recognizes ideas in which he believes), the (material) attitude of the subject concerned naturally follows.

The individual in question behaves in such and such a way, adopts such and such a practical attitude, and, what is more, participates in certain regular practices which are those of the ideological apparatus on which 'depend' the ideas which he has in all consciousness freely chosen as a subject. If he believes in God, he goes to Church to attend Mass, kneels, prays, confesses, does penance (once it was material in the ordinary sense of the term) and naturally repents and so on. If he believes in Duty, he will have the corresponding attitudes, inscribed in ritual practices 'according to the correct principles'. If he believes in justice, he will submit unconditionally to the rules of the Law, and may even protest when they are violated, sign petitions, take part in a demonstration, etc.

Throughout this schema we observe that the ideological representa-tion of ideology is itself forced to recognize that every 'subject' endowed with a 'consciousness' and believing in the 'ideas' that his 'consciousness' inspires in him and freely accepts, must 'act according to his ideas', must therefore inscribe his own ideas as a free subject in the actions of his material practice. If he does not do so, 'that is wicked'.

Indeed, if he does not do what he ought to do as a function of what he believes, it is because he does something else, which, still as a func-tion of the same idealist scheme, implies that he has other ideas in his head as well as those he proclaims, and that he acts according to these other ideas, as a man who is either 'inconsistent' ('no one is willingly evil') or cynical, or perverse.

In every case, the ideology of ideology thus recognizes, despite its imaginary distortion, that the 'ideas' of a human subject exist in his actions, or ought to exist in his actions, and, if that is not the case, it lends him other ideas corresponding to the actions (however perverse) that he does perform. This ideology talks of actions: I shall talk of actions inserted into *practices*. *And* I shall point out that these practices are governed by the *rituals* in which these practices are inscribed, within the *material existence of an ideological apparatus*, be it only a small part of that apparatus: a small mass in a small church, a funeral, a minor match at a sports club, a school day, a political party meeting, etc. [. . .]

And I shall immediately set down two conjoint theses:

- There is no practice except by and in an ideology.
- There is no ideology except by the subject and for subjects.

I can now come to my central thesis.

Ideology interpellates individuals as subjects

This thesis is simply a matter of making my last proposition explicit: there is no ideology except by the subject and for subjects. Meaning, there is no ideology except for concrete subjects, and this destination for ideology is made possible only by the subject: meaning, *by the category of the subject* and its functioning.

By this I mean that, even if it only appears under this name (the subject) with the rise of bourgeois ideology, above all with the rise of legal ideology, the category of the subject (which may function under other names: e.g., as the soul in Plato, as God, etc.) is the constitutive category of all ideology, whatever its determination (regional or class) and whatever its historical date – since ideology has no history.

I say: the category of the subject is constitutive of all ideology, but at the same time and immediately I add that *the category of the subject is constitutive of all ideology only in so far as all ideology has the function (which defines it) of 'constituting' concrete individuals as subjects.* In the interaction of this double constitution exists the functioning of all ideology, ideology being nothing but its functioning in the material forms of existence of that functioning.

In order to grasp what follows, it is essential to realize that both he who is writing these lines and the reader who reads them are themselves subjects, and therefore ideological subjects (a tautological proposition), i.e. that the author and the reader of these lines both live 'spontaneously' or 'naturally' in ideology in the sense in which I have said that 'man is an ideological animal by nature'.

That the author, in so far as he writes the lines of a discourse which claims to be scientific, is completely absent as a 'subject' from 'his' scientific discourse (for all scientific discourse is by definition a subject-less discourse, there is no 'Subject of science' except in an ideology of science) is a different question which I shall leave on one side for the moment.

As St Paul admirably put it, it is in the 'Logos', meaning in ideology, that we 'live, move and have our being'. It follows that, for you and for me, the category of the subject is a primary 'obviousness' (obviousnesses are always primary): it is clear that you and I are subjects (free, ethical, etc. . . .). Like all obviousnesses, including those that make a word 'name a thing' or 'have a meaning' (therefore including the obviousness of the 'transparency' of language), the 'obviousness' that you and I are subjects – and that that does not cause any problems – is an ideological effect, the elementary ideological effect. It is indeed a peculiarity of ideology that it imposes (without appearing to do so, since these are 'obviousnesses') obviousnesses as obviousnesses, which we cannot fail to recognize and before which we have the inevitable and natural reaction of crying out (aloud or in the 'still, small voice of conscience'): 'That's obvious! That's right! That's true!'

At work in this reaction is the ideological *recognition* function which is one of the two functions of ideology as such (its inverse being the function of *misrecognition – méconnaissance*).

To take a highly 'concrete' example, we all have friends who, when they knock on our door and we ask, through the door, the question 'Who's there?', answer (since 'it's obvious'), 'It's me'. And we recognize that 'it is him', or 'her'. We open the door, and 'It's true, it really was she who was there'. To take another example, when we recognize somebody of our (previous) acquaintance ((*re*)-*connaissance*) in the street, we show him that we have recognized him (and have recognized that he has recognized us) by saying to him 'Hello, my friend', and shaking his hand (a material ritual practice of ideological recognition in everyday life – in France, at least; elsewhere, there are other rituals).

In this preliminary remark and these concrete illustrations, I only wish to point out that you and I are *always already* subjects, and as such constantly practise the rituals of ideological recognition, which guarantee for us that we are indeed concrete, individual, distinguishable and (naturally) irreplaceable subjects. The writing I am currently executing and the reading you are currently performing are also in this respect rituals of ideological recognition, including the 'obviousness' with which the 'truth' or 'error' of my reflections may impose itself on you.

But to recognize that we are subjects and that we function in the practical rituals of the most elementary everyday life (the hand-shake, the fact of calling you by your name, the fact of knowing, even if I do not know what it is, that you 'have' a name of your own, which means that you are recognized as a unique subject, etc.) – this recognition only gives us the 'consciousness' of our incessant (eternal) practice of ideological recognition – its consciousness, i.e. its *recognition* – but in no sense does it give us the (scientific) *knowledge* of the mechanism of this recognition. Now it is this knowledge that we have to reach, if you will, while speaking in ideology, and from within ideology we have to outline a discourse which tries to break with ideology, in order to dare to be the beginning of a scientific (i.e. subject-less) discourse on ideology.

Thus in order to represent why the category of the 'subject' is constitutive of ideology, which only exists by constituting concrete subjects as subjects, I shall employ a special mode of exposition: 'concrete' enough to be recognized, but abstract enough to be thinkable and thought, giving rise to a knowledge.

As a first formulation I shall say: *all ideology hails or interpellates concrete individuals as concrete subjects*, by the functioning of the category of the subject.

This is a proposition which entails that we distinguish for the moment between concrete individuals on the one hand and concrete subjects on the other, although at this level concrete subjects exist only in so far as they are supported by a concrete individual.

I shall then suggest that ideology 'acts' or 'functions' in such a way that it 'recruits' subjects among the individuals (it recruits them all), or 'transforms' the individuals into subjects (it transforms them all) by that very precise operation which I have called *interpellation* or hailing, and which can be imagined along the lines of the most commonplace everyday police (or other) hailing: 'Hey, you there!'

Assuming that the theoretical scene I have imagined takes place in the street, the hailed individual will turn round. By this mere one-hundred-and-eighty-degree physical conversion, he becomes a *subject*. Why? Because he has recognized that the hail was 'really' addressed to him, and that 'it was *really him* who was hailed' (and not someone else). Experience shows that the practical telecommunication of hailings is such that they hardly ever miss their man: verbal call or whistle, the one hailed always recognizes that it is really him who is being hailed. And yet it is a strange phenomenon, and one which cannot be explained solely by 'guilt feelings', despite the large numbers who 'have something on their consciences'.

Naturally for the convenience and clarity of my little theoretical theatre I have had to present things in the form of a sequence, with a before and an after, and thus in the form of a temporal succession. There are individuals walking along. Somewhere (usually behind them) the hail rings out: 'Hey, you there!' One individual (nine times out of ten it is the right one) turns round, believing/suspecting/knowing that it is for him, i.e. recognizing that 'it really is he' who is meant by the hailing. But in reality these things happen without any succession. The existence of ideology and the hailing or interpellation of individuals as subjects are one and the same thing.

EXERCISE: Compare two newspaper articles, taken from different styles of publication but dealing with the same news item. Contrast their styles, emphases and methods of representation, the 'spin' they give to the material, to find the different political, social or moral positions at the root of their treatments. If they view the events negatively or positively, on the basis of what underlying values do they do so? Assuming that the articles are inviting you to adopt their own position – 'hailing' you as subject of their discourse – what view of the world are they asking you to take?

Having examined a 'communications ISA', now look at the 'cultural ISA' of theatre: compare two video productions of the same scene from a Shakespeare play and analyse the ideological assumptions made by each. How are characters and events interpreted, and what view of them is proffered as a result? What issues or areas or

---

themes are brought to the fore and how, and what value systems are thereby implied? Try to consider all components of the productions – set design, lighting, costume – examining them for the way they inflect the matter of the tale. Once again, your aim is to discern what view of the world each production is asking you to adopt. When you have decided this, consider how your adoption of it might be supportive or disruptive of the status quo.

2.2 Epic theatre

Bertolt Brecht, from 'The Street Scene', in *Brecht on Theatre: The Development of an Aesthetic*, ed. and trans. John Willett, London: Methuen, 1964 [originally published 1938]

[A playwright, poet and director, Brecht was also an active participant in key discussions on politics and aesthetics taking place in pre-Second World-War Europe (see Jameson (ed.) 1977), emerging as the twentieth century's leading theorist of radical political theatre. His programme for an 'epic theatre' comprises two general categories of proposal. He on the one hand suggests eschewing the usual depiction of human action as psychologically driven to show instead causes of a social, historical and political kind; thus representing the individual less as the agent of events than the focus of external forces. On the other hand, he proposes the rejection of theatrical illusion. Ideology 'naturalizes' its ideas, presenting them not as constructions of reality but as obvious and common sense (see **Althusser**, **Barthes**), and this finds its corollary in the stage's concealment of its own artifice. By revealing the mechanics by which performance manufactures its view of the world, epic theatre seeks to 'alienate' that view, offering it to the audience as extraordinary, to be addressed critically (see also **Gilbert**, **Diamond**). Brecht thus sought to alter not only theatre's representation of reality but also the politics of the auditorium, encouraging in the spectator an active, interrogative attitude to what is presented.]

In the decade and a half that followed the World War a comparatively new way of acting was tried out in a number of German theatres. Its qualities of clear description and reporting and its use of choruses and projections as a means of commentary earned it the name of 'epic'. The actor used a somewhat complex technique to detach himself from the character portrayed; he forced the spectator to look at the play's situations from such an angle that they necessarily became subject to his criticism. Supporters of this epic theatre argued that the new subject matter, the highly involved incidents of the class war in its acutest and most terrible stage, would be mastered more easily by such a method, since it would thereby become possible to portray social processes as seen in their causal relationships. But the result of these experiments was that aesthetics found itself up against a whole series of substantial difficulties.

It is comparatively easy to set up a basic model for epic theatre. For practical experiments I usually picked as my example of completely simple, 'natural' epic theatre an incident such as can be seen at any street corner: an eyewitness demonstrating to a collection of people how a traffic accident took place. The bystanders may not have observed what happened, or they may simply not agree with him, may 'see things a different way'; the point is that the demonstrator acts the behaviour of driver or victim or both in such a way that the bystanders are able to form an opinion about the accident. [. . .]

Consider: the incident is clearly very far from what we mean by an artistic one. The demonstrator need not be an artist. The capacities he needs to achieve his aim are in effect universal. Suppose he cannot carry out some particular movement as quickly as the victim he is imitating; all he need do is to explain that *he* moves three times as fast, and the demonstration neither suffers in essentials nor loses its point. On the contrary it is important that he should not be too perfect. His demonstration would be spoilt if the bystanders' attention were drawn to his powers of transformation. He has to avoid presenting himself in such a way that someone calls out 'What a lifelike portrayal of a chauffeur!' He must not 'cast a spell' over anyone. He should not transport people from normality to 'higher realms'. He need not dispose of any special powers of suggestion.

It is most important that one of the main features of the ordinary theatre should be excluded from our street scene: the engendering of illusion. The street demonstrator's performance is essentially repetitive. The event has taken place; what you are seeing now is a repeat. If the scene in the theatre follows the street scene in this respect then the theatre will stop pretending not to be theatre, just as the street-corner demonstration admits it is a demonstration (and does not pretend to be the actual event). The element of rehearsal in the acting and of learning by heart in the text, the whole machinery and the whole process of preparation: it all becomes plainly apparent. What room is left for experience? Is the reality portrayed still experienced in any sense?

The street scene determines what kind of experience is to be prepared for the spectator. There is no question but that the street-corner demonstrator has been through an 'experience', but he is not out to make his demonstration serve as an 'experience' for the audience. Even the experience of the driver and the victim is only partially communicated by him, and he by no means tries to turn it into an enjoyable experience for the spectator, however lifelike he may make his demonstration. The demonstration would become no less valid if he did not reproduce the fear caused by the accident; on the contrary it would lose validity if he did. He is not interested in creating pure emotions. It is important to understand that a theatre which follows his lead in this respect undergoes a positive change of function.

One essential element of the street scene must also be present in the theatrical scene if this is to qualify as epic, namely that the demonstration should have a socially practical significance. Whether our street demonstrator is out to show that one attitude on the part of driver or pedestrian makes an accident inevitable where another would not, or whether he is demonstrating with a view to fixing the responsibility, his demonstration has a practical purpose, intervenes socially.

The demonstrator's purpose determines how thoroughly he has to imitate. Our demonstrator need not imitate every aspect of his characters' behaviour, but only so much as gives a picture. Generally the theatre scene will give much fuller pictures, corresponding to its more extensive range of interest. How do street scene and theatre scene link up here? To take a point of detail, the victim's voice may have played no immediate part in the accident. Eyewitnesses may disagree as to whether a cry they heard ('Look out!') came from the victim or from someone else, and this may give our demonstrator a motive for imitating the voice. The question can be settled by demonstrating whether the voice was an old man's or a woman's, or merely whether it was high or low. Again, the answer may depend on whether it was that of an educated person or not. Loud or soft may play a great part, as the driver could be correspondingly more or less guilty. A whole series of characteristics of the victim ask to be portrayed. Was he absent-minded? Was his attention distracted? If so, by what? What, on the evidence of his behaviour, could have made him liable to be distracted by just that circumstance and no other? Etc., etc. It can be seen that our street-corner demonstration provides opportunities for a pretty rich and varied portrayal of human types. Yet a theatre which tries to restrict its essential elements to those provided by our street scene will have to acknowledge certain limits to imitation. It must be able to justify any outlay in terms of its purpose.

The demonstration may for instance be dominated by the question of compensation for the victim, etc. The driver risks being sacked from his job, losing his licence, going to prison; the victim risks a heavy hospital bill, loss of job, permanent disfigurement, possibly unfitness for work. This is the area within which the demonstrator builds up his characters. The victim may have had a companion; the driver may have had his girl sitting alongside him. That would bring out the social element better and allow the characters to be more fully drawn.

Another essential element in the street scene is that the demonstrator should derive his characters entirely from their actions. He imitates their actions and so allows conclusions to be drawn about them. A theatre that follows him in this will be largely breaking with the orthodox theatre's habit of basing the actions on the characters and having the former exempted from criticism by presenting them as an unavoidable consequence deriving by natural law from the characters who perform them. To the street demonstrator the character of the man being demonstrated remains a quantity that need not be completely defined. Within certain limits he may be like this or like that; it doesn't matter. What the demonstrator is concerned with are his accident-prone and accident-proof qualities. The theatrical scene may show more fully defined individuals. But it must then be in a position to treat their individuality as a special case and outline the field within which, once more, its most socially relevant effects are produced. Our street demonstrator's possibilities of demonstration are narrowly restricted (indeed, we chose this model so that the limits should be as narrow as possible). If the essential elements of the theatrical scene are limited to those of the street scene then its greater richness must be an enrichment only. The question of borderline cases becomes acute.

Let us take a specific detail. Can our street demonstrator, say, ever become entitled to use an excited tone of voice in repeating the driver's statement that he has been exhausted by too long a spell of work? (In theory this is no more possible than for a returning messenger to start telling his fellow-countrymen of his talk with the king with the words 'I saw the bearded king'.) It can only be possible, let alone unavoidable, if one imagines a street-corner situation where such excitement, specifically about this aspect of the affair, plays a particular part. (In the instance above this would be so if the king had sworn never to cut his beard off until . . . etc.) We have to find a point of view for our demonstrator that allows him to submit this excitement to criticism. Only if he adopts a quite definite point of view can he be entitled to imitate the driver's excited voice; e.g. if he blames drivers as such for doing too little to reduce their hours of work. ('Look at him. Doesn't even belong to a union, but gets worked up soon enough when an accident happens. "Ten hours I've been at the wheel."')

Before it can get as far as this, i.e. be able to suggest a point of view to the actor, the theatre needs to take a number of steps. By widening its field of vision and showing the driver in other situations besides that of the accident the theatre in no way exceeds its model; it merely creates a further situation on the same pattern. One can imagine a scene of the same kind as the street scene which provides a well-argued demonstration showing how such emotions as the driver's develop, or another which involves making comparisons between tones of voice. In order not to exceed the model scene the theatre only has to develop a technique for submitting emotions to the spectator's criticism. Of course this does not mean that the spectator must be barred on principle from sharing certain emotions that are put before him; none the less to communicate emotions is only one particular form (phase, consequence) of criticism. The theatre's demonstrator, the actor, must apply a technique which will let him reproduce the tone of the subject demonstrated with a certain reserve, with detachment (so that the spectator can say: 'He's getting excited – in vain, too late, at last . . .' etc.). In short, the actor must remain a demonstrator; he must present the person demonstrated as a stranger, he must not suppress the '*he* did that, *he* said that' element in his performance. He must not go so far as to be wholly transformed into the person demonstrated.

One essential element of the street scene lies in the natural attitude adopted by the demonstrator, which is twofold; he is always taking two situations into account. He behaves naturally as a demonstrator, and he lets the subject of the demonstration behave naturally too. He never forgets, nor does he allow it to be forgotten, that he is not the subject but the demonstrator. That is to say, what the audience sees is not a fusion between demonstrator and subject, not some third, independent, uncontradictory entity with isolated features of (1) demonstrator and (2) subject, such as the orthodox theatre puts before us in its productions. The feelings and opinions of demonstrator and demonstrated are not merged into one.

We now come to one of those elements that are peculiar to the epic theatre, the so-called A-effect (alienation effect). What is involved here is, briefly, a technique of taking the human social incidents to be portrayed and labelling them as something striking, something that calls for explanation, is not to be taken for granted, not just natural. The object of this 'effect' is to allow the spectator to criticize constructively from a social point of view. Can we show that this A-effect is significant for our street demonstrator?

We can picture what happens if he fails to make use of it. The following situation could occur. One of the spectators might say: 'But if the victim stepped off the kerb with his right foot, as you showed him doing . . .' The demonstrator might interrupt saying: 'I showed him stepping off with his left foot.' By arguing which foot he really stepped off with in his demonstration, and, even more, how the victim himself acted, the demonstration can be so transformed that the A-effect occurs. The demonstrator achieves it by paying exact attention this time to his movements, executing them carefully, probably in slow motion; in this way he alienates the little sub-incident, emphasizes its importance, makes it worthy of notice. And so the epic theatre's alienation effect proves to have its uses for our street demonstrator too; in other words it is also to be found in this small everyday scene of natural street-corner theatre, which has little to do with art. The direct changeover from representation to commentary that is so characteristic of the epic theatre is still more easily recognized as one element of any street demonstration. Wherever he feels he can, the demonstrator breaks off his imitation in order to give explanations. The epic theatre's choruses and documentary projections, the direct addressing of the audience by its actors, are at bottom just this.

EXERCISE: Choose a short scene from a realist play and, as a two-part practical exercise, turn it into a piece of epic theatre. First, view its events as social phenomena. Consider how economics, ideology, cultural or historical factors, or the class of its characters, might have determined its action and outcome as written. How might you make such factors evident to an audience? Consider creating other scenes which would illustrate the social forces you find in this one. If your deliberations suggest it should have a different outcome, try changing the end in line with what you have found. When you have altered the scene to your satisfaction, discuss what your explorations reveal about the underlying assumptions of the realist play.

Only when you have completed the first phase of the exercise should you begin the second, experimenting with ways of 'alienating' the scene. Seek techniques of acting which would signal the simultaneous presence of actor and character on stage, such that the piece is seen to be a construction. What design of set, kind of music, use of props, costume, etc., would make it evident that yours is merely *one view* of events? Try your ideas in practice and, most importantly, note

> their effect on spectators' readings of the scene. Now consider what your findings suggest about the effect of theatrical illusion in the play as originally written.

2.3 The postmodern avant-garde

Jean-François Lyotard, from *The Postmodern Condition: A Report on Knowledge*, trans. Geoff Bennington and Brian Massumi, Manchester: Manchester University Press, 1984 [originally published 1979]

[Like many other post-structuralist writings, the following essay by Lyotard is concerned less with the structures of representation *per se* than with the possibility of their failure or disruption, for this is at the heart of his model of postmodernism. Whereas most critics use the term to describe cultural developments from the 1960s or 1970s, the 'postmodern' is for Lyotard a product of modernity itself, from which it erupts as a radical but desirable crisis in signification. The rationalistic thought characteristic of modernity is inherently authoritarian, he argues, for, in claiming for itself the status of sole truth, it represses all other truths. Aesthetic forms such as realism are implicated; by reproducing the familiar, stable view of the world, realism both perpetuates the dominant construction of the real and confirms the viewer's identity as one who sees and understands reality in that way. To counter this, Lyotard champions the radical experiments of the avant-garde, which, in eschewing known aesthetic languages, defy available modes of understanding. By demonstrating that there are things beyond the limits of our concepts, such work reveals that our concepts *have* limits, and that the world is therefore something other than our conceptualization of it. His thesis thus offers a way of understanding the political impact of experimental performance, its destabilization of hegemonic forms of art and thought.]

Photography did not appear as a challenge to painting from the outside, any more than industrial cinema did to narrative literature. The former was only putting the final touch to the program of ordering the visible elaborated by the quattrocento; while the latter was the last step in rounding off diachronies as organic wholes, which had been the ideal of the great novels of education since the eighteenth century. That the mechanical and the industrial should appear as substitutes for hand or craft was not in itself a disaster – except if one believes that art is in its essence the expression of an individuality of genius assisted by an elite craftsmanship.

The challenge lay essentially in that photographic and cinemato-graphic processes can accomplish better, faster, and with a circulation a hundred thousand times larger than narrative or pictorial realism, the task which academicism had assigned to realism: to preserve various conscious-nesses from doubt. Industrial photography and cinema will be superior to painting and the novel whenever the objective is to stabilize the referent, to arrange it according to a point of view which endows it with a recog-nizable meaning, to reproduce the syntax and vocabulary which enable the addressee to decipher images and sequences quickly, and so to arrive easily at the consciousness of his own identity as well as the approval which he thereby receives from others – since such structures of images and sequences constitute a communication code among all of them. This is the way the effects of reality, or, if one prefers, the fantasies of realism, multiply.

If they too do not wish to become supporters (of minor importance at that) of what exists, the painter and novelist must refuse to lend them-selves to such therapeutic uses. They must question the rules of the art of painting or of narrative as they have learned and received them from their predecessors. Soon those rules must appear to them as a means to deceive, to seduce, and to reassure, which makes it impossible for them to be 'true'. Under the common name of painting and literature, an unprecedented split is taking place. Those who refuse to re-examine the rules of art pursue successful careers in mass conformism by communi-cating, by means of the 'correct rules', the endemic desire for reality with objects and situations capable of gratifying it. [. . .]

As for the artists and writers who question the rules of plastic and narrative arts and possibly share their suspicions by circulating their work, they are destined to have little credibility in the eyes of those concerned with 'reality' and 'identity'; they have no guarantee of an audience. Thus it is possible to ascribe the dialectics of the avant-gardes to the challenge posed by the realisms of industry and mass communication to painting and the narrative arts. Duchamp's 'ready made' does nothing but actively and parodistically signify this constant process of dispossession of the craft of painting or even of being an artist. As Thierry de Duve penetratingly observes, the modern aesthetic question is not 'What is beautiful?' but 'What can be said to be art (and literature)?'

Realism, whose only definition is that it intends to avoid the ques-tion of reality implicated in that of art, always stands somewhere between academicism and kitsch. When power assumes the name of a party, realism and its neoclassical complement triumph over the experimental avant-garde by slandering and banning it – that is, provided the 'correct' images, the 'correct' narratives, the 'correct' forms which the party requests, selects and propagates can find a public to desire them as the appropriate remedy for the anxiety and depression that public experiences. [. . .]

When power is that of capital and not that of a party, the 'trans-avantgardist' or 'postmodern' (in Jencks's sense) solution proves to be better adapted than the antimodern solution. Eclecticism is the degree zero of contemporary general culture: one listens to reggae, watches a western, eats McDonald's food for lunch and local cuisine for dinner, wears Paris perfume in Tokyo and 'retro' clothes in Hong Kong; knowledge is a matter for television games. It is easy to find a public for eclectic works. By becoming kitsch, art panders to the confusion which reigns in the 'taste' of the patrons. Artists, gallery owners, critics, and public wallow together in the 'anything goes', and the epoch is one of slackening. But this realism of the 'anything goes' is in fact that of money; in the absence of aesthetic criteria, it remains possible and useful to assess the value of works of art according to the profits they yield. Such realism accommodates all tendencies, just as capital accommodates all 'needs', providing that the tendencies and needs have purchasing power. [. . .]

The interpretation which has just been given of the contact between the industrial and mechanical arts, and literature and the fine arts is correct in its outline, but it remains narrowly sociologizing and historicizing – in other words, one-sided. Stepping over Benjamin's and Adorno's reticences, it must be recalled that science and industry are no more free of the suspicion which concerns reality than are art and writing [. . .] The objects and the thoughts which originate in scientific knowledge and the capitalist economy convey with them one of the rules which supports their possibility: the rule that there is no reality unless testified by a consensus between partners over a certain knowledge and certain commitments.

This rule is of no little consequence. It is the imprint left on the politics of the scientist and the trustee of capital by a kind of flight of reality out of the metaphysical, religious and political certainties that the mind believed it held. This withdrawal is absolutely necessary to the emergence of science and capitalism. No industry is possible without a suspicion of the Aristotelian theory of motion, no industry without a refutation of corporatism, of mercantilism and of physiocracy. Modernity, in whatever age it appears, cannot exist without a shattering of belief and without discovery of the 'lack of reality' of reality, together with the invention of other realities.

What does this 'lack of reality' signify if one tries to free it from a narrowly historicized interpretation? The phrase is of course akin to what Nietzsche calls nihilism. But I see a much earlier modulation of Nietzschean perspectivism in the Kantian theme of the sublime. I think in particular that it is in the aesthetic of the sublime that modern art (including literature) finds its impetus and the logic of avant-gardes finds its axioms.

The sublime sentiment, which is also the sentiment of the sublime, is, according to Kant, a strong and equivocal emotion: it carries with it both pleasure and pain. Better still, in it pleasure derives from pain. Within the tradition of the subject, which comes from Augustine and Descartes and which Kant does not radically challenge, this contradiction, which some would call neurosis or masochism, develops as a conflict between the faculties of a subject, the faculty to conceive of something and the faculty to 'present' something. Knowledge exists if, first, the statement is intelligible, and, second, if 'cases' can be derived from the experience which 'corresponds' to it. Beauty exists if a certain 'case' (the work of art), given first by the sensibility without any conceptual determination, the sentiment of pleasure independent of any interest the work may elicit, appeals to the principle of a universal consensus (which may never be attained).

[...] The sublime is a different sentiment. It takes place, on the contrary, when the imagination fails to present an object which might, if only in principle, come to match a concept. We have the Idea of the world (the totality of what is), but we do not have the capacity to show an example of it. We have the Idea of the simple (that which cannot be broken down, decomposed), but we cannot illustrate it with a sensible object which would be a 'case' of it. We can conceive the infinitely great, the infinitely powerful, but every presentation of an object destined to 'make visible' this absolute greatness or power appears to us painfully inadequate. Those are Ideas of which no presentation is possible. Therefore, they impart no knowledge about reality (experience); they also prevent the free union of the faculties which gives rise to the sentiment of the beautiful; and they prevent the formation and the stabilization of taste. They can be said to be unpresentable.

I shall call modern the art which devotes its 'little technical expertise' (son 'petit technique'), as Diderot used to say, to present the fact that the unpresentable exists. To make visible that there is something which can be conceived and which can neither be seen nor made visible: this is what is at stake in modern painting. But how to make visible that there is something which cannot be seen? Kant himself shows the way when he names 'formlessness, the absence of form', as a possible index to the unpresentable. He also says of the empty 'abstraction' which the imagination experiences when in search for a presentation of the infinite (another unpresentable): this abstraction itself is like a presentation of the infinite, its 'negative presentation'. He cites the commandment, 'Thou shalt not make graven images' (Exodus), as the most sublime passage in the Bible in that it forbids all presentation of the Absolute. Little needs to be added to those observations to outline an aesthetic of sublime paintings. As painting, it will of course 'present' something though negatively; it will therefore avoid figuration or representation. It will be 'white' like one of Malevitch's squares; it will enable us to see only by making it impossible to see; it will please only by causing pain. One recognizes in those instructions the axioms of avant-gardes in painting, inasmuch as they devote themselves to making an allusion to the unpresentable by means of visible presentations. [. . .]

The postmodern

What, then, is the postmodern? What place does it or does it not occupy in the vertiginous work of the questions hurled at the rules of image and narration? It is undoubtedly a part of the modern. All that has been received, if only yesterday (*modo, modo*, Petronius used to say), must be suspected. What space does Cézanne challenge? The Impressionists'. What object do Picasso and Braque attack? Cézanne's. What presupposition does Duchamp break with in 1912? That which says one must make a painting, be it cubist. And Buren questions that other presupposition which he believes had survived untouched by the work of Duchamp: the place of presentation of the work. In an amazing acceleration, the generations precipitate themselves. A work can become modern only if it is first postmodern. Postmodernism thus understood is not modernism at its end but in the nascent state, and this state is constant.

Yet I would like not to remain with this slightly mechanistic meaning of the word. If it is true that modernity takes place in the withdrawal of the real and according to the sublime relation between the presentable and the conceivable, it is possible, within this relation, to distinguish two modes (to use the musician's language). The emphasis can be placed on the powerlessness of the faculty of presentation, on the nostalgia for presence felt by the human subject, on the obscure and futile will which inhabits him in spite of everything. The emphasis can be placed, rather, on the power of the faculty to conceive, on its 'inhumanity' so to speak (it was the quality Apollinaire demanded of modern artists), since it is not the business of our understanding whether or not human sensibility or imagination can match what it conceives. The emphasis can also be placed on the increase of being and the jubilation which result from the invention of new rules of the game, be it pictorial, artistic or any other. What I have in mind will become clear if we dispose very schematically a few names on the chessboard of the history of avant-gardes: on the side of melancholia, the German Expressionists and on the side of *novatio*, Braque and Picasso, on the former Malevitch and on the latter Lissitsky, on the one Chirico and on the other Duchamp. The nuance which distinguishes these two modes may be infinitesimal; they often coexist in the same piece, are almost indistinguishable; and yet they testify to a difference (*un différend*) on which the fate of thought depends and will depend for a long time, between regret and assay.

The work of Proust and that of Joyce both allude to something which does not allow itself to be made present. Allusion, to which Paolo Fabbri recently called my attention, is perhaps a form of expression indispensable to the works which belong to an aesthetic of the sublime. In Proust, what is being eluded as the price to pay for this allusion is the identity of consciousness, a victim to the excess of time (*au trop de temps*). But in Joyce, it is the identity of writing which is the victim of an excess of the book (*au trop de livre*) or of literature.

Proust calls forth the unpresentable by means of a language unaltered in its syntax and vocabulary and of a writing which in many of its operators still belongs to the genre of novelistic narration. The literary institution, as Proust inherits it from Balzac and Flaubert, is admittedly subverted in that the hero is no longer a character but the inner consciousness of time, and in that the diegetic diachrony, already damaged by Flaubert, is here put in question because of the narrative voice. Nevertheless, the unity of the book, the odyssey of that consciousness, even if it is deferred from chapter to chapter, is not seriously challenged: the identity of the writing with itself throughout the labyrinth of the interminable narration is enough to connote such unity, which has been compared to that of *The Phenomenology of Mind*.

Joyce allows the unpresentable to become perceptible in his writing itself, in the signifier. The whole range of available narrative and even stylistic operators is put into play without concern for the unity of the whole, and new operators are tried. The grammar and vocabulary of literary language are no longer accepted as given; rather, they appear as academic forms, as rituals originating in piety (as Nietzsche said) which prevent the unpresentable from being put forward.

Here, then, lies the difference: modern aesthetics is an aesthetic of the sublime, though a nostalgic one. It allows the unpresentable to be put forward only as the missing contents; but the form, because of its recognizable consistency, continues to offer to the reader or viewer matter for solace and pleasure. Yet these sentiments do not constitute the real sublime sentiment, which is in an intrinsic combination of pleasure and pain: the pleasure that reason should exceed all presentation, the pain that imagination or sensibility should not be equal to the concept.

The postmodern would be that which, in the modern, puts forward the unpresentable in presentation itself; that which denies itself the solace of good forms, the consensus of a taste which would make it possible to share collectively the nostalgia for the unattainable; that which searches for new presentations, not in order to enjoy them but in order to impart a stronger sense of the unpresentable. A postmodern artist or writer is in the position of a philosopher: the text he writes, the work he produces are not in principle governed by preestablished rules, and they cannot be judged according to a determining judgement, by applying familiar categories to the text or to the work. Those rules and categories are what the work of art itself is looking for. The artist and the writer, then, are working without rules in order to formulate the rules of what *will have been done*. Hence the fact that work and text have the characters of an *event*; hence also, they always come too late for their author, or, what amounts to the same thing, their being put into work, their realization (*mise en oeuvre*) always begin too soon. *Post modern* would have to be understood according to the paradox of the future (*post*) *anterior* (*modo*).

EXERCISE: Choose a realist play and an avant-garde modernist play (e.g. Luigi Pirandello's *Six Characters in Search of an Author*, Eugene O'Neill's *The Emperor Jones*, Alfred Jarry's *Ubu Rex*) and, comparing the two, discuss how the historical emergence of the latter might be said to have challenged realism as a dramatic form. If the avant-garde work breaks the 'rules' of realism, what are those rules thereby revealed to be? What ideas or beliefs – about theatre *and* reality – underpin realism and how does the modernist work refute or 'shatter' them? How must the spectator read the objects or events or individuals of stage realism, and how is the mode of reading required by the modernist play different? You are seeking the assumptions underpinning the form itself.

Now include a recent piece of live art in your deliberations. What does it reveal about the modernist work's own form and under-lying assumptions, and the modes of interpretation it demands of an audience? Does live art represent the final Lyotardian 'shattering of reality' or does it too cling to rules of performance or representa-tion? Can you conceive of a form of performance which would challenge it?

Part three

Performing gender and sexual identity

The current phase of feminist thought may be dated back to the 1949 publication of Simone de Beauvoir's *The Second Sex* (published in English in 1953), a work which paved the way for some of the pioneering writings of the movement (e.g. Friedan 1963, Millett 1969, Greer 1970). But it was largely in the 1970s that, alongside feminist action of a directly political kind, the profound 'theorization' of feminism took place, laying the foundation for its current position as one of the most rigorous of critical perspectives. Instrumental in this was the impact of a number of French theorists – notably Hélène Cixous (b. 1937), Luce Irigaray (b. 1930) and Julia Kristeva (b. 1941) – who employed tools provided by structuralism, post-structuralism, semiotics and contemporary psychoanalysis to address questions of women's subjection and representation. Out of this period of development emerged three broad tendencies: *liberal* or *bourgeois feminism* is generally the least thoroughgoing in its analysis, critiquing the status quo for its failure to offer women the same opportunities as men; *radical feminism* usually operates with essentialist assumptions, seeking those qualities it deems inherent to women and, in an inversion of traditional value-systems, valorizing them; *socialist* or *materialist feminism* addresses the feminine as entirely of social and historical construction, interrogating

the terms and means of that construction in an effort to produce an empowering understanding of it (see Eagleton (ed.) 1986, Showalter (ed.) 1985). Despite such diversity, however, there is widespread agreement on two basic principles. The first is the firm distinction between biological sex and the *cultural* construct that is gender. The second is the recognition that, for women, 'the personal is political'; that women's oppression occurs not only in the traditional arenas of political conflict – governmental politics and the workplace – but in the home, within social relationships and day-to-day behaviours, and as a feature of cultural identity. Although it too was informed by political actions of the late 1960s and 1970s, the radical theorization of sexuality has a shorter history. Perhaps the most influential figure in its recent development was Michel Foucault (1926–84), whose three volumes of *The History of Sexuality* not only chart the formation of 'legitimate' sexual identities but also provide a conceptual framework within which sexuality *per se* can be seen as socially constructed. Owing to the obvious consonance between gender and sexual identity, which negotiate some of the same political structures, feminist theory and queer theory or theories of sexual dissidence have been placed together in this one, large section.

All the extracts chosen for Part three are arguably materialist in outlook, not least because its focus is the signification of gender and sexual identity via the emphatically material practice of performance. The pieces by Irigaray and Cixous exemplify two key tendencies in feminist theories of gender, the first dealing with the commodification of women by men, the second with the symbolic positioning of women within the hierarchical binaries of patriarchal thought. Judith Butler's (b.1956) work is central to the study of performance because of her conceptualization of gender and sexual identity as inherently performative. Elin Diamond (b. 1948) proposes a mode of resistance to hegemonic constructions of gender. Moe Meyer (b. 1951) analyses a performative regime which subverts given notions of sexual identity.

(In this volume, see also **Grosz, Mulvey.**)

Further reading: Austin 1990, Eagleton (ed.) 1986, Moi 1985 and Todd 1988 offer good, general introductions to feminist theory, accessible to the beginner; Aston 1995, Case (ed.) 1990 and Parker and Kosofsky Sedgwick (eds) 1995 bring feminist theory to bear on performance, while Goodman, de Gay and Shaw (eds) 1999 broaden the perspective to address gender *per se*; Jagose 1997 and Weeks 1989 are excellent introductions to queer theory and the study of sexuality, Dollimore 1991, Meyer (ed.) 1994, Sinfield 1994 and Weeks 1985, 1991 are more advanced studies, while Foucault's three-volume work (1979, 1987 and 1988) comprises what is perhaps the most comprehensive and influential exploration of sexuality to date, essential reading for anyone who intends to specialize in this area.

3.1 Constructing gender I: The property model

Luce Irigaray, from *This Sex Which Is Not One*, trans. Catherine Porter with Carolyn Burke, Ithaca: Cornell University Press, 1985 [originally published 1977]

[One of the most influential feminist theorists to emerge from France in the 1970s (along with Hélène Cixous and Julia Kristeva), Irigaray has consistently focused on the way women are excluded from both the cultural and the socio-economic systems of patriarchal society. Functioning according to what she terms 'the logic of sameness', such systems typically deploy Woman symbolically as Man's 'other', the negative mirror-image against which he defines himself (1985a). Represented only in relation to Man, women are thus denied any means of self-representation. In the following piece she extends this logic, employing concepts drawn from Marxist economics to critique those anthropological theories which hold that the social order *per se* is founded on the exchange of women (see also Rubin 1975). By governing whom one may marry, the rules of exogamy and endogamy effectively determine what relationships can be formed between and within social groups, and hence the pattern of social relations overall. But in thus reducing real women to tokens within a male symbolic or economic system, this exchange in fact constitutes a process of commodification, imposing on them identities which are a function of their value to men.]

The society we know, our own culture, is based upon the exchange of women. Without the exchange of women, we are told, we would fall back into the anarchy (?) of the natural world, the randomness (?) of the animal kingdom. The passage into the social order, into the symbolic order, into order as such, is assured by the fact that men, or gr_____ _____ ____ _____ late women among themselves, according to a rule k_____ taboo.

Whatever familial form this prohibition may ta_____ of society, its signification has a much broader impact. dation of the economic, social and cultural order tha_____ centuries.

Why exchange women? Because they are 'scarce [commodities] . . . essential to the life of the group', the anthropologist tells us.[1] Why this characteristic of scarcity, given the biological equilibrium between male and female births? Because the 'deep polygamous tendency, which exists among all men, always makes the number of available women seem insufficient. Let us add that, even if there were as many women as men, these women would not all be equally desirable . . . and that, by defini- tion . . ., the most desirable women must form a minority.'[2]

Are men all equally desirable? Do women have no tendency toward polygamy? The good anthropologist does not raise such questions. *A fortiori*: why are men not objects of exchange among women? It is because women's bodies – through their use, consumption and circulation – provide for the condition making social life and culture possible, although they remain an unknown 'infrastructure' of the elaboration of that social life and culture. The exploitation of the matter that has been sexualized female is so integral a part of our sociocultural horizon that there is no way to interpret it except within this horizon.

In still other words: all the systems of exchange that organize patri- archal societies and all the modalities of productive work that are recognized, valued and rewarded in these societies are men's business. The production of women, signs and commodities is always referred back to men (when a man buys a girl, he 'pays' the father or the brother, not the mother . . .), and they always pass from one man to another, from one group of men to another. The work force is thus always assumed to be masculine, and 'products' are objects to be used, objects of transaction among men alone.

Which means that the possibility of our social life, of our culture, depends upon a ho(m)mo-sexual monopoly? The law that orders our society is the exclusive valorization of men's needs/desires, of exchanges among men. What the anthropologist calls the passage from nature to culture thus amounts to the institution of the reign of hom(m)o-sexuality. Not in an 'immediate' practice, but in its 'social' mediation. From this point on, patriarchal societies might be interpreted as societies functioning in the mode of 'semblance'. The value of symbolic and imaginary produc- tions is superimposed upon, and even substituted for, the value of relations of material, natural, and corporal (re)production.

In this new matrix of History, in which man begets man as his own likeness, wives, daughters and sisters have value only in that they serve as the possibility of, and potential benefit in, relations among men. The use of and traffic in women subtend and uphold the reign of masculine hom(m)o-sexuality, even while they maintain that hom(m)o-sexuality in speculations, mirror games, identifications and more or less rivalrous appropriations, which defer its real practice. Reigning everywhere, although prohibited in practice, hom(m)o-sexuality is played out through the bodies of women, matter or sign, and heterosexuality has been up to now just an alibi for the smooth workings of man's relations with himself, of relations among men. Whose 'sociocultural endogamy' excludes the participation of that other, so foreign to the social order: woman. Exogamy doubtless requires that one leave one's family, tribe, or clan, in order to make alliances. All the same, it does not tolerate marriage with populations that are too far away, too far removed from the prevailing cultural rules. A sociocultural endogamy would thus forbid commerce with women. Men make commerce of them, but they do not enter into any exchanges *with* them. Is this perhaps all the more true because exogamy is an economic issue, perhaps even subtends economy as such? The exchange of women as goods accompanies and stimulates exchanges of other 'wealth' among groups of men. The economy – in both the narrow and the broad sense – that is in place in our societies thus requires that women lend themselves to alienation in consumption, and to exchanges in which they do not participate, and that men be exempt from being used and circulated like commodities.

Marx's analysis of commodities as the elementary form of capitalist wealth can thus be understood as an interpretation of the status of woman in so-called patriarchal societies. The organization of such societies, and the operation of the symbolic system on which this organization is based – a symbolic system whose instrument and representative is the proper name: the name of the father, the name of God – contain in a nuclear form the developments that Marx defines as characteristic of a capitalist regime: the submission of 'nature' to a 'labor' on the part of men who thus constitute 'nature' as use value and exchange value; the division of labor among private producer-owners who exchange their women-commodities among themselves, but also among producers and exploiters or exploitees of the social order; the standardization of women according to proper names that determine their equivalences; a tendency to accumulate wealth, that is, a tendency for the representatives of the most 'proper' names – the leaders – to capitalize more women than the others; a progression of the social work of the symbolic toward greater and greater abstraction; and so forth.

To be sure, the means of production have evolved, new techniques have been developed, but it does seem that as soon as the father-man was assured of his reproductive power and had marked his products with his

name, that is, from the very origin of private property and the patriarchal family, social exploitation occurred. In other words, all the social
regimes of 'History' are based upon the exploitation of one 'class' of
producers, namely, women. Whose reproductive use value (reproductive
of children and of the labor force) and whose constitution as exchange
value underwrite the symbolic order as such, without any compensation
in kind going to them for that 'work'. For such compensation would
imply a double system of exchange, that is, a shattering of the monopo-
lization of the proper name (and of what it signifies as appropriative
power) by father-men.

Thus the social body would be redistributed into producer-subjects
no longer functioning as commodities because they provided the standard
of value for commodities and into commodity-objects that ensured the
circulation of exchange without participating in it as subjects. [. . .]

On the status of women in such a social order

What makes such an order possible, what assures its foundation, is thus
the exchange of women. The circulation of women among men is what
establishes the operations of society, at least of patriarchal society. Whose
presuppositions include the following: the appropriation of nature by man;
the transformation of nature according to 'human' criteria, defined by
men alone; the submission of nature to labor and technology; the reduction of its material, corporeal, perceptible qualities to man's practical
concrete activity; the equality of women among themselves, but in terms
of laws of equivalence that remain external to them; the constitution of
women as 'objects' that emblematize the materialization of relations among
men, and so on.

In such a social order, women thus represent a natural value and a
social value. Their 'development' lies in the passage from one to the other.
But this passage never takes place simply.

As mother, woman remains on the side of (re)productive nature and,
because of this, man can never fully transcend his relation to the 'natural'.
His social existence, his economic structures and his sexuality are always
tied to the work of nature: these structures thus always remain at the
level of the earliest appropriation, that of the constitution of nature as
landed property, and of the earliest labor, which is agricultural. But this
relationship to productive nature, an insurmountable one, has to be denied
so that relations among men may prevail. This means that mothers, reproductive instruments marked with the name of the father and enclosed in

his house, must be private property, excluded from exchange. The *incest taboo* represents this refusal to allow productive nature to enter into exchanges among men. As both natural value and use value, mothers cannot circulate in the form of commodities without threatening the very existence of the social order. Mothers are essential to its (re)production (particularly inasmuch as they are (re)productive of children and of the labor force: through maternity, child-rearing, and domestic maintenance in general). Their responsibility is to maintain the social order without intervening so as to change it. Their products are legal tender in that order, moreover, only if they are recognized within his law: that is, only in so far as they are appropriated by him. Society is the place where man engenders himself, where man is born into 'human', 'super-natural' existence.

The virginal woman, on the other hand, is pure exchange value. She is nothing but the possibility, the place, the sign of relations among men. In and of herself, she does not exist: she is a simple envelope veiling what is really at stake in social exchange. In this sense, her natural body disappears into its representative function. *Red blood* remains on the mother's side, but it has no price, as such, in the social order; woman, for her part, as medium of exchange, is no longer anything but *semblance*. The ritualized passage from woman to mother is accomplished by *the violation of an envelope*: the hymen, which has taken on the value of *taboo*, the taboo of virginity. Once deflowered woman is relegated to the status of use value, to her entrapment in private property; she is removed from exchange among men.

The *prostitute* remains to be considered. Explicitly condemned by the social order, she is implicitly tolerated. No doubt because the break between usage and exchange is, in her case, less clear-cut? In her case, the qualities of woman's body are 'useful'. However, these qualities have 'value' only because they have already been appropriated by a man, and because they serve as the locus of relations – hidden ones – between men. Prostitution amounts to *usage that is exchanged*. Usage that is not merely potential: it has already been realized. The woman's body is valuable because it has already been used. In the extreme case, the more it has served, the more it is worth. Not because its natural assets have been put to use this way, but, on the contrary, because its nature has been 'used up', and has become once again no more than a vehicle for relations among men.

Mother, virgin, prostitute: these are the social roles imposed on women. The characteristics of (so-called) feminine sexuality derive from them: the valorization of reproduction and nursing; faithfulness; modesty, ignorance of and even lack of interest in sexual pleasure; a passive acceptance of men's 'activity'; seductiveness, in order to arouse the consumers' desire while offering herself as its material support without getting pleasure herself ... *Neither as mother nor as virgin nor as prostitute has woman any right to her own pleasure.*

Of course the theoreticians of sexuality are sometimes astonished by women's frigidity. But, according to them, this frigidity is explained more by an impotence inherent to feminine 'nature' than by the submission of that nature to a certain type of society. However, *what is required of a 'normal' feminine sexuality is oddly evocative of the characteristics of the status of a commodity.* With references to and rejections of the 'natural' – physiological and organic nature, and so on – that are equally ambiguous.

And, in addition:

- Just as nature has to be subjected to man in order to become a commodity, so, it appears, does 'the development of a normal woman'. A development that amounts, for the feminine, to subordination to the forms and laws of masculine activity. The rejection of the mother – imputed to woman – would find its 'cause' here.

- Just as, in commodities, natural utility is overridden by the exchange function, so the properties of a woman's body have to be suppressed and subordinated to the exigencies of its transformation into an object of circulation among men.

- Just as a commodity has no mirror it can use to reflect itself, so woman serves as reflection, as image of and for man, but lacks specific qualities of her own. Her value-invested form amounts to what man inscribes in and on its matter: that is, her body.

- Just as commodities cannot make exchanges among themselves without the intervention of a subject that measures them against a standard, so it is with women. Distinguished, divided, separated, classified as like and unlike, according to whether they have been judged exchangeable. In themselves, among themselves, they are amorphous and confused: natural body, maternal body, doubtless useful to the consumer, but without any possible identity or communicable value.

- Just as commodities, despite their resistance, become more or less autonomous repositories for the value of human work, so, as mirrors of and for man, women more or less unwittingly come to represent the danger of a disappropriation of masculine power: the phallic mirage.

- Just as a commodity finds the expression of its value in an equivalent – in the last analysis, a general one – that necessarily remains external to it, so woman derives her price from her relation to the male sex, constituted as a transcendental value: the phallus. And indeed the enigma of 'value' lies in the most elementary relation among commodities. Among women. For, uprooted from their 'nature', they no longer relate to each other except in terms of what they represent in men's desire, and according to the 'forms' that this imposes upon them. Among themselves, they are separated by his speculations.

This means that the division of 'labor' – sexual labor in particular – requires that woman maintain in her own body the material substratum of the object of desire, but that she herself never have access to desire. The economy of desire – of exchange – is man's business. And that economy subjects women to a schism that is necessary to symbolic operations: red blood/semblance; body/value-invested envelope; matter/medium of exchange; (re)productive nature/fabricated femininity ... That schism – characteristic of all speaking nature, someone will surely object – is experienced by women without any possible profit to them. And without any way for them to transcend it. They are not even 'conscious' of it. The symbolic system that cuts them in two this way is in no way appropriate to them. In them, 'semblance' remains external, foreign to 'nature'. *Socially*, they are 'objects' for and among men and furthermore they cannot do anything but mimic a 'language' that they have not produced; *naturally*, they remain amorphous, suffering from drives without any possible representatives or representations. For them, the transformation of the natural into the social does not take place, except to the extent that they function as components of private property, or as commodities.

Notes

1   Claude Lévi-Strauss (1969) *The Elementary Structures of Kinship*, trans. James Harle Bell, John Richard von Sturmer and Rodney Needham (Harmondsworth: Penguin, 1969), p. 36.
2   *Ibid.*, p. 38.

EXERCISE: Choose a performance text from the traditional canon which has at its centre relationships between men and women (e.g. Aphra Behn's *The Rover*, William Shakespeare's *Measure for Measure*, August Strindberg's *Miss Julie*, Frank Wedekind's 'Lulu' plays; alternatively, Giuseppe Verdi's *La Traviata*, or Peter Tchaikovsky and George Balanchine's *Swan Lake*). First, consider how the female characters are defined. To what extent are their roles within the drama a function of their relationships with men – as daughters, wives, lovers, etc.? How far do they conform to the stereotypes of mother, virgin, whore, and so on, or those of some other classificatory scheme based on male concerns or 'usage'? What moral or ethical 'value' is each woman granted in the piece, and on the basis of what underlying value system are they so judged?

Now examine the temporal figuring of women, in the unfolding story. When a female character undergoes changes in condition or state, what does she move from and to, and what themes or values underpin that movement – what is illustrated *by* it? Are her different states self-defined or is she 'exchanged', moving between different relationships with men? If there is a female character who refuses orthodox or male-defined roles, what is her fate in the tale?

3.2 Constructing gender II: The culture/nature model

Hélène Cixous, from 'Sorties: Out and Out: Attacks/Ways Out/Forays', in *The Newly Born Woman* (with Catherine Clément), trans. Betsy Wing, London: I. B. Tauris, 1996 [originally published 1975]

[Perhaps the most important influences bearing on Cixous's work are those of post-structuralist philosopher Jacques Derrida (b. 1930) and psychoanalyst Jacques Lacan (1901–81). For Lacan, gender is a fundamental component of subjectivity (see **Althusser**), entry into the realm of culture, 'the Symbolic', being conditional upon one's negotiation of the binary Man/Woman (1977). It is precisely binary conceptual structures of this kind that Derrida subjects to 'deconstruction', disrupting the ground of dominant forms of logic by demonstrating the instability of their founding oppositions

(1978). In a comparable movement, Cixous in the following piece critiques those dichotomies via which the masculine and feminine are constructed oppositionally, and in which Woman is always located at the negative pole, construed as passive in contrast to active Man. If Cixous's writing is poetic, emphatically non-theoretical in form, this is in line with her project. It is via the formations of theoretical, philosophical language, she argues, that gendered effects of power are produced, and, in rejecting such language, she denies the structures of thought derived from it.]

Where is she?
Activity/passivity
Sun/Moon
Culture/Nature
Day/Night

Father/Mother
Head/Heart
Intelligible/Palpable
Logos/Pathos.
Form, convex, step, advance, semen, progress.
Matter, concave, ground – where steps are taken, holding- and dumping-
    ground.
Man
——
Woman

Always the same metaphor: we follow it, it carries us, beneath all its figures, wherever discourse is organized. If we read or speak, the same thread or double braid is leading us throughout literature, philosophy, criticism, centuries of representation and reflection.
Thought has always worked through opposition,
Speaking/Writing
Parole/Écriture
High/Low

Through dual, hierarchical oppositions. Superior/Inferior. Myths, legends, books. Philosophical systems. Everywhere (where) ordering intervenes, where a law organizes what is thinkable by oppositions (dual, irreconcilable; or sublatable, dialectical). And all these pairs of oppositions are *couples*. Does that mean something? Is the fact that Logocentrism subjects thought – all concepts, codes and values – to a binary system, related to 'the' couple, man/woman?

Nature/History
Nature/Art
Nature/Mind
Passion/Action

Theory of culture, theory of society, symbolic systems in general – art, religion, family, language – it is all developed while bringing the same schemes to light. And the movement whereby each opposition is set up to make sense is the movement through which the couple is destroyed. A universal battlefield. Each time, a war is let loose. Death is always at work.

Father/son   Relations of authority, privilege, force.

The Word/Writing   Relations: opposition, conflict, sublation, return.

Master/slave   Violence. Repression.

We see that 'victory' always comes down to the same thing: things get hierarchical. Organization by hierarchy makes all conceptual organization subject to man. Male privilege, shown in the opposition between *activity* and *passivity*, which he uses to sustain himself. Traditionally, the question of sexual difference is treated by coupling it with the opposition: activity/passivity.

There are repercussions. Consulting the history of philosophy – since philosophical discourse both orders and reproduces all thought – one notices that it is marked by an absolute *constant* which orders values and which is precisely this opposition, activity/passivity.

Moreover, woman is always associated with passivity in philosophy. Whenever it is a question of woman, when one examines kinship structures, when a family model is brought into play. In fact, as soon as the question of ontology raises its head, as soon as one asks oneself 'what is it?', as soon as there is intended meaning. Intention: desire, authority – examine them and you are led right back . . . to the father. It is even possible not to notice that there is no place whatsoever for woman in the calculations. Ultimately the world of 'being' can function while precluding the mother. No need for a mother, as long as there is some motherliness: and it is the father, then, who acts the part, who is the mother. Either woman is passive or she does not exist. What is left of her is unthinkable, unthought. Which certainly means that she is not thought, that she does not enter into the oppositions, that she does not make a couple with the father (who makes a couple with the son). [. . .]

And if we consult literary history, it is the same story. It all comes back to man – to *his* torment, his desire to be (at) the origin. Back to the father. There is an intrinsic connection between the philosophical and the literary (to the extent that it conveys meaning, literature is under the command of the philosophical) and the phallocentric. Philosophy is constructed on the premise of woman's abasement. Subordination of the feminine to the masculine order, which gives the appearance of being the condition for the machinery's functioning. [...]

Once upon a time ...

One cannot yet say of the following history 'it's just a story'. It's a tale still true today. Most women who have awakened remember having slept, *having been put to sleep.*

Once upon a time ... once ... and once again.

Beauties slept in their woods, waiting for princes to come and wake them up. In their beds, in their glass coffins, in their childhood forests like dead women. Beautiful, but passive; hence desirable: all mystery emanates from them. It is men who like to play dolls. As we have known since Pygmalion. Their old dream: to be god the mother. The best mother, the second mother, the one who gives the second birth.

She sleeps, she is intact, eternal, absolutely powerless. He has no doubt that she has been waiting for him for ever.

The secret of her beauty, kept for him: she has the perfection of something finished. Or not begun. However, she is breathing. Just enough life – and not too much. Then he will kiss her. So that when she opens her eyes she will see only *him*; him in place of everything, all-him.

– This dream is so satisfying! Whose is it? What desire gets something out of it?

He leans over her ... Cut. The tale is finished. Curtain. Once awake (him or her), it would be an entirely different story. Then there would be two people, perhaps. You never know with women. And the voluptuous simplicity of the preliminaries would no longer take place.

Harmony, desire, exploit, search – all these movements are preconditions – of woman's arrival. Preconditions, more precisely, of her *arising*. She is lying down, he stands up. She arises – end of the dream – what follows is socio-cultural: he makes her lots of babies, she spends her youth in labor; from bed to bed, until the age at which the thing isn't 'woman' for him any more. [...]

Already I know all about the 'reality' that supports History's progress: everything throughout the centuries depends on the distinction between the Selfsame, the ownself (– what is mine, hence what is good) and that which limits it: so now what menaces my-own-good (good never being anything other than what is good-for-me) is the 'other.' What is the 'Other'? If it is truly the 'other', there is nothing to say; it cannot be theorized.

The 'other' escapes me. It is elsewhere, outside: absolutely other. It doesn't settle down. But in History, of course, what is called 'other' is an alterity that does settle down, that falls into the dialectical circle. It is the other in a hierarchically organized relationship in which the same is what rules, names, defines, and assigns 'its' other. With the dreadful simplicity that orders the movement Hegel erected as a system, society trots along before my eyes reproducing to perfection the mechanism of the death struggle: the reduction of a 'person' to a 'nobody' to the position of 'other' – the inexorable plot of racism. There has to be some 'other' – no master without a slave, no economico-political power without exploitation, no dominant class without cattle under the yoke, no 'Frenchmen' without wogs, no Nazis without Jews, no property without exclusion – an exclusion that has its limits and is part of the dialectic. If there were no other, one would invent it. Besides, that is what masters do: they have their slaves made to order. Line for line. They assemble the machine and keep the alternator supplied so that it reproduces all the oppositions that make economy and thought run.

The paradox of otherness is that, of course, at no moment in History is it tolerated or possible as such. The other is there only to be reappropriated, recap-tured, and destroyed as other. Even the exclusion is not an exclusion. Algeria was not France, but it was 'French'. [. . .]

The empire of the selfame
(empirically from bad to worse)

[. . .] All the ways of differently thinking the history of power, property, masculine domination, the formation of the State, and the ideological equipment have some effect. But the change that is in process concerns more than just the question of 'origin'. There is phallocentrism. History has never produced or recorded anything else – which does not mean that this form is destinal or natural. Phallocentrism is the enemy. Of everyone. Men's loss in phallocentrism is different from but as serious as women's. And it is time to change. To invent the other history.

There is 'destiny' no more than there is 'nature' or 'essence' as such. Rather, there are living structures that are caught and sometimes rigidly set within historico-cultural limits so mixed up with the scene of History that for a long time it has been impossible (and it is still very difficult) to think or even imagine an 'elsewhere'. We are presently living in a transitional period – one in which it seems possible that the classic structure might be split.

It is impossible to predict what will become of sexual difference – in another time (in two or three hundred years?). But we must make no mistake: men and women are caught up in a web of age-old cultural determinations that are almost unanalyzable in their complexity. One can no more speak of 'woman' than of 'man' without being trapped within an ideological theater where the proliferation of representations, images, reflections, myths, identifications, transform, deform, constantly change everyone's Imaginary and invalidate in advance any conceptualization.

Nothing allows us to rule out the possibility of radical transformation of behaviors, mentalities, roles, political economy – whose effects on libidinal economy are unthinkable – today. Let us simultaneously imagine a general change in all the structures of training, education, supervision – hence in the structures of reproduction of ideological results. And let us imagine a real liberation of sexuality, that is to say, a transformation of each one's relationship to his or her body (and to the other body), an approximation to the vast, material, organic, sensuous universe that we are. This cannot be accomplished, of course, without political transformations that are equally radical. (Imagine!) Then 'femininity' and 'masculinity' would inscribe quite differently their effects of difference, their economy, their relationship to expenditure, to lack, to the gift. What today appears to be 'feminine' or 'masculine' would no longer amount to the same thing. No longer would the common logic of difference be organized with the opposition that remains dominant. Difference would be a bunch of new differences.

But we are still floundering – with few exceptions – in Ancient History.

EXERCISE: Begin by briefly compiling a catalogue of those binary oppositions which structure gender in your culture, matching every 'natural' quality of the feminine with its masculine opposite. As you note each binary, try to think of a 'text' (play, film, painting, myth, anecdote) as illustration and evidence. Is there common ground in all or most of the terms attached to women, or to men? How consistently are the dichotomies you have found reproduced in society as a whole?

Now, choosing a production you have seen (or one for which you can find good documentation), analyse the men's and women's costumes to find the qualities they attribute to each gender. Bear in mind that a single item may suggest several things simultaneously: in hiding a woman's legs, a ball gown may declare her chastity, deny her corporeality to make her 'ethereal', hamper her movements to suggest her suitability to domestic settings only, and so on; try to be exhaustive. Now compare the men's and women's costumes to find those associated qualities which form dichotomous pairs. You are seeking the ways in which the objects which clad and obscure real bodies grant them cultural meaning.

3.3 The drag act

Judith Butler, from *Gender Trouble: Feminism and the Subversion of Identity*, London: Routledge, 1990

[Butler's theorization of gender and sexual identity is among the most challenging, for it demands a revision of the very philosophical assumptions on which more orthodox views rest. Derived in large part from philosopher René Descartes, our everyday conception of the self is fundamentally dualistic, insisting on the distinction between body and mind and granting the latter primacy. It is on this basis that we commonly view the behaviours associated with gender and sexual identity as expressions of an essence located in the individual psyche. Butler's reversal of this causality, however, presents 'essential' identity as a fiction, conjured by the socially coded actions of the body. Her evocative description of gender as contrived via a 'stylized repetition of acts' thus represents a thoroughgoing materialism, for it rejects the very possibility of a metaphysical explanation of selfhood in favour of one grounded in the signifying power of the concrete body.]

What is the prohibitive law that generates the corporeal stylization of gender, the fantasied and fantastic figuration of the body? We have already considered the incest taboo and the prior taboo against homosexuality as the generative moments of gender identity, the prohibitions that produce identity along the culturally intelligible grids of an idealized and compulsory heterosexuality. That disciplinary production of gender effects a false stabilization of gender in the interests of the heterosexual construction and regulation of sexuality within the reproductive domain. The construction of coherence conceals the gender discontinuities that run rampant within heterosexual, bisexual and gay and lesbian contexts in which gender does not necessarily follow from sex, and desire, or sexuality generally, does not seem to follow from gender – indeed, where none of these dimensions of significant corporeality express or reflect one another. When the disorganization and disaggregation of the field of bodies disrupt the regulatory fiction of heterosexual coherence, it seems that the expressive model loses its descriptive force. That regulatory ideal is then exposed as a norm and a fiction that disguises itself as a developmental law regulating the sexual field that it purports to describe.

According to the understanding of identification as an enacted fantasy or incorporation, however, it is clear that coherence is desired, wished for, idealized, and that this idealization is an effect of a corporeal signification. In other words, acts, gestures and desire produce the effect of an internal core or substance, but produce this *on the surface* of the body, through the play of signifying absences that suggest, but never reveal, the organizing principle of identity as a cause. Such acts, gestures, enactments, generally construed, are *performative* in the sense that the essence or identity that they otherwise purport to express are *fabrications* manufactured and sustained through corporeal signs and other discursive means. That the gendered body is performative suggests that it has no ontological status apart from the various acts which constitute its reality. This also suggests that, if that reality is fabricated as an interior essence, that very interiority is an effect and function of a decidedly public and social discourse, the public regulation of fantasy through the surface politics of the body, the gender border control that differentiates inner from outer, and so institutes the 'integrity' of the subject. In other words, acts and gestures, articulated and enacted desires create the illusion of an interior and organizing gender core, an illusion discursively maintained for the purposes of the regulation of sexuality within the obligatory frame of reproductive heterosexuality. If the 'cause' of desire, gesture and act can be localized within the 'self' of the actor, then the political regulations and disciplinary practices which produce that ostensibly coherent gender are effectively displaced from view. The displacement of a political and discursive origin of gender identity on to a psychological 'core' precludes an analysis of the political constitution of the gendered subject and its fabricated notions about the ineffable inferiority of its sex or of its true identity.

If the inner truth of gender is a fabrication and if a true gender is a fantasy instituted and inscribed on the surface of bodies, then it seems that genders can be neither true nor false, but are only produced as the truth effects of a discourse of primary and stable identity. In *Mother Camp: Female Impersonators in America*, anthropologist Esther Newton suggests that the structure of impersonation reveals one of the key fabricating mechanisms through which the social construction of gender takes place. I would suggest as well that drag fully subverts the distinction between inner and outer psychic space and effectively mocks both the expressive model of gender and the notion of a true gender identity. Newton writes:

> At its most complex, [drag] is a double inversion that says, 'appearance is an illusion.' Drag says [Newton's curious personification] 'my "outside" appearance is feminine, but my essence "inside" [the body] is masculine.' At the same time it symbolizes the opposite inversion; 'my appearance "outside" [my body, my gender] is masculine but my essence "inside" [myself] is feminine.'[1]

Both claims to truth contradict one another and so displace the entire enactment of gender significations from the discourse of truth and falsity.

The notion of an original or primary gender identity is often parodied within the cultural practices of drag, cross-dressing and the sexual stylization of butch/femme identities. Within feminist theory, such parodic identities have been understood to be either degrading to women, in the case of drag and cross-dressing, or an uncritical appropriation of sex-role stereotyping from within the practice of heterosexuality, especially in the case of butch/femme lesbian identities. But the relation between the 'imitation' and the 'original' is, I think, more complicated than that critique generally allows. Moreover, it gives us a clue to the way in which the relationship between primary identification – that is, the original meanings accorded to gender – and subsequent gender experience might be reframed. The performance of drag plays upon the distinction between the anatomy of the performer and the gender that is being performed. But we are actually in the presence of three contingent dimensions of significant corporeality: anatomical sex, gender identity and gender performance. If the anatomy of the performer is already distinct from the gender of the performer, and both of those are distinct from the gender of the performance, then the performance suggests a dissonance not only between sex and performance, but sex and gender, and gender and performance. As much as drag creates a unified picture of 'woman' (what its critics often oppose), it also reveals the distinctness of those aspects of gendered experience which are falsely naturalized as a unity through the regulatory fiction of heterosexual coherence. *In imitating gender, drag implicitly reveals the imitative structure of gender itself – as well as its contingency.* Indeed, part of the pleasure, the giddiness of the performance is in the recognition of a radical contingency in the relation between sex and gender in the face of cultural configurations of causal unities that are regularly assumed to be natural and necessary. In the place of the law of heterosexual coherence, we see sex and gender denaturalized by means of a performance which avows their distinctness and dramatizes the cultural mechanism of their fabricated unity.

The notion of gender parody defended here does not assume that there is an original which such parodic identities imitate. Indeed, the parody is of the very notion of an original; just as the psychoanalytic notion of gender identification is constituted by a fantasy of a fantasy, the transfiguration of an Other who is always already a 'figure' in that double sense, so gender parody reveals that the original identity after which gender fashions itself is an imitation without an origin. To be more precise, it is a production which, in effect – that is, in its effect – postures as an imitation. This perpetual displacement constitutes a fluidity of identities that suggests an openness to resignification and recontextualization; parodic proliferation deprives hegemonic culture and its critics of the claim to naturalized or essentialist gender identities. Although the gender meanings taken up in these parodic styles are clearly part of hegemonic, misogynist culture, they are nevertheless denaturalized and mobilized through their parodic recontextualization. As imitations which effectively displace the meaning of the original, they imitate the myth of originality itself. In the place of an original identification which serves as a determining cause, gender identity might be reconceived as a personal/cultural history of received meanings subject to a set of imitative practices which refer laterally to other imitations and which, jointly, construct the illusion of a primary and interior gendered self or parody the mechanism of that construction. [. . .]

If the body is not a 'being', but a variable boundary, a surface whose permeability is politically regulated, a signifying practice within a cultural field of gender hierarchy and compulsory heterosexuality, then what language is left for understanding this corporeal enactment, gender, that constitutes its 'interior' signification on its surface? Sartre would perhaps have called this act 'a style of being', Foucault, 'a stylistics of existence'. And in my earlier reading of Beauvoir, I suggest that gendered bodies are so many 'styles of the flesh'. These styles are never fully self-styled, for styles have a history, and those histories condition and limit the possibilities. Consider gender, for instance, as *a corporeal style*, an 'act', as it were, which is both intentional and performative, where '*performative*' suggests a dramatic and contingent construction of meaning. [. . .]

In what senses, then, is gender an act? As in other ritual social dramas, the action of gender requires a performance that is *repeated*. This repetition is at once a re-enactment and re-experiencing of a set of meanings already socially established; and it is the mundane and ritualized form of their legitimation.[2] Although there are individual bodies that enact these significations by becoming stylized into gendered modes, this 'action' is a public action. There are temporal and collective dimensions to these actions, and their public character is not inconsequential; indeed, the performance is effected with the strategic aim of maintaining gender within its binary frame – an aim that cannot be attributed to a subject, but, rather, must be understood to found and consolidate the subject.

Gender ought not to be construed as a stable identity or locus of agency from which various acts follow; rather, gender is an identity tenuously constituted in time, instituted in an exterior space through a *stylized repetition of acts*. The effect of gender is produced through the stylization of the body and, hence, must be understood as the mundane way in which bodily gestures, movements and styles of various kinds constitute the illusion of an abiding gendered self. This formulation moves the conception of gender off the ground of a substantial model of identity to one that requires a conception of gender as a constituted *social temporality*. Significantly, if gender is instituted through acts which are internally discontinuous, then the *appearance of substance* is precisely that, a constructed identity, a performative accomplishment which the mundane social audience, including the actors themselves, come to believe and to perform in the mode of belief.

Notes

1   E. Newton (1972) *Mother Camp: Female Impersonators in America* (Chicago: University of Chicago Press), p. 103.

2   See Victor Turner (1974) *Dramas, Fields and Metaphors: Symbolic Action in Human Society* (Ithaca: Cornell University Press). See also Clifford Geertz (1983) 'Blurred Genres: The Refiguration of Thought', in *Local Knowledge: Further Essays in Interpretive Anthropology* (New York: Basic Books).

EXERCISE: In small groups, briefly visit a public place (the cafeteria of your own college, perhaps) and covertly note the bodily behaviours characteristic of the men and the women there. Begin by describing the physical details of each posture, action or movement, only afterwards considering what qualities it symbolically attributes to its gendered performer. When you have sufficient material, compile short catalogues of those behaviours or qualities and discuss what constructions of the masculine and feminine they collectively proffer. Your aim is to fix the 'corporeal styles' unwittingly enacted by men and women in your culture.

Now choose and view a dance duet from a classic Hollywood musical, and analyse its movements for the 'stylized acts' expressive of each dancer's gender. Conduct your analysis in close detail (use the freeze-frame or 'pause' facility, if available), isolating both individuals' gestures, postures and movements, and the interactions between the partners. To what extent does the dance reproduce the behaviours you noted in the first part of the exercise, or their equivalents? Consider which dancer tends to lead and which follows, which displays the freest use of the performance space and which is spatially restrained, who supports and who is supported, and so on. As you proceed, try to link each figure you isolate with comparable actions from the world of everyday behaviour.

3.4 Gestic criticism

Elin Diamond, from 'Brechtian Theory/Feminist Theory: Towards a Gestic Feminist Criticism', in C. Martin (ed.), *A Sourcebook on Feminist Theatre and Performance: On and Beyond the Stage*, London: Routledge, 1996 [original version published 1988]

[Diamond's position in the following piece is somewhat unusual in that she does not regard the literary canon as inherently antagonistic to feminism but proposes the use of **Brecht**'s 'alienation-effect' to feminist theatrical ends. Just as Brecht's techniques were designed to reveal the play's viewpoint as a product of authorial invention, so alienating the female actor from her character, Diamond argues, will render the social constructedness of stage representations of Woman apparent. By enabling the spectator to see gender ideology *as* ideology in this manner, feminist performance is to redraw the relationship between auditorium and stage. Whereas orthodox theatrical strategies reproduce dominant images and gender relations, promoting the kinds of processes described by **Mulvey**, this new relationship is to produce a 'historicization' of character, performer and spectator alike. The ultimate effect, then, is on the viewer's perceptions, creating a triangular gaze in which all the women, real and fictional, are recognized as the focus of social and political forces.]

Now feminists in film studies have been quick to appropriate elements of Brecht's critique of the theatre apparatus.[1] In summer 1974, the British film journal *Screen* published a Brecht issue whose stated purpose was a consideration of Brecht's theoretical texts and the possibility of a revolutionary cinema. In autumn 1975, Laura Mulvey published her influential essay 'Visual Pleasure and Narrative Cinema' in which, employing psychoanalysis 'as a political weapon', she argues that Hollywood film conventions construct a specifically male viewing position by aligning or suturing the male's gaze to that of the fictional hero, and by inviting him thereby both to identify narcissistically with that hero and to fetishize the female (turning her into an object of sexual stimulation).[2] In rejecting this dominant cinematic tradition, Mulvey powerfully invokes Brechtian concepts:

> The first blow against the monolithic accumulation of traditional film conventions . . . is to free the look of the camera into its materiality in time and space and the look of the audience into dialectics, passionate detachment.[3]

Demystifying representation, showing how and when the object of pleasure is made, releasing the spectator from imaginary and illusory identifications – these are crucial elements in Brecht's theoretical project. Yet we feminists in drama and theatre studies have attended more to the critique of the gaze than to the Brechtian intervention that signals a way of dismantling the gaze. Feminist film theorists, fellow-traveling with psychoanalysis and semiotics, have given us a lot to think about, but we, through Brechtian theory, have something to give them: a female body in representation that resists fetishization and a viable position for the female spectator. [. . .]

Gender, *Verfremdungseffekt*

The cornerstone of Brecht's theory is the *Verfremdungseffekt*, the technique of defamiliarizing a word, an idea, a gesture so as to enable the spectator to see or hear it afresh: 'a representation that alienates is one which allows us to recognize its subject, but at the same time makes it seem unfamiliar';[4] 'the A-effect consists of turning an object from something ordinary and immediately accessible into something peculiar, striking, and unexpected'.[5] In performance the actor 'alienates' rather than impersonates her character; she 'quotes' or demonstrates the character's behavior instead of identifying with it. Brecht theorizes that if the performer remains outside the character's feelings, the audience may also, thereby remaining free to analyze and form opinions about the play's 'fable'. *Verfremdungseffekt* also challenges the mimetic property of acting that semioticians call iconicity, the fact that the performer's body conventionally resembles the object (or character) to which it refers. This is why gender critique in the theatre can be so powerful.

Gender refers to the words, gestures, appearances, ideas and behavior that dominant culture understands as indices of feminine or masculine identity. When spectators 'see' gender they are seeing (and reproducing) the cultural signs of gender, and by implication, the gender ideology of a culture. Gender in fact provides a perfect illustration of ideology at work since 'feminine' or 'masculine' behavior usually appears to be a 'natural' – and thus fixed and unalterable – extension of biological sex. Feminist practice that seeks to expose or mock the strictures of gender usually uses some version of the Brechtian A-effect. That is, by alienating (not simply rejecting) iconicity, by foregrounding the expectation of resemblance the ideology of gender is exposed and thrown back to the spectator. [. . .] When gender is 'alienated' or foregrounded, the spectator is enabled to see a sign system *as* a sign system – the appearance, words, gestures, ideas, attitudes, etc., that comprise the gender lexicon become so many illusionistic trappings to be put on or shed at will. Understanding gender as ideology – as a system of beliefs and behavior mapped across the bodies of females and males, which reinforces a social status quo – is to appreciate the continued timeliness of *Verfremdungseffekt*, the purpose of which is to denaturalize and defamiliarize what ideology makes seem normal, acceptable, inescapable.

Sexual difference, the 'not, but'

Gender critique in artistic and discursive practices is often and wrongly confused with another topos in feminist theory: sexual difference. I would propose that 'sexual difference' be understood not as a synonym for gender oppositions but as a possible reference to differences within sexuality. [. . .] Sexual *difference*, then might be seen to destabilize the bipolar oppositions that constitute gender identity.

[. . .] To paraphrase Gayle Rubin, women and men are certainly different, but gender coercively translates the nuanced differences within sexuality into a structure of opposition; male vs female, masculine vs feminine, etc.[6] In my reading of Rubin, the 'sex/gender system', the trace of the difference of sexuality is kept alive within the sterile opposition of gender. I am suggesting that sexual difference is where we imagine, where we theorize; gender is where we live, our social address, although most of us, with an effort, are trying to leave home. Let me put it another way: no feminist can ignore the fact that the language of the battlefield is a system based on difference whose traces contain our most powerful desires.

Keeping differences in view instead of conforming to stable representations of identity, and *linking those differences to a practical politics*, are key to Brecht's theory of the 'not, but', a feature of alienated acting that I read intertextually with the sex/gender system.

> When [an actor] appears on stage, besides what he actually is doing he will at all essential points discover, specify, imply what he is not doing; that is he will act in such a way that the alternative emerges as clearly as possible, that his acting allows the other possibilities to be inferred and only represents one of the possible variants . . . Whatever he doesn't do must be contained and conserved in what he does.[7]

Each action must contain the trace of the action it represses, thus the meaning of each action contains difference. The audience is invited to look beyond representation – beyond what is authoritatively put in view – to the possibilities of as yet unarticulated actions or judgements. [. . .]

The Brechtian 'not, but' is the theatrical and theoretical analog to the subversiveness of sexual difference, because it allows us to imagine the deconstruction of gender – and all other – representations. Such deconstructions dramatize, at least at the level of theory, the infinite play of difference that Derrida calls *écriture* – the superfluity of signification that places meaning beyond capture within the covers of the play or the hours of performance. This is not to deny Brecht's wish for an instructive, analytical theatre; on the contrary, it invites the participatory play of the spectator, and the possibility for which Brecht most devoutly wished, that signification (the production of meaning) continue beyond the play's end, congealing into choice and action after the spectator leaves the theatre.

History, historicization

The sex/gender system requires contextualization. The understanding of women's material conditions in history and the problematics of uncovering 'women's history' are topoi in feminist theory that Brecht's theory of historicization greatly informs. [...] There is a double movement in Brechtian historicization of preserving the 'distinguishing marks' of the past and acknowledging, even foregrounding, the audience's present perspective.[8] When Brecht says that spectators should become historians, he refers both to the spectator's detachment, her 'critical' position, *and* to the fact that she is writing her own history even as she absorbs messages from the stage. Historicization is, then, *a way of seeing* and the enemy of recuperation and appropriation. [...] Brechtian historicization challenges the presumed ideological neutrality of any historical reflection. Rather it assumes, and promotes, what historians are now claiming: that readers/spectators of 'facts' and 'events' will, like Gertrude Stein reading the clouds, translate what is inchoate into signs (and stories), a move that produces not 'truth,' but mastery and pleasure.

Spectator, body, historicization

Historicization in fact puts on the table the issue of spectatorship and the performer's body. According to Brecht, one way that the actor alienates or distances the audience from the character is to suggest the historicity of the character in contrast to the actor's own present-time self-awareness on stage. The actor must not lose herself in the character but rather *demonstrate* the character as a function of particular socio-historical relations, a conduit of particular choices. As Timothy Wiles puts it, actor and audience, both in present time, 'look back on' the historical character as she fumbles through choices and judgements.[9] This does not, however, endow the actor with superiority, for as Wiles later points out this present-time actor is also fragmented: 'Brecht separates the historical man who acts from the aesthetic function of the actor.'[10] [...]

It is at this point – at the point of conceptualizing an unfetishized female performer and a female spectator – that an intertextual reading of Brechtian and feminist theories works productively. If feminist theory sees the body as culturally mapped and gendered, Brechtian historicization insists that this body is not a fixed essence but a site of struggle and change. If feminist theory is concerned with the multiple and complex signs of a woman's life: her color, her age, her desires, her politics – what I want to call her *historicity* – Brechtian theory gives us a way to put that historicity on view – in the theatre. In its conventional iconicity, theatre laminates body to character, but the body in historicization stands visibly and palpably separate from the 'role' of the actor as well as the role of the character; it is always insufficient and open. I want to be clear about this important point: the body, particularly the female body, by virtue of entering the stage space, enters representation – it is not just *there*, a live, unmediated presence, but rather (1) a signifying element in a dramatic fiction; (2) a part of a theatrical sign system whose conventions of gesturing, voicing, and impersonating are referents for both performer and audience; and (3) a sign in a system governed by a particular apparatus, usually owned and operated by men for the pleasure of a viewing public whose major wage earners are male. [. . .]

Spectator, author, Gestus

The explosive (and elusive) synthesis of alienation, historicization and the 'not, but' is the Brechtian Gestus: a gesture, a word, an action, a tableau by which, separately or in series, the social attitudes encoded in the play-text become visible to the spectator. A gest becomes *social* when it 'allows conclusions to be drawn about social circumstances'.[11] [. . .] If we read feminist concerns back into this discussion, the social gest signifies a moment of theoretical insight into sex/gender complexities, not only the play's 'fable', but in the culture which the play, at the moment of reception, is dialogically reflecting and shaping.

But this moment of visibility or insight is the very moment that complicates the viewing process. Because the Gestus is effected by an historical actor/subject, what the spectator sees is not a mere miming of social relationship, but a *reading* of it, an interpretation by an historical subject who supplements (rather than disappears into) the production of meaning. As noted earlier, the historical subject playing an actor, playing a character, splits the gaze of the spectator, who, as a reader of a complex sign system, cannot consume or reduce the object of her vision to a monolithic projection of the self. In fact, Gestus undermines the stability of the spectatorial 'self', for in the act of looking the spectator engages with her own temporality. She, too, becomes historicized – in motion and at risk, but also free to compare the actor/character's signs to 'what is close and proper to [herself]' – her material conditions, her politics, her skin, her desires. Sitting not in the dark, but in the Brechtian semi-lit smoker's theatre, the spectator still has the possibility of pleasurable identification. This is effected not through imaginary projection on to an ideal but through a triangular structure of actor/subject-character-spectator. Looking at the character, the spectator is constantly intercepted by the actor/subject, and the latter, heeding no fourth wall, is theoretically free to look back. The difference, then, between this triangle and the familiar oedipal one is that no one side signifies authority, knowledge, or the law. Brechtian theatre depends on a structure of representation, on exposing and making visible, but what appears even in the Gestus can only be provisional, indeterminate, non-authoritative. [. . .]

A gestic feminist criticism would 'alienate' or foreground those moments in a play-text in which social attitudes about gender could be made visible. It would highlight sex/gender configurations as they conceal or disrupt a coercive or patriarchal ideology. It would refuse to appropriate and naturalize male or female dramatists, but rather focus on historical material constraints in the production of images. It would attempt to engage dialectically with, rather than master, the play-text. And in generating meanings, it would recover (specifically gestic) moments in which the historical actor, the character, the spectator, *and* the author enter representation, however provisionally.

Gestic feminist criticism, Aphra Behn

In the brief space remaining, it is impossible to flesh out this critical schema, but I want to draw attention to a gestic moment that Aphra Behn has provided. [. . .]

In the prolog of her first play [1670] Behn takes note of the factions in the audience and genders them. She writes lines for a performer (gender unclear, but I would guess male) who enjoins the males in the audience to be leery of 'spies' – by implication whores whom the author has planted 'to hold you in wanton Compliment / That so you may not censure what she'as writ, / Which done, they face you down 'twas full of Wit'.[12]

I come now, at last, to my second short text on pointing.

Within moments the stage directions read '*Enter an Actress*', who '*pointing to the ladies*' asks, 'Can any see that glorious Sight and say / A Woman shall not Victor prove today?' In that pointing gesture, the actress sets up a triangular structure – between historical performer, the role she is destined to play, and the female spectators in the audience. She also mentions 'A Woman', a potential victor, and that seems to have a referent: the writer Aphra Behn (although it could be one of the females in the play). In that shared look, actor-subject, character, spectator, and author are momentarily joined, and for perhaps the first time on the English stage all four positions are filled by women. But not for long. In casting a closer eye at the female spectators, the actress soon differentiates, and in specifically sexual terms. Insisting, ironically perhaps, that 'There's not a Vizard in our whole Cabal' she condemns the lower-class whores, the Pickeroons, 'that scour for prey', but ends by promising total female 'sacrifice' to 'pleasure you'.[13]

Whom that 'you' now designates has become fully undecidable. In the sexual slang of the day, actress meant whore, authoress was soon to mean whore, and both were commodities in a pleasure market whose major consumers were male. Still, before conventional representation resumes, the signifying space is dominated by the interlocking look of women. I would call the actress's pointing, and the entire prolog, a Gestus, a moment when the sex/gender system, theatre politics, and social history cathect and become visible. For the feminist critic and theorist this Gestus marks a first step toward recovering a woman playwright in her sexual, historical, and theatrical specificity.

Notes

1   See B. Byg (1986) 'Brecht on the Margins: Film and Feminist Theory', paper presented at the annual convention of the Modern Language Association, New York, December.
2   L. Mulvey (1975) 'Visual Pleasure and Narrative Cinema', *Screen* 16/3 (autumn): 6.
3   *Ibid.*, p. 18.
4   B. Brecht (1964) *Brecht on Theatre: The Development of an Aesthetic*, ed. and trans. John Willett (New York: Hill & Wang), p. 192.
5   *Ibid.*, p. 143.
6   G. Rubin (1975) 'The Traffic in Women: Notes on the "Political Economy" of Sex', in *Toward an Anthropology of Women*, ed. Rayna Reiter (New York: Monthly Review Press), pp. 157–210.
7   *Brecht on Theatre*, p. 137.
8   *Ibid.*, p.190.

9   T. Wiles (1980) *The Theatre Event: Modern Theories of Performance* (Chicago: University of Chicago Press), p. 72.

10 *Ibid.*, p. 85.

11 *Brecht on Theatre*, p. 105.

12 A. Behn (1915) *The Forced Marriage, or The Jealous Bridegroom*, in *The Works of Aphra Behn*, vol. 3, ed. Montague Summers (London: Heinemann), pp. 285–381, p. 286.

13 *Ibid.*, p. 286.

EXERCISE: Choose a modern play by a woman playwright which renders constructions of gender visible (e.g. Caryl Churchill's *Cloud 9* or *Top Girls*, Adrienne Kennedy's *The Owl Answers*, Sarah Daniels's *Beside Herself*, Holly Hughes's *World Without End* or Holly Hughes, Lois Weaver and Peggy Shaw's *Dress Suits to Hire*) and consider how it punctures or refutes orthodox representations of Woman. Try to be precise about the effect of each technique used. How does the interpretative relationship established between viewer and viewed differ from that of more conventional dramas?

Armed with what you have learned, now attempt some historicist (gestic) feminist criticism. Choose a historical (post-Renaissance) play and, focusing on its female characters, first consider what assumptions it makes as to the nature of femininity. Then search for moments in the play with potential for a disruption of those assumptions. Consider for example passages in which the nature of Woman is discussed, offering actresses opportunities to dissent from that view in performance; where women are portrayed stereotypically, making space for ironic delivery; where female characters contradict the piece's construction of the feminine; where the character is clearly at odds with the historical reality of the actress; where ideas or discourses of the period provide for alternative interpretations of events or characters: that is, seek moments in which the actress might engage the female spectator in a shared, critical understanding of the play's construction of her character. As you do so, refer to the modern play you first examined, seeking comparable moments and effects. You are not attempting to claim an originally radical status for the piece; rather, you are trying to engage a *modern* viewer or reader dialectically in a discussion of its meanings.

3.5 Acting camp

Moe Meyer, from the Introduction to *The Politics and Poetics of Camp*, London and New York: Routledge, 1994

[Drawing on Judith **Butler**'s theories of gender and Linda Hutcheon's writings on postmodernism, Meyer in the following piece argues that Camp performance possesses an inherent political potency. Central to his thesis is the proposition that, although dominant ideology holds it to be a biological given, gender identity is in reality performed, a role enacted using behaviours which are already socially coded. With no such ready-made conventions available with which to express his or her identity, the culturally marginalized 'queer' of necessity reuses existing behaviours, but does so in a self-conscious and parodic fashion. This postmodern parody is possible because of gender's 'textual' character – the fact that it consists of no more than symbols – and the opportunities it therefore offers for 'intertextual' play (see **Barthes**). Its effect is to reveal the absence at the heart of orthodox modes of gender performance, for in showing such behaviours to be constructive of identity, queer performance undermines their claim to express an essence. It thereby subverts not merely given conceptions of gender or sexuality but the very assumptions on which ideological models of selfhood are built.]

The use of the word 'queer' to designate what is usually referred to as 'gay and lesbian' marks a subtle, ongoing and not yet stabilized renomination. [. . .] 'Queer' does not indicate the biological sex or gender of the subject. More importantly, the term indicates an ontological challenge to dominant labeling philosophies, especially the medicalization of the subject implied by the word 'homosexual', as well as a challenge to discrete gender categories embedded in the divided phrase 'gay and lesbian'. Because Camp, as we are defining it in this volume, gains its political validity as an ontological critique, and because its reconceptualization was initiated by observations of queer activist practices, the term 'queer' may be the best descriptor of this parodic operation.

The reappropriation of the once derogatory term 'queer', and its contemporary use as an affirmative self-nominated identity label, is far from clear in its current applications. Two writers who have attempted to define this term, Teresa de Lauretis and Simon Watney,[1] both do so by juxtaposing it with and in opposition to the labels of 'gay and lesbian'. I think that this logic is inadequate to the task of clarifying the meaning of 'queer'. Watney, in particular, identifies the emergence of the label as a generational phenomenon, one used by younger gay men and lesbians to differentiate themselves from what appears to be the bourgeois assimilationism rampant among some segments of the gay and lesbian community and to signify that those who have come out in the era of AIDS are somehow different from those who have not. The flaws in this kind of argument should be apparent: first, it indicates that what is at stake is a critique of class, not of sex/gender; second, it conflates middle class with middle age and assumes a unified understanding of the terms gay and lesbian and a singular lifestyle on the part of those who have reached a certain age; and third, it reveals itself as based in the ageism that has been so detrimental within the gay community. If the term 'queer' is indeed based within imagined generational difference, then I would suggest that it signifies nothing more than a potentially destructive, divisive and ageist maneuver that, in the end, serves to interrupt the continuity of political struggle through an ahistoricizing turn. But once the uncritiqued ageism of current definitions has been revealed and discarded, what remains – the critique of class – is of definite value and can be used to formulate what might be at stake in both the terms 'queer' and 'Camp'.

What I would offer as a definition of queer is one based on an alternative model of the constitution of subjectivity and of social identity. The emergence of the queer label as an oppositional critique of gay and lesbian middle-class assimilationism is, perhaps, its strongest and most valid aspect. In the sense that the queer label emerges as a class critique, then what is opposed are bourgeois models of identity. What 'queer' signals is an ontological challenge that displaces bourgeois notions of the Self as unique, abiding and continuous while substituting instead a concept of the Self as performative, improvisational, discontinuous and processually constituted by repetitive and stylized acts. Rather than some new kind of subject constitution that emerges as the result of a generation-specific response to the AIDS crisis, queer identity is more accurately identified as the praxical response to the emergence of social constructionist (sex/gender as ideologically interpellated) models of identity and its, by now overly rehearsed, oppositional stance to essentialist (sexual orientation as innate) models, thus historically situating queer identity in an epistemological rift that predates the advent of AIDS.

Queerness can be seen as an oppositional stance not simply to essentialist formations of gay and lesbian identities, but to a much wider application of the depth model of identity which underwrites the epistemology deployed by the bourgeoisie in their ascendancy to and maintenance of dominant power. As such, the queer label contains a critique of a more vast and comprehensive system of class-based practices of which sex/gender identity is only a part. The history of queer practices, as Thomas A. King charts in chapter one of this volume,[2] is a critical maneuver not limited to sexualities, but is one that has valuable applications for marginal social identities in general. Broadening the scope of the queer critique in this manner also constitutes a radical challenge to the entire concept of an identity based upon sexual orientation or sexual desire because the substitution of a performative, discontinuous Self for one based upon the unique individual actually displaces and voids the concept of sexual orientation itself by removing the bourgeois epistemological frames that stabilize such identifications. Queer sexualities become, then, a series of improvised performances whose threat lies in the denial of any social identity derived from participation in those performances. As a refusal of sexually defined identity, this must also include the denial of the difference upon which such identities have been founded. And it is precisely in the space of this refusal, in the deconstruction of the homo/hetero binary, that the threat and challenge to bourgeois ideology is queerly executed.

As the rejection of a social identity based upon the differentiation of sexual practices, queer identity must be more correctly aligned with various gender, rather than sexual, identities because it is no longer based, and does not have to be, upon material sexual practice. Perhaps emerging as a response to certain unaccountable and uncontainable sexualities – such as celibate gay men and lesbians; heterosexuals who engage in same-sex sexual activity without taking on an identity based on that activity; or even closeted gays who maintain multiple, exclusive and discrete social identities by switching back and forth between performative signifying codes – queer identity is not just another in an inventory of available sexual identities. Because sexual behavior is clearly not the determining factor in finalizing a self-nomination, even for conventional gays and lesbians, queerness contains the knowledge that social identities, including those of sex, but especially those of gender, are always accompanied by some sort of public signification in the form of specific enactments, embodiments or speech acts which are non-sexual or, in the very least, extrasexual. Accordingly, Judith Butler has theorized that

> gender is in no way a stable identity or locus of agency from which various acts proceed; rather, it is an identity tenuously constituted in time – an identity instituted through a *stylized repetition of acts*. Further, gender is instituted through the stylization of the body and, hence, must be understood as the mundane way in which bodily

gestures, movements, and enactments of various kinds constitute the illusion of an abiding gendered self.[3]

Butler's definition of gender can provide an explanation of queer identity that not only locates that identity within a performative nexus but also solves the problems of identity formation involving celibate gay men, etc., listed above.

Because gender identity is instituted by repetitive acts, then queer performance is not expressive of the social identity but is, rather, the reverse – the identity is self-reflexively constituted by the performances themselves. Whether one subscribes to an essentialist or constructionist theory of gay and lesbian identity, it comes down to the fact that, at some time, the actor must do something in order to produce the social visibility by which the identity is manifested. Postures, gestures, costume and dress, and speech acts become the elements that constitute both the identity and the identity performance. When we shift the study of gay and lesbian identity into a performance paradigm, then every enactment of that identity depends, ultimately, upon extrasexual performative gestures. Even the act of 'coming out', that is, the public proclamation of one's self-nomination as gay or lesbian, is constituted by an institutionalized speech act. I suggest that queer identity emerges as self-consciousness of one's gay and lesbian performativity sets in.

In the sense that queer identity is performative, it is by the deployment of specific signifying codes that social visibility is produced. Because the function of Camp, as I will argue, is the production of queer social visibility, then the relationship between Camp and queer identity can be posited. Thus I define Camp as the total body of performative practices and strategies used to enact a queer identity, with enactment defined as the production of social visibility. This expanded definition of Camp, one based on identity performance and not solely in some kind of unspecified cognitive identification of an ironic moment, may come as a bit of a jolt to many readers. It means that all queer identity performative expressions are circulated within the signifying system that is Camp. In other words, queer identity is inseparable and indistinguishable from its processual enactment, or Camp. [...]

Processing the Notes

[...] In order to produce a new reading of Camp, one that can account for its recent politicization, we need to jettison objectivist methodologies.

Objectivism, as I am using it here, refers to an empiricist route to knowledge that 'posits a real world which is independent of consciousness and theory, and which is accessible through sense-experience'.[4] This real world can be 'discovered' by a knowing subject who is the 'source of the sense data which validates knowledge'.[5] An objectivist methodology becomes extremely problematic in theories of social behavior where the human subjects of study are unavoidably transformed into 'objects' of knowledge that are used to generate sense-experience for the observer. As a result, human actors are reduced to 'thinglike' status as their own knowledge and experience become rendered as a structure of neutral surfaces readable only by the observer. As a mode for interpretation of queer cultural expressions, the one-way dynamic of objectivism most often results in the erasure of gay and lesbian subjects through an anti-dialogic turn that fails to acknowledge a possibly different ontology embodied in queer signifying practices. Instead, we need to develop a performance-centered methodology that takes into account and can accommodate the particular experience of the individual social actors under study, one which privileges process, the agency of knowledgeable performers, and the constructed nature of human realities. This approach provides a space for individual authority and experience that, regardless of different perceptions of sexual identity, envisions a power – albeit decentered – that is able to resist, oppose and subvert. Working with a theory of agency and performance, I will attempt the sacrilegious: to produce a definition of Camp. Such a definition should be stable enough to be of benefit to the reader, yet flexible enough to account for the many actions and objects that have come to be described by the term. Following Bredbeck's cue[6] (that it would be more productive to approach the project through a study of the workings of the Camp sign), I will suggest a definition of Camp based upon the delineation of a praxis formed at the intersection of social agency and postmodern parody.

Broadly defined, Camp refers to strategies and tactics of queer parody. The definition of parody I use is that of Linda Hutcheon.[7] Her postmodern redefinition of parody differs sharply from conventional usages that conflate parody with irony or satire. Rather, as elaborated by Hutcheon, parody is an intertextual manipulation of multiple conventions, 'an extended repetition with critical difference'[8] that 'has a hermeneutic function with both cultural and even ideological implications'.[9] Hutcheon explains that 'Parody's overt turning to other art forms',[10] its derivative nature, and its dependence upon an already existing text in order to fulfill itself are the reason for its traditional denigration, a denigration articulated within a dominant discourse that finds value only in an 'original'.

Hutcheon clears a space for a reconsideration of parody through its very contestation of ideas of Romantic singularity because it 'forces a reassessment of the process of textual production'.[11] At the same time, her redefinition provides the opportunity for a reassessment of Camp, when Camp is conceptualized as parody. Hutcheon's theory of parody is valuable for providing the terms needed to differentiate Camp from satire, irony and travesty; and to terminate, finally, the conflation of Camp with kitsch and schlock, a confusion that entered the discourse as a result of the heterosexual/Pop colonization of Camp in the 1960s. When subjected to Hutcheon's postmodern redefinition, Camp emerges as specifically queer parody possessing cultural and ideological analytic potential, taking on new meanings with implications for the emergence of a theory that can provide an oppositional queer critique.

While Hutcheon's theory is capable of locating the address of a queer parodic praxis, it still needs to be queerly adjusted in order to plumb its potential for a Camp theory. By employing a performance-oriented methodology that privileges process, we can restore a knowledgeable *queer* social agent to the discourse of Camp parody. While dominant discursive formations of Camp maintain a social agent, that agent is implied, and thus taken for granted to be heterosexual. Camp theorizing has languished since the 1960s when Sontag's appropriation banished the queer from the discourse, substituting instead an un-queer bourgeois subject under the banner of Pop.[12] It is this changeling that transformed Camp into the apolitical badge of the consumer whose status-quo 'sensibility' is characterized by the depoliticizing Midas touch, and whose control over the apparatus of representation casts the cloak of invisibility over the queer at the moment it appropriates and utters the C-word. Yet, in order to reclaim Camp-as-critique, the critique silenced in the 1960s, which finds its voice solely when spoken by the queer, we cannot reverse the process of banishment by ejecting the un-queer from the discourse. That kind of power does not belong to the queer. All we can do, perhaps, is to produce intermittent queer visibility in our exile at the margins long enough to reveal a terminus at the end of a pathway of dominant power with the goal of foregrounding the radical politic of parodic intertextuality.

When parody is seen as process, not as form, then the relationship between texts becomes simply an indicator of the power relationships between social agents who wield those texts, one who possesses the 'original', the other who possesses the parodic alternative. Anthony Giddens has argued that structures of signification can be understood only in relation to power and domination.[13] In fact, he defines power and domination as the ability to produce codes of signification.[14] Accordingly, value production is the prerogative of the dominant order, dominant precisely because it controls signification and which is represented by the privilege of nominating its own codes as the 'original'. The 'original', then, is the signifier of dominant presence and, because dominance can be defined as such only by exercising control over signification, it is only through the 'original' that we can know and touch that power. In that case, parody becomes the process whereby the marginalized and disenfranchised advance their own interests by entering alternative signifying codes into discourse by attaching them to existing structures of signification. Without the process of parody, the marginalized agent has no access to representation, the apparatus of which is controlled by the dominant order.[15] Camp, as specifically queer parody, becomes, then, the only process by which the queer is able to enter representation and to produce social visibility.

Notes

1   T. de Lauretis (1991) 'Queer Theory: Lesbian and Gay Sexualities/An Introduction', *Differences* 3/2: iii–xvii; S. Watney (1991) 'Troubleshooters: Simon Watney on Outing', *Artforum* 30/3: 16–18.
2   T. A. King (1994) 'Performing "Akimbo": Queer Pride and Epistemological Prejudice', in Moe Meyer (ed.), *The Politics and Poetics of Camp* (London and New York: Routledge).
3   J. Butler (1990) 'Performative Acts and Gender Constitution: An Essay in Phenomenology and Feminist Theory', in Sue-Ellen Case (ed.), *Performing Feminisms: Feminist Critical Theory and Theatre* (Baltimore: Johns Hopkins University Press). The same argument is outlined in the excerpt by Butler included in this volume.
4   T. Lovell (1983) *Pictures of Reality: Aesthetics, Politics and Pleasure* (London: British Film Institute), p. 10.
5   *Ibid.*, p. 11.
6   G. Bredbeck (1993) 'B/O – Barthes's Text/O'Hara's Trick: The Phallus, the Anus, and the Text', *PMLA* 108/2 (March): 268–82.
7   L. Hutcheon (1985) *A Theory of Parody: The Teachings of Twentieth-century Art Forms* (New York: Methuen).
8   *Ibid.*, p. 7.
9   *Ibid.*, p. 2.
10 *Ibid.*, p. 5.
11 *Ibid.*, p. 5.
12 S. Sontag (1983) 'Notes on Camp', in *A Susan Sontag Reader* (New York: Vintage Books).
13 A. Giddens (1984) *The Constitution of Society: Outline of the Theory of Structuration* (Berkeley: University of California Press).
14 *Ibid.*, p. 31.
15 S.-E. Case (1991) 'Tracking the Vampire', *Differences* 3/2: 1–20, p. 9.

EXERCISE: View a camp performance (consider television documentaries on subjects such as voguing or films such as *The Adventures of Priscilla, Queen of the Desert* or *La Cage aux Folles*). First, isolating a short, illustrative sequence, discuss what behaviours constitutive of orthodox gender and sexual identities are being reused. If a male performer is employing behavioural signatures usually associated with women, for example, consider where they are drawn from (where and by whom would you find them used without irony?), and what characteristics – what components of gender or sexual *identity* – they are ordinarily deemed to express. Then analyse how the performer parodies such behaviours. For this you will probably need to work in considerable detail, focusing on individual gestures, postures, vocal inflections, etc.; use the freeze-frame or 'pause' facility if available. How does such parody change your view of those behaviours – what do they suggest as a consequence of it? In your group, has everyone's view of 'normal' behaviour changed? If there are now a variety of views, how do you account for this?

Part four

Performing ethnicity

Cultural identity is one of the bases of social organization, reproducing and/or reinforcing patterns of allegiance and opposition, and so has, historically, coincided with structures of social power. The concept of 'race', for example, was established in the late eighteenth and nineteenth centuries as a way of classifying individuals on supposedly 'biological' grounds. In doing so, it actually functioned ideologically, attributing to other peoples innately inferior qualities of temperament, personality, intellect, and so on, as justification for Western Europe's colonization of their lands. Current critiques of ethnically orientated power structures of this kind draw on diverse sources: the Francophone 'négritude' movement of the 1930s and 1940s; the ideas born out of African American struggles for self-determination; the analyses of proponents of colonial independence such as Aimé Césaire (b. 1913), Amilcar Cabral (1924–73), C. L. R. James (1901–89) and Frantz Fanon (1925–61). It was Fanon in particular who explored the role played by representations of 'otherness' in colonial relations, the way images of non-dominant peoples both characterized them in the gaze of the colonizing power and became internalized, shaping the way those peoples saw themselves (see Fanon 1968). The ongoing analysis of such representations, the forms they take and the functions they serve, is central to fields such as African American Studies, Cultural Studies and, most recently, Post-colonial Studies. In a groundbreaking work which all but founded Post-colonial Studies as a discipline, Edward Said coined the term 'colonial discourse' (1978) to describe that Foucauldian complex of images, practices and 'knowledges' via which colonizers justified and naturalized their domination of the colonized. At stake in such representations is more than the sensibilities of those depicted, for the meanings fixed to the bodies and cultures of non-dominant peoples work to validate the conditions of real, material disadvantage in which they live.

Although the following pieces focus on different kinds of 'subaltern' group, both the indigenous people of colonized lands and descendants of the African diaspora, the perspectives they provide are relevant to the representation of non-dominant peoples generally. Abdul JanMohamed (b. 1945) theorizes the basic binary structure of thought operating in dominant representations of the non-dominant. The piece by Eric Lott (b. 1959) examines the way real lives and bodies are repressed in favour of a performed image inscribed with the meanings of the dominant culture. The second pair of excerpts outline possible modes of resistance. bell hooks (b. 1952) argues that apparently neutral representations of black people in the mass media actually function in support of white power structures; she thereby offers a perspective from which representations of the subaltern may be critiqued. Helen Gilbert (b. 1956) explores ways in which a quality fundamental to performance, its liveness, can be deployed to explode such representations in practice.

Further reading: probably the best introduction to ethnicity and performance is Gilbert and Tompkins 1996; Gilroy 1987, LaCapra (ed.) 1991, Hiller (ed.) 1991, Malik 1996, Miles 1989 and Said 1978 each take a different approach to issues of ethnicity and representation, and so may usefully be posed against one another for an in-depth exploration of the field; Ashcroft *et al.* 1989 and (eds) 1995, Barker *et al.* (eds) 1994, Loomba 1998 and Williams and Chrisman (eds) 1994 all offer clear, comprehensive surveys of post-colonial theory, although Ashcroft *et al.* 1998 is hard to beat in terms of concise explanations; for accessible introductions to African American studies see Gates (ed.) 1984 and 1986; for ethnicity viewed from a Cultural Studies perspective, see Gilroy 1993, Mercer 1994 and, especially, Hall 1980, 1996a, 1996b.

4.1 The Other

Abdul JanMohamed, from 'The Economy of Manichean Allegory: The Function of Racial Difference in Colonialist Literature', *Critical Inquiry* 12: 59–87, 1985

[In this influential essay post-colonial theorist JanMohamed employs a principle drawn from the psychoanalytical theories of Jacques Lacan to explain the forms in which colonizing cultures perceive and represent colonized peoples. Subjectivity is for Lacan formed over two stages of an individual's development. In the first, the precultural stage of the 'imaginary', the child defines itself in opposition to the world around it, organizing its perceptions and experiences via terms which form dichotomous pairs: subject versus object, self versus other, etc. (see also **Grosz**). This provides the basis for its entry into the second stage, the 'symbolic', where it assimilates its culture's signifying systems, learning to negotiate a world composed of other social subjects. The basis of our relations with others, it is the psychic structures born out of these stages of development, JanMohamed argues, which condition the colonizer's conception and representation of the 'native'. It is on this basis that he offers a two-part classification of colonial texts, the imaginary and symbolic versions of the binary, 'manichean' principle at the root of our sense of self.]

1. The perception of racial difference is, in the first place, influenced by economic motives. For instance, as Dorothy Hammond and Alta Jablow have shown, Africans were perceived in a more or less neutral and benign manner before the slave trade developed; however, once the triangular trade became established, Africans were newly characterized as the epitome of evil and barbarity.[1] The European desire to exploit the resources of the colonies (including the natives, whom Europeans regarded as beasts of burden) drastically disrupted the indigenous societies. Through specific policies of population transfers, gerrymandering of borders and forced production, to mention only a few such measures, European colonialists promoted the destruction of native legal and cultural systems and, ultimately, the negation of non-European civilizations. These measures produce pathological societies, ones that exist in a state of perpetual crisis.

To appreciate the function of colonialist fiction within this ambience, we must first distinguish between the 'dominant' and the 'hegemonic' phases of colonialism as well as between its material and discursive ideological practices. Throughout the dominant phase, which spans the period from the earliest European conquest to the moment at which a colony is granted 'independence', European colonizers exercise direct and continuous bureaucratic control and military coercion of the natives: during this phase the 'consent' of the natives is primarily passive and indirect. Although we shouldn't overlook the various forms of native 'co-operation' – for example, in the traffic of slaves – the point remains that such co-operation testifies less to a successful interpellation of the native than to the colonizer's ability to exploit pre-existing power relations of hierarchy, subordination and subjugation within native societies. Within the dominant phase (to which I will confine the scope of this paper), the indigenous peoples are subjugated by colonialist material practices (population transfers, and so forth), the efficacy of which finally depends on the technological superiority of European military forces. Colonialist discursive practices, particularly its literature, are not very useful in controlling the conquered group at this early stage: the native is not subjugated, nor does his culture disintegrate, simply because a European characterizes both as savage.

By contrast, in the hegemonic phase (or neocolonialism) the natives accept a version of the colonizers' entire system of values, attitudes, morality, institutions, and, more important, mode of production. This stage of imperialism does rely on the active and direct 'consent' of the dominated, though, of course, the threat of military coercion is always in the background. The natives' internalization of Western cultures begins before the end of the dominant phase. The nature and the speed of this internalization depend on two factors. The many local circumstances and the emphasis placed on interpellation by various European colonial policies. But in all cases, the moment of 'independence' – with the natives' obligatory, ritualized acceptance of Western forms of parliamentary government – marks the formal transition to hegemonic colonialism.

Distinguishing between material and discursive practices also allows us to understand more clearly the contradictions between the covert and overt aspects of colonialism. While the covert purpose is to exploit the colony's natural resources thoroughly and ruthlessly through the various imperialist material practices, the overt aim, as articulated by colonialist discourse, is to 'civilize' the savage, to introduce him to all the benefits of Western cultures. Yet the fact that this overt aim, embedded as an assumption in all colonialist literature, is accompanied in colonialist texts by a more vociferous insistence, indeed by a fixation, upon the savagery and the evilness of the native should alert us to the real function of these texts: to justify imperial occupation and exploitation. If such literature can demonstrate that the barbarism of the native is irrevocable, or at least very deeply ingrained, then the European's attempt to civilize him can continue indefinitely, the exploitation of his resources can proceed without hindrance, and the European can persist in enjoying a position of moral superiority.

Thus a rigorous subconscious logic defines the relations between the covert and overt policies and between the material and discursive practices of colonialism. The ideological functions of colonialist fiction within the dominant phase of imperial control, then, must be understood not in terms of its putative or even real effects on the native but in terms of the exigencies of domestic – that is, European and colonialist – politics and culture; and the function of racial difference, of the fixation on and fetishization of native savagery and evil, must be mapped in terms of these exigencies and ideological imperatives. I do not wish to suggest, however, that racial denigration has no effect whatsoever on colonized intellectuals and literature. It does – but only during the late stages of the dominant phase and, more particularly, during the hegemonic phase.

Before turning to the question of racial difference in the works I will discuss, we need to note the relation of the individual author to the field of colonialist discourse. The dominant pattern of relations that controls the text within the colonialist context is determined by economic and political imperatives and changes, such as the development of slavery, that are external to the discursive field itself. The dominant model of power- and interest-relations in all colonial societies is the manichean opposition between the putative superiority of the European and the supposed inferiority of the native. This axis in turn provides the central feature of the colonialist cognitive framework and colonialist literary representation: the manichean allegory – a field of diverse yet interchangeable oppositions between white and black, good and evil, superiority and inferiority, civilization and savagery, intelligence and emotion, rationality and sensuality, self and Other, subject and object. The power relations underlying this model set in motion such strong currents that even a writer who is reluctant to acknowledge it and who may indeed be highly critical of imperialist exploitation is drawn into its vortex. The writer is easily seduced by colonial privileges and profits and forced by various ideological factors (that I will examine below) to conform to the prevailing racial and cultural preconceptions. Thus the 'author-function' in such texts, as elsewhere, 'is tied to the legal and institutional systems that circumscribe, determine, and articulate the realm of discourses'.[2] And since this 'function' in the imperialist context confers on the author all the moral and psychological pleasures of manichean superiority, a 'native' writer, such as V. S. Naipaul, can also be inducted, under the right circumstances, to fulfill the author-function of the colonialist writer.

Another significant feature of the system governing colonialist fiction is the nature of its audience. Since the object of representation – the native – does not have access to these texts (because of linguistic barriers) and since the European audience has no direct contact with the native, imperialist fiction tends to be unconcerned with the truth-value of its representation. In fact, since such literature does not so much represent as present the native for the first time, it is rarely concerned with overtly affirming the reader's experience of his own culture and therefore does not really solicit his approval: it exists outside the dialogic class discourse of European literature. The value of colonialist statements is consequently all the more dependent on their place in colonialist discourse and on 'their capacity for circulation and exchange, their possibility of transformation, not only in the economy of discourse, but, more generally, in the administration of scarce resources'.[3]

Just as imperialists 'administer' the resources of the conquered country, so colonialist discourse 'commodifies' the native subject into a stereotyped object and uses him as a 'resource' for colonialist fiction. The European writer commodifies the native by negating his individuality, his subjectivity, so that he is now perceived as a generic being that can be exchanged for any other native (they all look alike, act alike and so on). Once reduced to his exchange-value in the colonialist signifying system, he is fed into the manichean allegory, which functions as the currency, the medium of exchange, for the entire colonialist discursive system. The exchange function of the allegory remains constant, while the generic attributes themselves can be substituted infinitely (and even contradictorily) for one another. As Said points out in his study of Orientalism, such strategies depend on a 'flexible *positional* superiority, which puts the Westerner in a whole series of possible relationships with the Orient without ever losing him the relative upper hand'.[4] Within such a representational economy, the writer's task is 'administer' the relatively scarce resources of the manichean opposition in order to reproduce the native in a potentially infinite variety of images, the apparent diversity of which is determined by the simple machinery of the manichean allegory.

Hence we can observe a profound symbiotic relationship between the discursive and the material practices of imperialism: the discursive practices do to the symbolic, linguistic presence of the native what the material practices do to his physical presence; the writer commodifies him so that he can be exploited more efficiently by the administrator, who, of course, obliges by returning the favor in kind. In fact, at any given point within a fully developed dominant imperialism, it is impossible to determine which form of commodification takes precedence, so entirely are the two forms intertwined.

2. Colonialist literature is an exploration and a representation of a world at the boundaries of 'civilization', a world that has not (yet) been domesticated by European signification or codified in detail by its ideology. That world is therefore perceived as uncontrollable, chaotic, unattainable and ultimately evil. Motivated by his desire to conquer and dominate, the imperialist configures the colonial realm as a confrontation based on differences in race, language, social customs, cultural values and modes of production.

Faced with an incomprehensible and multifaceted alterity, the European theoretically has the option of responding to the Other in terms of identity or difference. If he assumes that he and the Other are essentially identical, then he would tend to ignore the significant divergences and to judge the Other according to his own cultural values. If, on the other hand, he assumes that the Other is irremediably different, then he would have little incentive to adopt the viewpoint of that alterity: he would again tend to turn to the security of his own cultural perspective. Genuine and thorough comprehension of Otherness is possible only if the self can somehow negate or at least severely bracket the values, assumptions, and ideology of his culture. As Nadine Gordimer's and Isak Dinesen's writings show, however, this entails in practice the virtually impossible task of negating one's very being, precisely because one's culture is what formed that being. Moreover, the colonizer's invariable assumption about his moral superiority means that he will rarely question the validity of either his own or his society's formation and that he will not be inclined to expend any energy in understanding the worthless alterity of the colonized. By thus subverting the traditional dialectic of self and Other that contemporary theory considers so important in the formation of self and culture, the assumption of moral superiority subverts the very potential of colonialist literature. Instead of being an exploration of the racial Other, such literature merely affirms its own ethnocentric assumptions; instead of actually depicting the outer limits of 'civilization', it simply codifies and preserves the structures of its own mentality. While the surface of each colonialist text purports to represent specific encounters with specific varieties of the racial Other, the subtext valorizes the superiority of European cultures, of the collective process that has mediated that representation. Such literature is essentially specular: instead of seeing the native as a bridge toward syncretic possibility, it uses him as a mirror that reflects the colonialist's self-image.

Accordingly, I would argue that colonialist literature is divisible into two broad categories: the 'imaginary' and the 'symbolic'.[5] The emotive as well as the cognitive intentionalities of the 'imaginary' text are structured by objectification and aggression. In such works the native functions as an image of the imperialist self in such a manner that it reveals the latter's self-alienation. Because of the subsequent projection involved in this context, the 'imaginary' novel maps the European's intense internal rivalry. The 'imaginary' representation of indigenous people tends to coalesce the signifier with the signified. In describing the attributes or actions of the native, issues such as intention, causality, extenuating circumstances, and so forth, are completely ignored; in the 'imaginary' colonialist realm, to say 'native' is automatically to say 'evil' and to evoke immediately the economy of the manichean allegory. The writer of such texts tends to fetishize a nondialectical, fixed opposition between the self and the native. Threatened by a metaphysical alterity that he has created, he quickly retreats to the homogeneity of his own group. Consequently, his psyche and text tend to be much closer to and are often entirely occluded by the ideology of his group.

Writers of 'symbolic' texts, on the other hand, are more aware of the inevitable necessity of using the native as a mediator of European desires. Grounded more firmly and securely in the egalitarian imperatives of Western societies, these authors tend to be more open to a modifying dialectic of self and Other. They are willing to examine the specific individual and cultural differences between Europeans and natives and to reflect on the efficacy of European values, assumptions and habits in contrast to those of the indigenous cultures. 'Symbolic' texts, most of which thematize the problem of colonialist mentality and its encounter with the racial Other, can in turn be subdivided into two categories.

The first type, represented by novels like E. M. Forster's *A Passage to India* and Rudyard Kipling's *Kim*, attempts to find syncretic solutions to the manichean opposition of the colonizer and the colonized. This kind of novel overlaps in some ways with the 'imaginary' text: those portions of the novel organized at the emotive level are structured by 'imaginary' identification, while those controlled by cognitive intentionality are structured by the rules of the 'symbolic' order. Ironically, these novels – which are conceived in the 'symbolic' realm of intersubjectivity, heterogeneity, and particularity but are seduced by the specularity of 'imaginary' Otherness – better illustrate the economy and power of the manichean allegory than do the strictly 'imaginary' texts.

The second type of 'symbolic' fiction, represented by the novels of Joseph Conrad and Nadine Gordimer, realizes that syncretism is impossible within the power relations of colonial society because such a context traps the writer in the libidinal economy of the 'imaginary'. Hence, becoming reflexive about its context, by confining itself to a rigorous examination of the 'imaginary' mechanism of colonialist mentality, this type of fiction manages to free itself from the manichean allegory.

Notes

1   D. Hammond and A. Jablow (1970) *The Africa That Never Was: Four Centuries of British Writing About Africa* (New York: Waveland Press), pp. 20–3.
2   M. Foucault (1977) 'What Is an Author?', in *Language, Counter-memory, Practice: Selected Essays and Interviews*, ed. Donald F. Bouchard and Sherry Simon (Oxford: Blackwell), p. 130.
3   M. Foucault (1972) *The Archaeology of Knowledge*, trans. A. M. Sheridan Smith (London and New York: Tavistock), p. 120.
4   E. W. Said (1978) *Orientalism* (London and New York: Routledge & Kegan Paul), p. 7.
5   See J. Lacan (1977) 'The Mirror Stage as Formative of the Function of the I as Revealed in Psychoanalytic Experience', in *Écrits: A Selection*, trans. Alan Sheridan (London: Tavistock/Routledge & Kegan Paul).

EXERCISE: Choose a non-dominant ethnic group resident in your country and, down one side of a sheet of paper, briefly list the characteristics traditionally attributed to it by the dominant group (you should do this frankly, with the understanding that it is not your views but those of the dominant culture which you are recording). As you do so, try to give examples of each attribution (from anecdotes, newspaper articles, political speeches, jokes, etc.). Only when you have completed your list should you start the next phase: write next to each entry its opposite – pairing 'lazy' with 'hard-working', for example – to compile a second list. What overall images of the non-dominant and dominant groups do the lists conjure, and what do the lists together suggest about the relations between them? How do your binaries compare with those you compiled for the **Cixous** exercise? If there are similarities, what do they suggest?

Now choose a historical play in which characters from another or subaltern culture feature alongside characters from the author's own (e.g. William Shakespeare's *Othello* or *The Merchant of Venice*, Dion

Boucicault's *The Octoroon*, George L. Aiken's version of *Uncle Tom's Cabin*). Comparing the two kinds of character, discuss what manichean dichotomies are operating in the piece, always supporting your ideas with concrete examples from the text. Is emotion posed against reason, or barbarity against civilization? Is the piece in JanMohamed's sense 'imaginary' or 'symbolic'? If it displays elements of both, consider how and where each occurs, and which view dominates.

4.2 Blackface

Eric Lott, from *Love and Theft: Blackface Minstrelsy and the American Working Class*, New York and Oxford: Oxford University Press, 1995

[Much of the force of Lott's account of American blackface minstrelsy derives from his examination of the complex socio-historical circumstances in which such acts were performed, and the dense, often conflicting meanings they negotiated. Central to his reading of the tale of Juba is the notion of the 'seeming counterfeit'. Although the dancer was black and his dance authentic, both were presented as imitations, for it was only when construed as copies that the images of black culture which minstrelsy conjured were distanced from the reality of African American lives. This production of 'blackness' in order to contain it, to neutralize the subversive power of black bodies and practices, resulted in its mobilization as a multivalent symbol in a *white* cultural landscape. But such containment was ambiguous, the performances vulnerable to recontextualization, and Lott charts the way in which minstrelsy's stereotypical imagery drew its pleasures and powers from realities which retained a potential to disturb.]

Until the first blackface band formed in 1843, minstrelsy was an interstitial art: performers appeared between the acts of 'respectable' theatrical productions, or as afterpieces to them; they also shared the stage with many comic acts in the pleasure gardens, circuses, museums and 'vaudevilles' newly sprung up to meet the demands of a growing urban working population. Accordingly, the phenomenon consisted largely of solo dancers, banjoists, singers, burlesque playlets, comic impersonations and various kinds and combinations of duos.

Yet we have seen that for all their scattered presentation, minstrel acts immediately secured 'blackness' a public hearing. The urgency that attended its appearance is notable in P. T. Barnum's tussle with the black-face convention in 1841. Thomas Low Nichols (Walt Whitman's editor at the *New York Aurora* in the early 1840s) tells the story of the black-face dancer John Diamond's quitting Barnum's organization and leaving the cultural entrepreneur, early in his career, with a problem:

> In New York, some years ago, Mr. P. T. Barnum had a clever boy who brought him lots of money as a dancer of negro break-downs; made up, of course, as a negro minstrel, with his face well black-ened, and a woolly wig. One day Master Diamond, thinking he might better himself, danced away into the infinite distance.
>
> Barnum, full of expedients, explored the dance-houses of the Five Points and found a boy who could dance a better break-down than Master Diamond. It was easy to hire him; but he was a genuine negro; and there was not an audience in America that would not have resented, in a very energetic fashion, the insult of being asked to look at the dancing of a real negro. To any man but the origi-nator of Joyce Heth, the venerable negro nurse of Washington, and the manufacturer of the Fiji Mermaid, this would have been an insuperable obstacle.
>
> Barnum was equal to the occasion. Son of the State of white oak cheeses and wooden nutmegs, he did not disgrace his lineage. He greased the little 'nigger's' face and rubbed it over with a new blacking of burnt cork, painted his thick lips with vermillion, put on a woolly wig over his tight curled locks, and brought him out as the 'champion nigger-dancer of the world'. Had it been suspected that the seeming counterfeit was the genuine article, the New York Vauxhall would have blazed with indignation.[1]

It is easy to remark here that blackface was simply less objectionable than the appearance of black people onstage, particularly given the caricatures that resulted. Yet I would emphasize two things: not only that the idea of black representation had definite limits, was considered offensive or outrageous, worked against the grain; but also that it was possible for a black man in blackface, without a great deal of effort, to offer credible imitations of white men imitating him. That is to say, some blackface impersonations may not have been as far from this period's black theatrical self-presentation as we tend to believe – and so much the worse, the reader might add: no doubt the standard was set by whites. On this occasion, however, far from easily falling into a prefitted stereotype, the hired black 'boy' seems to have been Juba (William Henry Lane), who would a few years later become the most famous – and, significantly, nearly the only – black performer to appear in white theaters in the mid-1840s. Dickens celebrated him in chapter 6 of *American Notes* (1842) as the best popular dancer of the day; even 'Master Diamond' (after an 1844 dance competition with Juba that left Diamond the loser) believed him to be the pre-eminent dancer in antebellum America.[2]

The primary purpose of the mask, then, may have been as much to maintain control over a potentially subversive act as to ridicule, though the double bind was that blackface performers' attempts at regulation were also capable of producing an aura of 'blackness'. The incident suggests the danger of the simple public display of black practices, the offering of them for white enjoyment. The moments at which the intended counterfeit broke down and failed to 'seem', when the fakery evaporated, could (as we have seen) result in acts of unsettling authenticity, even if a white man were inside. From this perspective we might say that the elements of derision involved in blackface performance were not so much its raison d'être as an attempt to 'master' the power and interest of black cultural practices it continually generated. As a figure for early blackface acts, 'the seeming counterfeit' is perfectly apt. To the extent that such acts merely *seemed*, they kept white involvement in black culture under control, indeed facilitated that involvement; but the power disguised by the counterfeit was also often invoked by it, suggesting the occasional ineffectiveness, the mere seeming, of the counterfeit itself.

It is well known that Diamond, Rice and other early blackface performers laid claim to such power through the predominantly black dances in their acts. Even those most skeptical of the blackface phenomenon commonly accepted the authenticity of the dances (though these too, as we have seen, were predictably miscegenated). We should notice, however, that whites subtly acknowledged the greater power of the genuine article, a fact that also illuminates the purpose of the diminished copy. Again, the counterfeit was a means of exercising white control over explosive cultural forms as much as it was an avenue of racial derision (though to say the one is perhaps also to say the other). Advertising himself as the 'BEST DANCER LIVING', Diamond boasted in early 1840s playbills of his 'skill at Negro Dancing', which audiences surely enjoyed more than mocked. But in challenge dance contests he would tempt only 'any other *white* person' (perhaps foreseeing his defeat by the expert Juba), a particularly good way of regulating the black threat to his own reputation and to that of his profession while making a living from just that threat. It was paramount that the culture constantly being called up also be kept safely under wraps. This was made plain in a playbill for a New York performance in 1845, by which time Juba's already legendary stature allowed him to appear regularly on the stage:

> The entertainment to conclude with the Imitation Dance, by Mast. Juba, in which he will give correct Imitation Dances of all the principal Ethiopian Dancers in the United States. After which he will give an imitation of himself – and then you will see the vast difference between those that have heretofore attempted dancing and this WONDERFUL YOUNG MAN.[3]

This performance seems, and probably was, astonishingly bold: the trusted counterfeiters mocked in return by a representative of those from whom they had stolen; a public display of black irony toward whites, all stammers and jerks and gracelessness, who had tried to become better blacks. Yet it also foregrounds minstrelsy as a safely imitative form: the notion of the black dancer 'imitating himself' indicates minstrelsy's fundamental consequence for black culture, the dispossession and control by whites of black forms that would not for a long time be recovered. Dickens catches this simulacral dilemma almost unawares in his account of Juba when he says, in a final flourish, that the dancer 'finishes by leaping gloriously on the bar-counter, and calling for something to drink, with the chuckle of a million of counterfeit Jim Crows, in one inimitable sound!'[4] It was hard to see the real thing without being reminded, even unfavorably, of the copy, the 'cover version' that effectively did its work of cultural coverage. Nor, just as surely, could the copy be seen without reminding one of the real thing; as Eileen Southern has remarked, 'No one forgot that the black man was behind it all.'[5] This simultaneous production and subjection of black maleness may have been more than a formal consequence of wearing blackface; it may indeed have been the minstrel show's main achievement, articulating precisely a certain structure of racial feeling. The very real instability of white men's investment in black men, however, seems often to have exceeded this happy ambiguity, giving rise to a good deal of trouble. Much of the trouble, as in Dickens's account, had to do with the black male body.

Dickens, among many others, marked the male body as the primary site of the power of 'blackness' for whites. All that separates his record of Juba from other such commentary (on both white and black performers) is literary skill, by which I mean the ability to disguise his own skittish attraction to the dancer's body. In New York City, circling toward the center of the wretched Five Points district, Dickens 'descends' into Almack's, 'assembly-room of the Five Point fashionables'. A lively scene of dancing begins to flag, when Juba makes his appearance:

> Suddenly the lively hero dashes in to the rescue. Instantly the fiddler grins, and goes at it tooth and nail; there is new energy in the tambourine; new laughter in the dancers; new smiles in the land-lady; new confidence in the landlord; new brightness in the very candles. Single shuffle, double shuffle, cut and cross-cut; snapping his fingers, rolling his eyes, turning in his knees, presenting the backs of his legs in front, spinning about on his toes and heels like nothing but the man's fingers on the tambourine; dancing with two left legs, two right legs, two wooden legs, two wire legs, two spring legs – all sorts of legs and no legs – what is this to him?[6]

The brilliant dancing calls forth a brilliant mimetic escalation: a sharp focus on simple steps of the feet shifts to jump cuts of fingers, eyes, knees, legs and bodies that blur into fingers, then to curious industrial metaphors (legs of wood, wire, spring) for the dynamo energy of this 'heroic' display. All of it is of course a tribute to such display; the escalation is one of enlarging circles or areas of kinesis. But the energy and artistry are finally distanced; the escalation is *away* from the dancing; the metaphors dwarf what they are called on to describe. The whole passage reads as though Dickens did not really know what to do with such energy, where to put it. He ends up producing an account that lacks an immanent purpose. All he will venture is that the dance is so dazzling that everything finally seems like something else, not itself – body into fingers, legs into no legs. And once this move is made, the black man's body has been contained even as it is projected into public, something minstrel performers them-selves had somehow to accomplish.

The 'black' body's dangerous power was remarked by nearly all observers of the minstrel phenomenon; it was probably mainly responsible for minstrelsy's already growing reputation for 'vulgarity'. Those conscious of minstrelsy's counterfeit, for example, resorted to suggestive language to describe its distance from the true coin. The actress Fanny Kemble, in her plantation memoirs of the 1830s, clinched such an observation – that 'all the contortions, and springs, and flings, and kicks, and capers you have been beguiled into accepting as indicative of [blacks] are spurious' – by ending the list of adjectives with the inevitable sexual parry 'faint, feeble, impotent – in a word, pale Northern reproductions of that ineffable black conception'.[7] It required little imagination from the audience to make

blackface itself 'ineffable', for dancers made much of the sexual exaggeration that came so easily to such performances, and song sheet illustrations
unfailingly registered, in muted form, this recurring preoccupation. Dancers
relied on vigorous leg- and footwork, twists, turns and slaps of toe and
heel. The body was always grotesquely contorted, even when sitting; stiff-
ness and extension of arms and legs announced themselves as unsuccessful
sublimations of sexual desire. (In 'Coal Black Rose' [1827], the cuckolded
lover sings, 'Make haste, Rosa, lubly dear, / I froze tiff as poker waitin
here.')[8] Banjos were deployed in ways that anticipated the phallic suggestions of rock 'n' roll. Kemble's frank fascination with what 'these people
[slaves] did with their bodies'[9] was carried to the stage, where, for instance,
dancers would exploit the accents of sexuality and of sexual ambiguity;
the 'jaybird wing', perhaps similar to a frontier dance of the same name,
was considered highly indecent for someone in skirts – perhaps even more
so if this someone were male.[10]

We are justified in seeing early blackface performance as one of the
very first constitutive discourses of the body in American culture. Certainly
minstrelsy's commercial production of the black male body was a fundamental source of its threat and its fascination for white men, anticipating
Harriet Beecher Stowe's famous 'vision' that the whipping of Tom would
prove the most potent image of *Uncle Tom's Cabin*. The problem this
cultural form faced was how to ensure that what it invoked was safely
rerouted, not through white *meanings* – for even the anarchic, threatening
associations of black male sexuality were created by white cultural meanings – but through a kind of disappearing act in which blackface made
'blackness' flicker on and off so as simultaneously to produce and disintegrate the body. Nineteenth-century observers of the minstrel show offer
a clue to this dialectic. After a flurry of evidence documenting the authentic
nature of early minstrel songs, theater historian T. Allston Brown suggests
that most of them ('Long Tail Blue', 'Sich a Getting up Stairs') 'were taken
from hearing the darkies of the South singing after the labor of the day
was over on the plantation. The verses and airs were altered, written and
arranged as I have described.'[11] Another commentator believed minstrel
songs to be the 'veritable tunes and words which have lightened the labor
of some weary negro in the cotton fields, amused his moonlight hours as
he fished, or waked the spirits of the woods as he followed in the track
of the wary racoon'.[12] The fact is that minstrel songs and dances conjured
up not only the black body but its labor, not only its sexuality but its
place and function in a particular economy.

The body, Richard Dyer has argued, becomes a central problem in
justifying or legitimating a capitalist (or indeed slave) economy. The

rhetoric of these economics must insist either that capital has the magical power of multiplying itself or that slaves are contented, tuneful children in a plantation paradise; in reality, of course, it is *human labor* that must reproduce itself as well as create surplus value. In these societies the body is a potentially subversive site because to recognize it fully is to recognize the exploitative organization of labor that structures their economies. Cultural strategies must be devised to occlude such a recognition: reducing the body purely to sexuality is one strategy; colonizing it with a medical discourse in which the body is dispersed into discrete parts or organs is another. Shackling the body to a discourse of racial biology is still another, and in western societies the black body in particular has, in Dyer's words, served as the site of both '*remembering and denying* the inescapability of the body in the economy', a figuration of the world's body and its labor, easily called up and just as easily denied.[13] In antebellum America it was minstrelsy that performed this crucial hegemonic function, invoking the black male body as a powerful cultural sign of sexuality as well as a sign of the dangerous, guilt-inducing physical reality of slavery but relying on the derided category of race finally to dismiss both.

Notes

1   T. L. Nichols (1874) *Forty Years of American Life* [1864], 2nd edn (London: Longmans Green), pp. 369–70.

2   M. H. Winter (1948) 'Juba and American Minstrelsy', in *Chronicles of the American Dance*, ed. Paul Magriel (New York: Henry Holt), p. 47.

3   Uncatalogued playbills in the Harvard Theatre Collection.

4   C. Dickens (1972) *American Notes* [1842] (New York: Penguin), p. 139.

5   E. Southern (1975) 'Black Musicians and Early Ethiopian Minstrelsy', *The Black Perspective in Music* 3/1: 77–83.

6   Dickens, *American Notes*, p. 139.

7   F. A. Kemble (1969) *Journal of a Residence on a Georgian Plantation 1838–1839* [1863] (Chicago: Afro-American Press), p. 96.

8   S. F. Damon (1936) *Series of Old American Songs* (Providence: Brown University Library).

9   Kemble, *Journal*, p. 96.

10   H. Nathan (1977) *Dan Emmett and the Rise of Early Negro Minstrelsy* [1962] (Norman: University of Oklahoma Press).

11   T. A. Brown (1874) 'The Origin of Negro Minstrelsy', in *Fun in Black; or, Sketches of Minstrel Life*, ed. Charles H. Day (New York: De Witt), pp. 5–10, p. 6.

12   'Negro Minstrelsy – Ancient and Modern', in *ibid.*, p. 73.

13   R. Dyer (1986) *Heavenly Bodies: Film Stars and Society* (New York: St Martin's), pp. 138–9.

EXERCISE: Choose two performances in which characters from a non-dominant ethnic group are enacted by performers from the dominant; the depiction of Native Americans, say, in two classic Westerns. Analysing the means used to conjure them – dress, demeanour, acting conventions, the 'typical' activities they are shown undertaking, etc. – consider what characteristics are attributed to that people, and what discourses or 'knowledges' are drawn upon in doing so. Does their depiction invoke ideas of the Noble Savage, or of Edenic innocents? Does it suggest views grounded in notions of religious condemnation, or moral, medical or evolutionary inferiority? Is the group identified in sexual, biological or historical/anthropological terms? You are seeking the meanings which dominant culture fixes to the image of the subaltern.

Now relate those images to their social and political context, and consider what function they serve(d). Can you locate the terms and meanings you have found in contemporary texts, theories or discourses? What does the dominant culture or group gain by representing the subaltern in this manner? What reality is obscured by the images, and why must they be contained – what and/or whom does it threaten?

4.3 The resisting viewer

bell hooks, from 'Teaching Resistance: The Racial Politics of Mass Media', in *Killing Rage: Ending Racism*, Harmondsworth: Penguin, 1996

[One of the USA's leading black feminist critics, bell hooks has consistently advocated the crossing of boundaries, both political and racial, in order to repudiate the all-pervasive values of what she terms 'white supremacy'. Frequently positioning herself as an outsider, she uses that 'otherness' as a vantage from which to critique popular culture, exploring the ways in which it functions as an instrument of ideological interpellation (see **Althusser**). In the following essay she offers an uncompromising analysis of mainstream culture's representation of African Americans. If today's mass media rarely adopt an overtly racist stance, she argues, the images of racial harmony or equality they provide nevertheless work to indoctrinate viewers from a racist standpoint. It is her recognition of the *covert* freight carried by such representations, the assumptions underlying even 'positive images', which lends hooks's argument much of its power. It is not that racism flourishes *despite* the apparently liberal visions they offer; rather, those images themselves serve colonialist ideology, obliquely reproducing ideas which support a racially ordered social hierarchy.]

In the beginning black folks were most effectively colonized via a structure of ownership. Once slavery ended, white supremacy could be effectively maintained by the institutionalization of social apartheid and by creating a philosophy of racial inferiority that would be taught to everyone. This strategy of colonialism needed no country, for the space it sought to own and conquer was the minds of whites and blacks. As long as a harsh brutal system of racial apartheid was in place, separating blacks from whites by laws, coercive structures of punishment, and economic disenfranchisement, many black people seemed to intuitively understand that our ability to resist racist domination was nurtured by a refusal of the colonizing mindset. Segregation enabled black folks to maintain oppositional world views and standpoints to counter the effects of racism and to nurture resistance. The effectiveness of those survival strategies was made evident by both civil rights movements and the militant resistance that followed in their wake. This resistance to colonialism was so fierce, a new strategy was required to maintain and perpetuate white supremacy. Racial integration was that strategy. It was the setting for the emergence of neocolonial white supremacy.

Placed in positions of authority in educational structures and on the job, white people could oversee and eradicate organized resistance. The new neocolonial environment gave white folks even greater access and control over the African American mind. Integrated educational structures were the locations where whites could best colonize the minds and imaginations of black folks. Television and mass media were the other great neocolonial weapons. [. . .] While the Eurocentric biases taught to blacks in the educational system were meant to socialize us to believe in our inherent inferiority, it was ultimately the longing to have access to material rewards granted whites (the luxury and comfort represented in advertising and television) that was the greatest seduction. Aping whites, assimilating their values (i.e., white supremacist attitudes and assumptions) was clearly the way to achieve material success. And white supremacist values were projected into our living rooms, into the most intimate spaces of our lives by mass media. Gone was any separate space apart from whites where organized militant resistance could emerge. Even though most black communities were and remain segregated, mass media bring white supremacy into our lives, constantly reminding us of our marginalized status.

With the television on, whites were and are always with us, their voices, values, and beliefs echoing in our brains. It is this constant presence of the colonizing mindset passively consumed that undermines our capacity to resist white supremacy by cultivating oppositional world views. Even though most African Americans do not identify with the experiences of whites in real life or have intimate relationships with them, these boundaries are crossed when we sit facing the television. [...] Constantly and passively consuming white supremacist values both in educational systems and via prolonged engagement with mass media, contemporary black folks, and everyone else in this society, are vulnerable to a process of overt colonization that goes easily undetected. Acts of blatant racism are rarely represented in mass-media images. Most television shows suggest via the liberal dialogues that occur between white characters, or racially integrated casts, that racism no longer serves as a barrier. Even though there are very few black judges in the United States, television courtroom dramas cast black characters in these roles in ways so disproportionate to the reality that it is almost ludicrous. Yet the message sent to the American public and folks all over the world watching American television is that our legal system has triumphed over racial discrimination, that not only is there social equality but that black folks are often the ones in power. I know of no studies that have examined the role television has played in teaching white viewers that racism no longer exists. Many white folks who never have intimate contact with black folks now feel that they know what we are like because television has brought us into their homes. Whites may well believe that our presence on the screen and in their intimate living spaces means that the racial apartheid that keeps neighborboods and schools segregated is the false reflection and that what we see on television represents the real. [...]

Movies also offer us the vision of a world where white folks are liberal, eager to be social equals with blacks. The message of films like *Grand Canyon*, *Lethal Weapon*, *The Bodyguard*, and a host of other Hollywood films is that whites and blacks live together in harmony. Contemporary Hollywood films that show strife between races situate the tension around criminal behavior where black characters may exist as good or bad guys in the traditional racist cowboy scenario but where most whites, particularly heroic ones, are presented as capable of transcending the limitations of race.

For the most part television and movies depict a world where blacks and whites coexist in harmony although the subtext is clear; this harmony is maintained because no one really moves from the location white supremacy allocates to them on the race–sex hierarchy. Denzel Washington and Julia Roberts may play opposite one another in *The Pelican Brief* but there will not be a romance. True love in television and movies is almost always an occurrence between those who share the same race. When love happens across boundaries as in *The Bodyguard*, *Zebrahead* or *A Bronx Tale*, it is doomed for no apparent reason and/or has tragic consequences. White and black people learning lessons from mass media about racial bonding are taught that curiosity about those who are racially different can be expressed as long as boundaries are not actually crossed and no genuine intimacy emerges. Many television viewers of all races and ethnicities were enchanted by a series called *I'll Fly Away* which highlighted a liberal white family's struggle in the South and the perspective of the black woman who works as a servant in their home. Even though the series is often centered on the maid, her status is never changed or challenged. Indeed she is one of the 'stars' of the show. It does not disturb most viewers that at this moment in history black women continue to be represented in movies and on television as the servants of whites. The fact that a black woman can be cast in a dramatically compelling leading role as a servant does not intervene on racist/sexist stereotypes, it reinscribes them. [...] Mass media consistently depict black folks either as servants or in subordinate roles, a placement which still suggests that we exist to bolster and caretake the needs of whites. Two examples that come to mind are the role of the black female FBI agent in *The Silence of the Lambs*, whose sole purpose is to bolster the ego of the white female lead played by Jodie Foster. And certainly in all the *Lethal Weapon* movies Danny Glover's character is there to be the buddy who because he is black and therefore subordinate can never eclipse the white male star. Black folks confront media that include us and subordinate our representation to that of whites, thereby reinscribing white supremacy.

While superficially appearing to present a portrait of racial social equality, mass media actually work to reinforce assumptions that black folks should always be cast in supporting roles in relation to white characters. That subordination is made to appear 'natural' because most black characters are consistently portrayed as a little less ethical and moral than whites, not given to rational reasonable action. It is not surprising that it is those black characters represented as didactic figures upholding the status quo who are portrayed as possessing positive characteristics. They are rational, ethical, moral peacemakers who help maintain law and order.

Significantly, the neocolonial messages about the nature of r:
are brought to us by mass media do not just shape whites' mii
imaginations. They socialize black and other non-white minds .
Understanding the power of representations, black people have in both
the past and present challenged how we are presented in mass media,
especially if the images are perceived to be 'negative', but we have not
sufficiently challenged representations of blackness that are not obviously
negative even though they act to reinforce white supremacy. Concurrently,
we do not challenge the representations of whites. We were not outside
movie theaters protesting when the white male lead character in *Paris
Trout* brutally slaughters a little black girl (even though I can think of
no other image of a child being brutally slaughtered in a mainstream film)
or when the lead character in *A Perfect World* played by Kevin Costner
terrorizes a black family who gives him shelter. Even though he is a
murderer and an escaped convict, his character is portrayed sympatheti-
cally whereas the black male father is brutally tortured presumably because
he is an unloving, abusive parent. In *A Perfect World* both the adult white
male lead and the little white boy who stops him from killing the black
man are shown to be ethically and morally superior to black people.

Films that present cinematic narratives that seek to intervene in and
challenge white supremacist assumption, whether they are made by black
or white folks, tend to receive negative attention or none at all. John
Sayles's film *The Brother from Another Planet* successfully presented a
black male role. Rather than portraying a black male as a sidekick of a
more poweful white male, or as a brute and sex fiend, he offered us the
image of a gentle, healing, angelic black male spirit. John Waters's film
Hairspray was able to reach a larger audience. In this movie, white people
choose to be anti-racist, to critique white privilege. Jim Jarmusch's film
Mystery Train is incredibly deconstructive of racist assumptions. When
the movie begins we witness a young Japanese couple arriving at the bus
station in Memphis who begin to speak Japanese with a black man who
superficially appears to be indigent. Racist stereotypes and class assumptions are challenged at this moment and throughout the film. White
privilege and lack of understanding of the politics of racial difference are
exposed. Yet most viewers did not like this film and it did not receive
much attention. Julie Dash's film *Daughters of the Dust* portrayed black
folks in ways that were radically different from Hollywood conventions.
Many white viewers and even some black viewers had difficulty relating
to these images. Radical representations of race in television and movies
demand that we be resisting viewers and break our attachment to conventional representations. These films, and others like them, demonstrate that

film and mass media in general can challenge neocolonial representations that reinscribe racist stereotypes and perpetuate white supremacy. If more attention were given these films, it would show that aware viewers long for mass media that act to challenge and change racist domination and white supremacy.

Until all Americans demand that mass media no longer serve as the biggest propaganda machine for white supremacy, the socialization of everyone to subliminally absorb white supremacist attitudes and values will continue. Even though many white Americans do not overtly express racist thinking, it does not mean that their underlying belief structures have not been saturated with an ideology of difference that says white is always, in every way, superior to that which is black.

EXERCISE: Choose and view an episode of a television soap (preferably one which some of you already know) in which both dominant and subaltern groups are represented. Begin by describing each of the major characters in three dimensions, detailing (1) their social characteristics (profession, social class, etc.), (2) their personal qualities (moral or ethical status, positive or negative personality traits) and (3) their roles (central or secondary, active or reactive) in the narrative. Then consider to what degree these reproduce notional hierarchies such as are posited by racist ideology. Should this initially prove difficult, try mentally swapping the ethnicity of the characters; if the result seems implausible or 'unnatural', consider why the actual casting appears *natural* – that is, what assumptions have been naturalized by ideology to appear 'obvious' or 'commonsense'. Does characterization in the piece tend to reinforce racial stereotypes, or produce an integrationist vision which obscures the social reality?

4.4 Orality

Helen Gilbert, from 'De-scribing Orality: Performance and the Recuperation of Voice', in *De-scribing Empire: Post-colonialism and Textuality*, eds Chris Tiffin and Alan Lawson, London and New York: Routledge, 1994

[In the following extract Gilbert, a leading theorist of post-colonial performance, examines orality as an instrument of political resistance. Central to her thesis is the distinction made by linguist Émile Benveniste (1902–76) between two possible modes of utterance, *discours* and *histoire*. In effacing the role of the speaking subject, *histoire* claims for itself the authority of objectivity, thereby attributing to its claims the status of a past, self-evident truth: in contrast, *discours* situates itself in the here and now, acknowledging that it is by and for someone, and that its meanings are therefore the work of a specific speaker. Gilbert draws an implicit parallel between *histoire* and colonialist forms of representation, including Western illusionistic theatre, for the latter not only reproduces ideological images of the colonial world and its people but also effaces its process of 'telling' to present only the 'told'. But operating in the mode of *discours*, she argues, indigenous oral performance is able to puncture such illusions and their meanings (see also **Diamond**), posing the irreducible physical reality of Aboriginal peoples against hegemonic constructions of them to produce a **Brechtian** alienation-effect in which meaning becomes subject to contest.]

Language itself is obviously paramount in the articulation of hitherto muted indigenous voices, and it is widely accepted that the appropriation and abrogation of the colonizers' linguistic codes are essential to post-colonial writing. Like their literary counterparts, Aboriginal performance texts have incorporated these processes in varying degrees by using words (indigenous and creolized), syntax and grammar that differ from those of standard English. Kevin Gilbert's *The Cherry Pickers* (1988), initially performed in 1971 and regarded as the 'first Aboriginal play' in the European sense, makes a point of 'bastardizing' ([Kevin] Gilbert's own term) conventional English beyond the limits of the purely colloquial by using words like 'tremendaciously' and 'rememberising', as well as neologisms such as 'kunstidonus' or 'amphiskkulus', to satirize the pretentiousness of white speech and signal its inappropriateness to an Aboriginal context. This strategy is not specific to drama; what is specific, and particularly empowering, are the possibilities for enunciating such discourses orally and with recognizably Aboriginal inflections. Aspects of speech like tonality, diction, rhythm, and accent are clearly important performative tools here, as are associated metalinguistic features. Jimmy Chi's *Bran Nue Dae* (1991), for example, makes abundant use of such devices to produce a distinctive performance which, while conforming structurally and thematically to the popular musical genre, simultaneously subverts and extends its conventions. Opportunities for individual characters to articulate multiple identities abound in this text, which uses different *voices* for dialogue, story-telling and singing. Some of the most politically humorous moments in the play also arise from the deployment of voice. Willie's aping of Father Benedictus as the mission boys raid the school tuck-shop is a case in point: 'Yah it is gut to eat at der Lord's table. First ve haff made un inwentory of der spoils. Den ve haff to partake of der fruits ov our labours. Thankyou Lord!'[1] Although I can't recreate the specificity of the performance I attended, this quotation perhaps gives some idea of how accent might be used subversively to produce colonial mimicry which, as Homi Bhabha has shown, 'is at once a mode of appropriation and resistance' that reveals the ambivalence of colonial discourse and turns the 'insignia of its authority [into] a mask, a mockery'.[2]

Plays by Jack Davis, Bob Maza and others introduce substantial dialogues in Nyoongah and Boandik with minimal or no glossing, in attempts to recuperate Aboriginal languages as viable codes of communication. Because these languages are performed rather than inscribed, they proclaim radical alterity in a context where non-Aboriginal audience members can neither 'look up' the meaning nor quite imagine how such words might be scripted. If, as Ong suggests, the literate mind's 'sense of control over language is closely tied to the visual transformations of language',[3] this alterity, which prevents the seamless application of writing to the oral, enacts an important mode of resistance for oral cultures against the hegemony of literate ones. Bill Ashcroft's discussion of unglossed foreign languages in the written text illuminates this point:

> Signifiers of alterity are not necessarily inaccessible; rather they explicitly establish a distance between the writer and reader functions in the text as a cultural gap. The gap of silence reaffirms the parameters of meanability as cultural parameters, and the language use offers its own hybridity as the sign of an absence which cannot be simply traversed by an interpretation. It directly intercepts notions of 'infinite transmissibility' to protect its difference from the incorporating universalism of the centre.[4]

The oral text, I would argue, politicizes the signs of absence enacted through indigenous language usage even further by intensifying the ambivalent 'fear and desire' responses which codes of difference evoke in a majority audience. Whereas a reader will rarely read or sound out each word of an unglossed text, preferring simply to skip over to the familiar, an audience member experiences difference in complicated ways. On the one hand, aural signifiers, along with gesture and facial expression, make meaning more tantalizingly accessible and thus attach a promise of some understanding, and hence control, to the effort required to decipher the foreign. Nevertheless, at the same time, the verbal mode of communication conjures an 'other' that occupies theatrical time and space through a series of implosive sounds which cannot be ignored or fully appropriated.

The articulation of oppositional voices also raises the problem of translation, which is further complicated when one attempts to describe and/or enact a performative mode in a written text. Louis Nowra's *Capricornia* (1988) invalidates this activity by illustrating the comic effect of the reverse when Tocky, his part-Aboriginal protagonist, 'translates' the Bible into an oral performance in pidgin for her classmates while her teacher reads in a flat voice:

> MRS HOLLOWER: 'And the Philistine said unto David, "Am I a dog and thou comest to me with staves?" '
> TOCKY: The Philistine was a mongrel.
> MRS HOLLOWER: 'And the Philistine cursed David by his gods.'
> TOCKY: He told him to fuck off.
> MRS HOLLOWER: 'Then said David to the Philistine, "Thou comest to me with a sword, and with a spear, and with a shield ..." '
> TOCKY: He had sword, nulla nulla and woomera.[5]

This passage only begins to suggest the subversive possibilities in such a scene; more striking in dramatization are the particular inflections of a pidgin dialect and the rigidity of Mrs Hollower's voice and stance as opposed to the fluidity of Tocky's. As she translates, Tocky incorporates more and more gestures into her narrative until finally it becomes a full-blown carnivalesque performance when she *'mimes cutting off [Goliath's] head and shows it to the crowd, strutting as would David'*.[6] Mrs Hollower intervenes at this point and her comment that Tocky's translation is 'More than sufficient' is an uncomfortable recognition of the subversive power of the mode of excess created in the performance.

What she objects to most is Tocky's over-literal enactment of a text which largely derives its authority and 'truth value' (in the Foucauldian sense) from the historical contingency of its closure in written form. For Tocky, however, translating involves more than simply substituting one linguistic code for another. The differences between the two narratives can be discussed according to Émile Benveniste's notions of *histoire* and *discours*,[7] though these terms should not be set up as absolute binaries. Mrs Hollower's reading, which avoids interpretive nuances, attempts to abstract the narrative from any enunciative context and to suggest that meaning is fixed in the priority of language. Tocky's performance, on the other hand, foregrounds the role of the interlocutor and the specific context of utterance in the creation of meanings unfixed in *discours*. Aware of her audience (both onstage and in the auditorium) and her own position as entertainer, she undermines the agency of Mrs Hollower's *histoire* by refusing to represent the story symbolically or take its supposed message seriously. While Mrs Hollower insists that 'the word of God requires no translation', Nowra's text makes a quite different point: that translation is never a neutral act but a political one which involves operations of power, usually of the translator over the translated. [. . .]

In performance contexts, the truth, if any, is in the telling. By offering a wide range of potential articulations, dramatic texts amplify the splitting and hybridization of dominant discourses. The acoustic variability of actors' voices and the specific spaces they resonate in become significant sites of meaning. In particular, irony, mimicry and ambivalence, key linguistic strategies in post-colonial texts, can be inflected in diverse ways in performance. Discord, harmony, synchronicity, simultaneity and other auditory signifiers also offer possible ways of creating a performative heteroglossia that demonstrates the dialogic interactions between voices which Bakhtin outlines. Hence, whereas indigenous *writing* has been termed necessarily 'double-voiced since it must partake of the colonizing discourses in the process of literary decolonization',[8] Aboriginal *drama* could be more appropriately called voluntarily 'multi-voiced'.

In its multiple dissembling of axiomatic meanings, performance also opens up the possibility of enacting silence as a viable vocal mode of expression. As one of the framing devices for *The Cake Man*'s mission narrative, silence is the Aborigines' audible response to the colonizing moment when three white men attempt to 'civilize' a tribal family by proffering the Bible. The Aborigines' mute rejection of the 'gift' can be interpreted as an active protest against imposed languages, as can the increasingly frequent Pinteresque pauses in Sweet William's epilogue to the play. In performative contexts, silence enacts more than a problematic absence of voice which marks an untraversable gap between Aboriginal and white discourses. Unlike readers who must imagine silence through the words which evoke it, and who then fill this potential gap with plenitude as they read on, an audience experiences silence as a code of speech with its own illocutionary and perlocutionary effects. These emerge through the length and depth of the silence in the specific spaces of its enunciation, through its tenor in relation to the volume, tone and intent of the speech which circumscribes or interrupts it, and through the gestures and postures of the silent. And since an audience will normally respond to silence with more of the same, amplifying the initial presence/absence with multiple echoes, this collective silence marks an unusual chiasmus, a moment of discursive conjunction of Aboriginal and non-Aboriginal voices that is both democratic and anarchic.

In apposition to the silent voices in the initial scene, Merritt reintroduces the father of the tribal family as Sweet William, a particularly loquacious contemporary Aborigine who, in a long monologue or, more accurately, series of dialogues, alternately adopts the guises of story-teller, singer, biblical interpreter, drunken yarn-spinner, amateur philosopher and cultural mediator. The effectiveness of these voices, which articulate the rhetoric of a paradigmatic trickster figure, clearly relies on performative contexts and the vocal virtuosity of the actor to convey diverse subjectivities. Hence, although Sweet William sets himself up as a kind of souvenir, 'the Australian Aborigine ... made in England',[9] this identity is a 'rort' in more ways than one. As trickster, his adoption of different voices can be seen as a series of verbal rorts which are particularly theatrical in the sense that acting always implies deception in the notion of role. Continually shifting subjectivities are important here because they forestall attempts to fix the actor/character as the reified object of the viewer's gaze. [. . .]

I have outlined the specifically linguistic functions of a performative orality as the endless deferral of the authority of writing, the political intervention in translating processes, and the deployment of culturally inflected voices with which Aborigines can truly speak their differences, their partialities and their silences. The results are a Brechtian defamiliarization of language as a transparent signifier and a focus on 'voice' itself as a site of contestation. Also important in the performance of oral discourses are the specificities of their enunciative occasions, which will vary according to the actors involved, the spaces they perform in and the audiences with whom they interact. Ong argues that orality relegates meaning largely to context whereas writing concentrates meaning in language itself.[10] Current reader-response theories and studies in communication clearly show that writing as a signifier is not so unproblematic; however performance does utilize a wider range of semiotic systems in the production of meaning. Many of these systems, clearly influenced by culturally specific artistic conventions, are far too complex to be discussed in this paper except in so far as they evoke the oral in ways that an unperformed text cannot approximate.

The opportunity to build on speech with movement further revivifies oral traditions and aids the production of Aboriginal subjectivities. Terry Goldie has argued that since 'history awarded semiotic control to the invaders . . . the image of native peoples has functioned as a constant source of semiotic reproduction, in which each textual image refers back to those offered before'.[11] Performance intervenes in this object-signifying process through what Isidore Okpewho calls an 'expansion and ventilation of the body'.[12] In performance, the Aboriginal body has three functions. First, as a physical body, it is a sign of otherness that resists appropriation through the metaphysics of its insistent presence on stage. As a social body, however, it becomes a site of contestation showing the historical inscriptions of indigenous and colonizer cultures and their competing ideologies. Finally, as an artistic body, it bridges the gap between physical and social, grounding Aboriginal voices in speaking, moving subjects. [. . .]

If 'rhetoric . . . is essentially antithetical [because] the orator speaks in the face of at least implied adversaries',[13] Merritt's Sweet William is perhaps the paradigmatic Aboriginal orator. His rhetoric is designed to unsettle audience members, to make them aware of their prejudices, and to intervene in the illusionistic signifying processes of realist theatre. To a certain extent, his oratory 'alienates' Aboriginality, thus exposing it as an ideology that is mapped across the body as a system of beliefs and behaviours. This ideology reflects the dominant group's expectations and status quo as much as any essential identity. Sweet William's disingenuous pose as an 'authentic' boomerang-throwing Aborigine, for example, explicitly makes the audience complicit in the discourses of tourism, at the same time as it *im*plicitly subverts the voyeuristic conventions of both tourism and theatre.

Notes

1   J. Chi and Kuckles (1991) *Bran Nue Dae: A Musical Journey* (Sydney: Currency/Broome: Magabala Books), p. 7.
2   H. Bhabha (1985) 'Signs Taken for Wonders: Questions of Ambivalence and Authority under a Tree outside Delhi, May 1817', in F. Barker *et al.* (eds), *Europe and its Others: Proceedings of the Essex Conference on the Sociology of Literature, July 1984*, vol. 1 (Colchester: University of Essex), p. 103.
3   W. J. Ong (1982) *Orality and Literacy: The Technologizing of the Word* (London: Methuen), p. 14.
4   B. Ashcroft, G. Griffiths and H. Tiffin (1989) *The Empire Writes Back: Theory and Practice in Post-colonial Literatures* (London: Routledge), p. 72.
5   L. Nowra (1988) *Capricornia* (Sydney: Currency), p. 30.
6   *Ibid.*, p. 31.
7   É. Benveniste (1966) *Problems of General Linguistics* (Miami: University of Miami Press). See K. Elam (1980) *The Semiotics of Theatre and Drama* (London: Methuen), pp. 144–8, for a discussion of these distinctions in dramatic discourse; and S. Muecke (1983) 'Discourse, History, Fiction:

Language and Aboriginal History', *Australian Journal of Cultural Studies* 1/1: 71–80, who applies Benveniste's theories to Aboriginal oral narrative.

8   K. O. Arthur (1990) 'Neither Here Nor There: Towards Nomadic Reading', *New Literatures Review* 17: 31–44.

9   R. Merritt (1978) *The Cake Man* (Sydney: Currency), p. 12.

10   Ong, *Orality*, p. 106.

11   T. Goldie (1988) 'Signifier Resignified: Aborigines in Australian Literature', *Aboriginal Culture Today*, Special Issue of *Kunapipi* 10/1–2: 59–75.

12   I. Okpewho (1979) *The Epic in Africa: Towards a Poetics of the Oral Performance* (New York: Columbia University Press), p. 181.

13   Ong, *Orality*, p. 111.

EXERCISE: Have one of your number prepare for the session by choosing a short, simple story (one with a moral message or a hero-and-villain narrative) and writing a one-paragraph synopsis of it: do not be concerned about the literary merit of story or synopsis. Have them tell the tale at the start of the class, 'bringing it to life' as far as possible, only afterwards providing copies of the synopsis. Then compare story and performance to consider what the act of story-telling itself added to the tale. Did it offer additional meanings, emphasize or alter its moral import? If it fostered particular responses to characters, how did this inflect the audience's overall reaction to the events recounted? Using the results of your deliberations, plan and practise ways of modifying the story-telling so that the tale's moral would be reversed without altering the tale itself.

Now choose a scene from a play in which a member of a non-dominant ethnic group is represented in a conventional or stereotypical manner (you might use the play you analysed in the **JanMohamed** exercise). Enact the piece experimentally, looking for ways in which the performer playing that character might counter its given textual representation. How can the representation be rendered ironic, offered up for critical reflection? Consider the use of asides, 'mugging', miming or mimicking (of other characters, or of the discourses or behaviours of the dominant group generally) to undermine the scene's assumptions. How might you emphasize the real physical presence of the performer to mark his or her distance from the stereotypical character? You are seeking ways of establishing a *discours* to puncture and subvert the *histoire* of the text.

Part five

The performing body

In this case : ←they get to experience what the dancers are conveying

The body of live performance is unique in that, unlike the bodies represented *by* other media, it occupies the same time and space as the audience. Whereas mainstream film, say, presents only the fictional character, the live performer's emphatic physical presence has the capacity to remind viewers of the outside of the fiction, juxtaposing the body which is signified, performed, with the real, signif*ying* body of the performer. The theorization of the performer is dealt with elsewhere in this volume (see **Brecht**, **Diamond**, **Gilbert**): the following selection of pieces deals primarily with the cultural, signified body, that which is performed. The current, very widespread critical focus on the culturally coded body is informed by work from a range of different disciplines. Anthropology has long recognized the cultural specificity of posture and gesture and their meanings (LeBarre 1947, Mauss 1974) [1935], and of the symbolic prescriptions and prohibitions that surround corporeal processes (Douglas 1966). Recent sociology has highlighted the body's institutional and discursive construction (Turner 1996). Varied structuralist and post-structuralist writings have viewed it as the locus of signification or of signification's failure (e.g. Barthes 1972b, Foucault 1977a, 1979), while allied psychoanalytical theories have explored its role in the inauguration of selfhood (Lacan 1977, Kristeva

1982). Perhaps the greatest impact in recent decades has been made by feminist scholarship, which has, for example, examined the role of the body in the construction of gendered and sexual identity (**Butler** 1990a), explored how the everyday practices it undertakes reproduce patriarchal systems (Walum 1974) and viewed it as the possible site of resistance (**Cixous** 1996). If there is a central tendency in such varied perspectives, it is an insistence on the body's materiality while simultaneously asserting that this materiality is also the basis for signification, and hence cultural meaning. Such meanings, already inscribed on the bodies of performers and in the gaze of spectators, are inevitably mobilized and negotiated on the stage.

The following excerpts examine various aspects of the symbolic coding of the body. Michel Foucault (1926–84) considers political investments in the body and its actions. Patrice Pavis (b. 1947) provides a semiotic analysis of the kinesics of mime which can be extended to other kinds of perform-ance movement. Only the piece by Elizabeth Grosz (b. 1952) addresses the eruption of the real body through signification, looking at the ways in which corporeality is hedged about with taboos, and how transgressing these can challenge symbolic systems. Elizabeth Wilson (b. 1936) explores bodily adornment as the canvas on which multiple meanings meet and find resolution.

(In this volume, see also **Butler, Bakhtin, Lott.**)

Further reading: Contrasting perspectives on the socialized or politicized body are offered by Elias 1978, **Foucault** 1977a, 1979 and Polhemus (ed.) 1978, which as a group provide a good introduction to its possibilities; for examples of the various ways Dance Studies has approached the moving body see Foster 1986, (ed.) 1996, Franco 1995 and Manning 1993; Warner 1985 is an excellent introduction to representation and the gendered body generally, while Adair 1992, Burt 1995 and Phelan 1993 consider that body in performance; Douglas 1966, **Grosz** 1995, Russo 1994 and Schneider 1997 all explore the significance of bodily transgression; for the adorned body see **Barthes** 1967, Hollander 1975, Lurie 1981 and, partic-ularly, **Wilson** 1985.

5.1 Political bodies

Michel Foucault, from *Discipline and Punish: The Birth of the Prison*, Harmondsworth: Penguin, 1977 [originally published 1975]

[In works dealing with topics as diverse as psychopathology, sexuality, medicine and prisons, Foucault consistently examines society's oppressive definition of the individual. With a formulation which owes much to Nietzsche, in the following piece he argues that, as part of modernity, political power came to be exerted over bodies less by direct coercion than by a diffuse, invisible 'discipline'. Underlying this is his concept of 'power-knowledge'. When an individual is defined and quantified via a given form of knowledge – the science of psychiatry, say, or sexology – a relation of power, that of knower to known, is formed. Placing the inmate of a penitentiary under surveillance establishes the same kind of power-relation, with the gaoler made the watcher, the holder of knowledge, and the prisoner induced to enact the corresponding role of the watched. The impact on behaviour is direct, for in 'disciplining' their activity in accordance with knowledge's conception of them, individuals inscribe power on their own bodies, in effect performing hegemonic models of the human subject. Thus in a variety of institutions, ranging from the school to the prison, asylum, factory and army, forms of power-knowledge effected a literal shaping of bodily actions, articulating a 'micro-physics of power' which would disseminate into the wider social whole.]

Historians long ago began to write the history of the body. They have studied the body in the field of historical demography or pathology; they have considered it as the seat of needs and appetites, as the locus of physiological processes and metabolisms, as a target for the attacks of germs or viruses; they have shown to what extent historical processes were involved in what might seem to be the purely biological base of existence; and what place should be given in the history of society to biological 'events' such as the circulation of bacilli, or the extension of the life-span. But the body is also directly involved in a political field; power relations have an immediate hold upon it; they invest it, mark it, train it, torture it, force it to carry out tasks, to perform ceremonies, to emit signs. [. . .] This subjection is not only obtained by the instruments of violence or ideology; it can also be direct, physical, pitting force against force, bearing on material elements, and yet without involving violence; it may be calculated, organized, technically thought out; it may be subtle, make use neither of weapons nor of terror and yet remain of a physical order. That is to say, there may be a 'knowledge' of the body that is not exactly the science of its functioning, and a mastery of its forces that is more than the ability to conquer them: this knowledge and this mastery constitute what might be called the political technology of the body. Of course, this technology is diffuse, rarely formulated in continuous, systematic discourse; it is often made up of bits and pieces; it implements a disparate set of tools or methods. In spite of the coherence of its results, it is generally no more than a multiform instrumentation. Moreover, it cannot be localized in a particular type of institution or state apparatus. For they have recourse to it; they use, select or impose certain of its methods. But, in its mechanisms and its effects, it is situated at a quite different level. What the apparatuses and institutions operate is, in a sense, a micro-physics of power, whose field of validity is situated in a sense between these great functionings and the bodies themselves with their materiality and their forces.

Now, the study of this micro-physics presupposes that the power exercised on the body is conceived not as a property but as a strategy, that its effects of domination are attributed not to 'appropriation', but to dispositions, manoeuvres, tactics, techniques, functionings; that one should decipher in it a network of relations, constantly in tension, in activity, rather than a privilege that one might possess; that one should take as its model a perpetual battle rather than a contract regulating a transaction or the conquest of a territory. In short this power is exercised rather than possessed; it is not the 'privilege', acquired or preserved, of the dominant class, but the overall effect of its strategic positions – an effect that is manifested and sometimes extended by the position of those who are dominated. [. . .] This means that these relations go right down into the depths of society, that they are not localized in the relations between the state and its citizens or on the frontier between classes and that they do not merely reproduce, at the level of individuals, bodies, gestures and behaviour, the general form of the law or government. [. . .]

Perhaps, too, we should abandon a whole tradition that allows us to imagine that knowledge can exist only where the power relations are suspended and that knowledge can develop only outside its injunctions, its demands and its interests. [. . .] We should admit rather that power produces knowledge (and not simply by encouraging it because it serves power or by applying it because it is useful); that power and knowledge directly imply one another; that there is no power relation without the correlative constitution of a field of knowledge, nor any knowledge that does not presuppose and constitute at the same time power relations. These 'power-knowledge relations' are to be analysed, therefore, not on the basis of a subject of knowledge who is or is not free in relation to the power system, but, on the contrary, the subject who knows, the objects to be known and the modalities of knowledge must be regarded as so many effects of these fundamental implications of power-knowledge and their historical transformations. In short, it is not the activity of the subject of knowledge that produces a corpus of knowledge, useful or resistant to power, but power-knowledge, the processes and struggles that traverse it and of which it is made up, that determines the forms and possible domains of knowledge. [. . .]

Docile bodies

Let us take the ideal figure of the soldier as it was still seen in the early seventeenth century. To begin with, the soldier was someone who could be recognized from afar; he bore certain signs: the natural signs of his strength and his courage, the marks, too, of his pride; his body was the blazon of his strength and valour; and although it is true that he had to learn the profession of arms little by little – generally in actual fighting – movements like marching and attitudes like the bearing of the head belonged for the most part to a bodily rhetoric of honour; 'The signs for recognizing those most suited to this profession are a lively, alert manner, an erect head, a taut stomach, broad shoulders, long arms, strong fingers, a small belly, thick thighs, slender legs and dry feet, because a man of such a figure could not fail to be agile and strong'; when he becomes a pike-bearer, the soldier 'will have to march in step in order to have as much grace and gravity as possible, for the pike is an honourable weapon, worthy to be borne with gravity and boldness'.[1] By the late eighteenth century, the soldier has become something that can be made; out of a formless clay, an inapt body, the machine required can be constructed; posture is gradually corrected; a calculated constraint runs slowly through each part of the body, mastering it, making it pliable, ready at all times, turning silently into the automatism of habit; in short, one has 'got rid of the peasant' and given him 'the air of a soldier' (ordinance of 20 March 1764). Recruits become accustomed to

> holding their heads high and erect; to standing upright, without bending the back, to sticking out the belly, throwing out the chest and throwing back the shoulders; and, to help them acquire the

habit, they are given this position while standing against a wall in such a way that the heels, the thighs, the waist and the shoulders touch it, as also do the backs of the hands, as one turns the arms outwards, without moving them away from the body ... Likewise, they will be taught never to fix their eyes on the ground, but to look straight at those they pass ... to remain motionless until the order is given, without moving the head, the hands or the feet ... lastly to march with a bold step, with knee and ham taut, on the points of the feet, which should face outwards.

(ordinance of 20 March 1764) [...]

What was so new in these projects of docility that interested the eighteenth century so much? It was certainly not the first time that the body had become the object of such imperious and pressing investments; in every society, the body was in the grip of very strict powers, which imposed on it constraints, prohibitions or obligations. However, there were several new things in these techniques. To begin with, there was the scale of the control: it was a question not of treating the body, *en masse*, 'wholesale', as if it were an indissociable unity, but of working it 'retail', individually; of exercising upon it a subtle coercion, of obtaining holds upon it at the level of the mechanism itself – movements, gestures, attitudes, rapidity: an infinitesimal power over the active body. Then there was the object of the control: it was not or was no longer the signifying elements of behaviour or the language of the body, but the economy, the efficiency of movements, their internal organization; constraint bears upon the forces rather than upon the signs; the only truly important ceremony is that of exercise. Lastly, there is the modality: it implies an uninterrupted, constant coercion, supervising the processes of the activity rather than its result and it is exercised according to a codification that partitions as closely as possible time, space, movement. These methods, which made possible the meticulous control of the operations of the body, which assured the constant subjection of its forces and imposed upon them a relation of docility-utility, might be called 'disciplines'. [...] The historical moment of the disciplines was the moment when an art of the human body was born, which was directed not only at the growth of its skills, nor at the intensification of its subjection, but at the formation of a relation that in the mechanism itself makes it more obedient as it becomes more useful, and conversely. What was then being formed was a policy of coercions that act upon the body, a calculated manipulation of its elements, its gestures, its behaviour. The human body was entering a machinery of power that explores it, breaks it down and rearranges it. A 'political anatomy', which was also a 'mechanics of power', was being born; it defined how one may have a hold over others' bodies, not only so that they may do what one wishes, but so that they may operate as one wishes, with the techniques, the speed and the efficiency that one determines. Thus discipline produces subjected and practised bodies, 'docile' bodies. Discipline increases the forces of the body (in economic terms of utility) and diminishes these same forces (in political terms of obedience). In short, it dissociates power from the body; on the one hand, it turns it into an 'aptitude', a 'capacity' which it seeks to increase; on the other hand, it reverses the course of the energy, the power that might result from it, and turns it into a relation of strict subjection. If economic exploitation separates the force and the product of labour, let us say that disciplinary coercion establishes in the body the constricting link between an increased aptitude and an increased domination.

The 'invention' of this new political anatomy must not be seen as a sudden discovery. It is rather a multiplicity of often minor processes, of different origin and scattered location, which overlap, repeat or imitate one another, support one another, distinguish themselves from one another according to their domain of application, converge and gradually produce the blueprint of a general method. They were at work in secondary education at a very early date, later in primary schools; they slowly invested the space of the hospital; and, in a few decades, they restructured the military organization. They sometimes circulated very rapidly from one point to another (between the army and the technical schools or secondary schools), sometimes slowly and discreetly (the insidious militarization of the large workshops). On almost every occasion, they were adopted in response to particular needs: an industrial innovation, a renewed outbreak of certain epidemic diseases, the invention of the rifle or the victories of Prussia. This did not prevent them being totally inscribed in general and essential transformations, which we must now try to delineate.

There can be no question here of writing the history of the different disciplinary institutions, with all their individual differences. I simply intend to map on a series of examples some of the essential techniques that most easily spread from one to another. These were always meticulous, often minute, techniques, but they had their importance: because they defined a certain mode of detailed political investment of the body, a 'new microphysics' of power; and because, since the seventeenth century, they had constantly reached out to ever broader domains, as if they tended to cover the entire social body. Small acts of cunning endowed with a great power of diffusion, subtle arrangements, apparently innocent, but profoundly suspicious, mechanisms that obeyed economies too shameful to be acknowledged, or pursued petty forms of coercion – it was nevertheless they that brought about the mutation of the punitive system, at the threshold of the contemporary period. Describing them will require great attention to detail: beneath every set of figures, we must seek not a meaning but a precaution; we must situate them not only in the inextricability of a functioning but in the coherence of a tactic. They are the acts of cunning, not so much of the greater reason that works even in its sleep and gives meaning to the insignificant, as of the attentive 'malevolence' that turns everything to account. Discipline is a political anatomy of detail.

Note

1   J. de Montgomery (1636) *La Milice français*, p. 6 and p. 7.

EXERCISE: Choose two institutional situations, one in which the operation of power is overt (e.g. an officer interviewing a private soldier or a lesson in a classroom) and one in which it is not (a visit to a hospital, a day's work in an office, a church service). Record the 'rules' governing individual bodily behaviour in both (posture, demeanour, dress, kinds of movement or injunctions to be still) and the larger arrangements in which they are located (positioning of bodies in space, differences in elevation, organization of lines of sight, etc.). Now consider how those situations express power. Who is the knower (present or absent) and what knowledge does he or she operate? Who are the known and what do they present themselves *as* – in effect, what knowledge or conception of themselves do they enact in another's gaze – by behaving in the required way? Pin down modes of knowledge by naming them as precisely as you can – e.g. 'Christian theology', 'rules of politeness' – and exploring the model of the individual implicit to their 'discipline'.

Now select a scene from a play in which socio-political power is central; a trial scene, perhaps, or one set in a king's court. First, determine its three-part formula of power – known, knower and form of knowledge – as before. Then, as a practical exercise, have one of your group speak all the lines while others mime the action, experimenting with ways of expressing that power-knowledge via the body alone. Do not be content to signal, say, high and low status; rather, ask how the specific mode of knowledge characterizes each individual (what does it mean to be a serf? a criminal defendant? a private soldier?) and seek ways of signifying that social identity.

5.2 Moving bodies: the mime

Patrice Pavis, from 'The Discourse of (the) Mime', in
Languages of the Stage: Essays in the Semiology of Theatre,
trans. Susan Melrose and Barbara Behar, New York:
Performing Arts Journal, 1982 [originally published 1980]

[One of Theatre Studies' most influential semioticians, Pavis has in his writings addressed topics ranging from Brechtian acting to drama criticism, intercultural performance and the mechanics of theatrical signification. His semiotic approach in the following piece bears comparison with Saussure's, for he sees each mime as creating what is in effect a system. It is not via individual gestures, he argues, that the mimodrama images its object; rather, this is achieved when its initial actions provide the key (in **Goffman**'s sense) to the logic underpinning that object's 'gestural universe'. The resulting performance not only conjures the quoted regime of movement, it offers the audience additional meaning in the form of an attitude expressed towards that movement, a perspective upon it that emerges from the tension between the mime and the realm of ordinary gestures it quotes. Perhaps the key term in the essay is 'coherence', for in Pavis's use two meanings come together: it is in *cohering*, combining to form a kinesic language, that individual movements become intelligible, *coherent*. In choosing mime, a form in which the body operates independently of dialogue, set and other performance media, he offers a way of understanding how bodily movement itself signifies.]

The inaction of the Earth

What does the mime's body say? [. . .] To speak of mime – or, worse still, to write on mime – is to dwell awkwardly on a few moments of gesture. All that remains of what Amiel[1] does are a few shots that allow us, after the event, to spin out what he says.

Fortunately, mime lends itself to being captured by the photographic lens, for it is made up more of attitudes and poses than of movements; like the eye of the camera, the human eye chooses privileged moments when the body, even in the midst of agitation and transformation, discovers flashes of eternity. People in the theatre call it the *presence* of the body; they point to this paradox of the art of gesture, namely that: 'in the discourse of mime, the poetic attitude-image has first priority, over-shadowing the movement-translation'.[2] But this silence of the body is deceptive. It precedes and prepares for the imperceptible unfolding of the hand, the arm, the torso: the hands seem to seize hold of a sphere, they know no rest, they concentrate and encompass the world of the story to be created. All that can be read for the moment is the crossing of the forearms and feet, the curve of the back that precludes the temptation to identify the body with something. The mime often begins his evolution with the image of an unusual position, of an artifically produced form, controlled by a rigid body whose center seems masked and displaced.

But before the evolution can actually begin, the key to the reading of the whole sequence must be provided. This key indicates the modality of the body in action, the distance separating normal gesture (ours, the one we normally experience) from the gestural mode in which what follows must be 'read'. A gap almost makes itself felt, strangely preparing a new vision of gesture. At the beginning of his mimodrama, Amiel embodies an astronaut moving through weightlessness according to laws that have nothing to do with those of our everyday world and to which we have become accustomed through the NASA films. Walking by slow hops on the moon – or on any other planet discovered by our astronaut – the mime elaborates a new system of gesture which, once mapped out, must retain its coherence. Any system or gestural modality is possible, provided it is sustained. The spectator's pleasure comes from his understanding, accepting and finally becoming accustomed to this new convention. The difficulty for Amiel is to play this ease of movement, to produce through a slight bending of the knees the illusion that he will fly away if he steps a little too heavily on the ground. The slightest muscular error and the modal key to the gesture would be accidentally destroyed and, with it, the sense of sequence and the logic of the gestural narrative.

Even more than for verbal discourse, modality indicates the actor's attitude toward his text: persuasion, doubt, irony, play. This is not merely a psychological pointer to the action but a piece of information on the very nature of the gesture: in the case of mime, gestural enunciation is immediately poured back into its text, it becomes one with it and consti-tutes it in a narrative of a mode other than the one of 'everyday' gestures.

Hence we can feel the paradox of gesture in the theatre of the body. In 'real life' our gestures are often superimposed on our verbal discourse to complement it, contradict it or add nuances to it. In the case of silent mime, it is very difficult to produce gestures that comment on a gestural sequence: any metagestural commentary is in fact reduced to the same level as the other gestures. It is difficult to separate the one from the other, for we grant the same importance to all gestures without seeking to distinguish a substratum of gestures that will be submitted to a metagestural commentary.

The coherence of a mime sequence, which occurs when the same modality is maintained, also seriously limits the possibilities of mime. Thus the spectator is troubled by the intervention of the spoken word in gesture, for the universe of gesture is then contaminated by meaning of a different sort. No exchange, other than a distancing one, can be established between the body and the shock of the sound it utters. Similarly, a mute gestural dialogue between two mimes is very difficult for they would have to find the gestural equivalent in terms of the gestures of the other person. At this point, the mime dialogue quickly results in a cross-coding of two discourses, as when two mutes 'discuss' something by means of a common code of equivalences between words and gestures.

That is why the gestural dialogues in the sketches where two characters are playing together are always a little disappointing: thus, in the orchestra-conductor sketch Amiel plays a conductor constantly interrupted by a facetious violinist. If there is a dialogue, it takes place only at the level of psychological reactions and anecdote; we have no problem imagining the words that could he exchanged between the two men. Immediately, the 'musician clown gag' ruins the work of the body; it is at once too recognizably anecdotal and banal. When the body tries to say too much, and with too much wit, the body is 'talkative', overstated by an overly precise story and discourse.

The mime should therefore be left alone, and his only dialogue should be the one established between what he does and what he does not do, between normative gestures and their poetic deviation: the comparison between two universes of differing coherence and modality, between our immobility and the limits of our body, and his movements and original mode of existence creates the dialogue in the spectator.

But this dialogue is only initiated – with Amiel as with all mimes – when the body begins to unfold, tears itself from inert matter and sketches in a narrative.

The unfolding of the human narrative

The narrative takes place in time and in the unfolding of the whole body. The body is in a vertical position, available for movement, ready to evolve and to adjust to all the shifts of weight. The face looking towards the camera seems the only fixed relationship. The arms are undecided between support and rejection. The angle of perspective deforms the body's symmetry and elongates the mime's stature. As soon as it is freed from weight and inert matter, the body is open to all metamorphoses. Amiel takes as a theme for his variations on creation the genesis of various species of animals: the frog, the spider, the eagle, the gorilla . . . and man. (The last two are difficult to distinguish.) Each gestural narrative takes shape before our eyes, starting from that flash which indicates to us what animal and what action is being presented to us. Some reality effect, no matter how tenuous, is therefore essential to the identification of the sequence being mimed. Even the most abstract mimodrama does not escape this mimetic recognition; indeed, it relies on it to construct the phases of its story.

But it is not by mere imitation of an object that mime recreates the reality it seeks to symbolize. Gestural narrativity proceeds musically: the mime produces first an easily identifiable sequence, a basic theme that will then be varied and clarified until the gestural action of this basic theme appears sufficiently autonomous and clear. The body secretes an impression of recognition and strangeness, then sculpts it and pushes it to the work boundaries of cliché. The important thing is that the minimal sequence be clearly understood and that the spectator be able to graft on to it all the different improvisations: it will be quickly understood that the astronaut is absent-mindedly manipulating various levers and that the frog is croaking and puffing itself up through the periodic movement of arms and curved back.

The minimal narrative includes only a few characteristic phases of the evolution of the mime: for example, it may be created by the association of certain movements which, taken in the same sequential order, refer unmistakably to the same story.

In fact, the gesture does not have to be recognizable as a theme or have a precise meaning: gestural narrativity is organized syntactically rather than semantically – for example, by systems of thematic or meaningful oppositions (movement/attitude; speed/slowness; jerky movements/smooth movements; life/death; animate/inanimate, etc.). Mimes have often, in their theoretical writings, tried to pinpoint this quality of gesture that distinguishes their gestures from mere 'mechanical and geometrical movement in space'.[3] For Marcel Marceau, 'the mime-actor vibrates like the strings of a harp. He is lyrical: his gesture seems crowned with a poetic halo.'[4] Beyond these metaphors, we must know how to interpret these intuitions as the metalanguage proper to the gesture of mime: not, as Marceau states, a happy marriage of form (gestural architecture) and content (the social meaning of gesture), but knowledge by the mime of a codification proper to the 'normal' gesture, and the art of transposing gesture by extracting from it certain pertinent signs, knowing how to combine them in a contrived sequence that, nevertheless, appears natural.

The gesture of such a sequence can be spaced out and broken down into a precise program. It is always clearly 'framed' by a mark indicating the beginning and end of one action so that it appears quoted like a word in quotation marks emerging clearly from the surrounding text. This 'framing' of gestural moments clearly structures the spatio-temporal continuum and isolates several phases from everyday gesture and real movement. That is why we often have the impression, when we see the mime, of watching several clearly separated 'gestural jerks'. Within each phase, the gestural space is modeled, compressed, stretched out, broken down, according to the mime's attitude to his narrative.

The attitudes which many mimes consider to be the result and quintessence of the mimodrama crystallize the whole sequence and form the armature of the story: 'what the mime must do is to juxtapose the numerous attitudes that he has constructed'.[5]

These privileged moments of mime – the moments of a certain attitude – suggest by contrast all that is left unsaid or rather 'undone' by the body, conspicuous by its absence but actively participating in the construction of meaning. We know that the dramatic text (also the poetic text and that of everyday conversations) deliberately says only a tiny part of what we understand through extratextual elaboration, the play of presuppositions and cultural references. In the same way, the 'gestural text' very often gives evidence of a very great economy of means: to signify the vanity of the pig sunbathing on the beach, for example, it is enough to have him delicately rub his skin with cream. What is left 'undone' in gesture is everything the mime boasts of being able to do without establishing his character or sketching in an action; this makes him all the better perceived. It is this 'undone', just as much as the perceivable gesture, which produce the illusion of a new being and a new world, of an endless metamorphosis of mime. [. . .]

137

The quotations of the little pig in leotards

This little pig is even more lovable for putting on very human airs. He is obviously obsessed with his skin. He performs very delicate little movements with his hands to remove body hair, stretch negligently, pose his elbow on his knee to express idleness and the desire for seduction. But, while indicating to us the importance of quotation in the discourse of mime, he does us a particular epistemological service. [. . .] For it is only by reference to everyday gesture that we find the delicacy of the little pig's gestures comic: he is quoting a cultural code, and in the theatre the recognition of the ideological effect makes us understand and smile. The quoted gesture is always clearly detachable from the continuum; it only needs a few signs to be recognized (the astronaut's gum chewing; the coquette's nose in the air; the cowboy taken from a Sergio Leone spaghetti western; the pose of Rodin's thinker in the blind man sketch; etc.). Quotation also very frequently functions as self-quotation: gesture enlarges and clarifies the basic sequence that provided the key to the object being imitated. The 'musical' nature of the story and the gestural narrative explains this taste for thematic repetition, quotation and variation.

That is the charm of mime, but also its worst enemy: there is nothing more tedious than a mime repeating himself over and over again, bringing to our notice an action that we have long ago identified and which is purely and simply replayed in the same version. Thus any gesture is quotation of a gesture, i.e., an 'inter-gesture' (a fact partly discerned by the Brechtian theory of the *Gestus*). We would, therefore, be tempted to contradict Etienne Decroux when he states that 'mime is a succession of present actions' and that 'the word alone can evoke absent things'.[6]

Moreover, this is also a quotation, by contrast or absence, of a gestural norm systematically violated by the mime: that of our own body and our own way of moving. The mime challenges this norm and only seems to obey his own laws and conventions: he frequently makes us forget the law of gravity, leans forward dangerously without falling, simulates movements while walking on the spot. The spectator's pleasure is to contemplate himself in this body which always seems to have its own way, free from physical laws, malleable, and capable of shaping and being shaped at will. This explains why we so frequently see a mimodrama whose hero is struggling with an insurmountable physical obstacle (a ball to be picked up, a man to be pushed away, support to be achieved in order to get one out of a sticky situation).

As for poetic language, it is the deviation from a norm, a theoretically neutral set of gestures that enhances the originality of the gestural image, and indicates the artistic procedure being used. Sometimes, without its being essential, the mime (Decroux, Jerry de Giacomi in his 'exercises in the style of Decroux') is seeking an ideal plasticity, a body with the proportions and poses of a classical statue. Of course, this ideally harmonious model does not exist, but haunts the sculptor and remains an inaccessible archetype.

The pleasure of quoting with one's body the discourse of others, and, for the spectator, of deciphering these allusive charades, is the whole charm of the theatre of gesture. Gestural discourse is so full of quotations that in the end it becomes an original and autonomous text, making us forget that it is made up of a host of lucky finds, so perfect is the illusion of a body coinciding with the object being imitated.

Notes

1   This article analyses a performance by mime artist Amiel at the festival 'Mime and Mask', *Porte de la Suisse*, on 27 January 1979.
2   Jean Dorcy (undated) *J'aime la mime* (Paris: Editions Denoel), p. 60.
3   M. Marceau (1958) 'Le halo poétique', in Jean Dorcy (ed.), *À la recherche de la mime* (Neuilly-sur-Seine: Les Cahiers de Danse et Culture), p. 140.
4   *Ibid.*, p. 138.
5   E. Decroux (1963) *Paroles sur le mime* (Paris: Gallimard), p. 125.
6   *Ibid.*, p. 135.

EXERCISE: Choose a short sequence of dance (or mime or movement-theatre, if preferred); a performance on video, which you can rerun during analysis, might be preferable. First, list the kinds of movement that make up its kinesic vocabulary. Is there a consistent use of sudden, ragged or 'spontaneous' gestures, or do movements which are evenly paced, 'dignified' or hieratic dominate? Do performers reach up and stand on points, seeking elevation, or hug the floor? Choose your descriptive terms carefully, for they must be broad enough to encompass movements which are different but precise enough to encapsulate the qualities they share. Then consider how these elements relate to each other. Are ragged movements posed *against* the fluid, or do earthbound and elevating actions counterpoint each other? Do sudden gestures of the hands parallel violent movements of the whole body? You are seeking the logic underpinning the piece's coherence.

Now analyse the performance's relationship to the realm of non-performance movement. Consider what recognizable regimes of movement it quotes and, in doing so, what 'attitude' it takes towards them – that is, what is indicated by its particular deviation or distance from, or inflection of those movements. If it depicts a soldier marching, what do its gestural forms say about that soldier or his march? If it quotes recognizably masculine or feminine behaviours, what perspective upon them or the figure performing them does it offer? You are seeking those meanings which the performance itself generates.

5.3 Transgressive bodies

Elizabeth Grosz, from 'The Body of Signification', in *Abjection, Melancholia and Love: The Works of Julia Kristeva*, eds John Fletcher and Andrew Benjamin, London and New York: Routledge, 1990

[In the following essay Grosz explores the foundation of the symbolic coding of the body, a consistent topic of her work, as figured in the writings of structuralist polymath Julia Kristeva (b. 1941). Following psychoanalist Jacques Lacan, Kristeva asserts that it is the body's surface, acting as a notional border, which initially enables us to see ourselves as distinct entities, defining us as 'subjects' by marking our separation from the 'objects' of the surrounding world (1982). Although this occurs during the 'Mirror Stage', before our entry into the realm of culture (see **JanMohamed**), cultures subsequently remobilize that experience symbolically, policing the body's perimeter with signs and rituals so that acts or materials which cross or question it are defined as 'abject', to be viewed with disgust. The body is thereby invested with cultural meanings, its materiality obscured by signs, so that our conception of our bodies reflects and reinforces the ruling socio-symbolic order. But if abjection guards the borders of the subject and society, abject materials and acts can also be used to affirm our corporeality, subverting those symbolic systems in which our sense of self is enmeshed. This theory thus provides a framework in which to analyse the impact of contemporary transgressive performance.]

Corporeality and subjectivity

For writers as diverse as Lyotard, Irigaray, Deleuze, Derrida and Foucault, the body is conceived as a fundamentally historical and political object; indeed, for many it is the central object over and through which relations of power and resistance are played out. Although clearly the interests, methods and frameworks of these writers are extremely diverse, each is concerned to challenge the ways in which the body has been relegated to a subordinate or secondary position relative to the primacy of the mind, consciousness or reason. Each is committed to a non-reductive materialism, a materialism which, rather than mere brute physicality, also includes the materiality of discourses, as well as psychical drives and unconscious processes. Each develops a materialism which, while refusing prevailing biologistic, naturalistic and physicalist reductions of the body to the status of brute, given object, nevertheless accepts its irreducible materiality and corporeality as a condition of subjectivity. The subject is produced as such by social and institutional practices and techniques, by the inscriptions of social meanings, and by the attribution of psychical significance to body parts and organs. The interlocking of bodies and signifying systems is the precondition both of an ordered, relatively stable identity for the subject and of the smooth, regulated production of discourses and stable meanings. It also provides the possibility of a disruption and breakdown of the subject's, and discourses', symbolic registration.

In place of the mind/body dichotomy, the fundamental connectedness of the mind to the body, the creation of a psychical 'interior' for the bodies' object-like status, the mapping of the body's interior on its exterior and its exterior on its interior, all need to be theorized. Kristeva's conception of the body's role in psychical development and in signification provides a major, if undeveloped, contribution to such an understanding. Only if the body's psychical interior is projected outwards, and its material externality is introjected as necessary conditions of subjectivity, can the dualism of our Cartesian heritage be challenged. [. . .]

For Lacan, the development of the infant's ego is dependent on its ability to identify with an image of its corporeal unity. [. . .] His notion of the imaginary anatomy is derived from his understanding of the mirror stage. The imaginary anatomy is a psychical map or *image* of the body which is internalized by the subject and lived as real. It is a specular and psychical construct, a representation of the subject's lived experiences of its bodily parts and organs. It is not a photographic or realist representation of the body, nor is it a scientifically valid representation, one capable of accounting for the body's physiological functions. Rather, it is a fantasized image, the complex result of the subject's internalization of its specular image and its acceptance of everyday social and familiar belief about the body's organic structure – a product, that is, of cultural and libidinal investments in the body:

> If the hysterical symptom is a symbolic way of expressing a conflict between different forces ... to call these symptoms functional is but to confess our ignorance, for they follow a pattern of a certain imaginary Anatomy which has typical forms of its own ... I would emphasise here that the imaginary anatomy referred to here varies with the ideas (clear or confused) about bodily functions which are prevalent in a given culture. It all happens as if the bodily-image had an autonomous existence of its own, and by autonomous I mean here independent of objective structure. All the phenomena we've been discussing seem to exhibit the laws of *gestalt*.[1]

Lacan explicitly refers to the formative work of Roger Caillois and Paul Schilder in developing his notion of the imaginary anatomy.[2] Both stress that the subject's acquisition of a sense of self, of continuous identity, is the result of the child's ability to locate itself within a body in space, and thus to have a spatial comportment. Incidentally, the mirror stage not only presents the subject with an image of itself, it also duplicates in representational form the environment, enabling real and virtual space to be directly compared. For Lacan the imaginary anatomy it provides is the 'threshold of the visible world'.[3]

Freud's cortical homunculus [the 'little man in the head'] is literalized in Lacan's model. Lacan claims that 'the cerebral cortex functions like a mirror' and that 'it is the site where the images are integrated into the libidinal relationship which is hinted at in the theory of narcissism'.[4] This 'cortical mirror' is not however a neuro-physiological but a psychological postulate. Lived in an external, 'natural' space – a space, incidentally, which is acquired and not innate – the body must also gain a conceptual and psychical spatiality in order for it to be lived as the subject's own, for the subject to reside in or as its body.

From these psychoanalytic indications, it seems that the subject is not an unanchored, disembodied physical entity – whether it is conceived only in terms of consciousness or split between a consciousness and an unconsciousness. It is a subject, an ego, only with reference to the mapping and signification of its corporeality. Although this occurs through the mediation of the image of the body and the degree of erotogenicity of its surface in the mirror stage and the pre-oedipal period, it is clear that the child's particular mode of corporeality – its sex and concrete corporeality – is also relevant to the kind of symbolic and oedipal identity it comes to acquire. The child is positioned as a symbolic subject with reference to the (patriarchal) meaning of its anatomy: this is what Freud calls the 'oedipus complex' and Lacan defines as the 'Law of the Father'. The body's sexual specificity – or rather, the social meaning of its sexual organs – will position the subject either as having (for men) or being (for women) the phallus, and through its relation to the phallic signifier, positions it as a subject or object in the symbolic. [. . .]

Abject bodies

Kristeva's notion of abjection provides a sketch of that period which marks the threshold of the child's acquisition of language and a relatively stable enunciative position. In *Powers of Horror* she argues that it is only through the delimitation of the 'clean and proper' body that the symbolic order, and the acquisition of a sexual and psychical identity within it, becomes possible.[5] Abjection attests to the perilous and provisional nature of the symbolic control over the dispersing impulses of the semiotic drives, which strive to break down and through identity, order, and stability. Through abjection, bodily processes become enmeshed bit by bit in significatory processes in which images, perceptions and sensations become linked to and represented by 'ideational representatives' or signifiers.

Kristeva explores the ways in which the inside and the outside of the body, the spaces between the subject and object, and the self and other become structured and made meaningful through the child's taking up a position in the symbolic order. These pairs need to be oppositionally coded in order for the child's body to be constituted as a unified whole and for its subjectivity to be definitively tied to the body's form and limits. They are the conditions under which the child may claim the body as its own, and thus also the conditions under which it gains a place as a speaking being and point of enunciation.

Kristeva is fascinated by the ways in which 'proper' sociality and subjectivity are based on the expulsion or exclusion of the improper, the unclean, and the disorderly elements of its corporeal existence that must be separated from its 'clean and proper' self. The ability to take up a symbolic position as a social and speaking subject entail the disavowal of its modes of corporeality, especially those representing what is considered unacceptable, unclean or anti-social. The subject must disavow part of itself in order to gain a stable self, and this form of refusal marks whatever identity it acquires as provisional, and open to breakdown and instability.

Kristeva's claim is not entirely new. It is a variation of Freud's position in *Totem and Taboo* and *Civilisation and its Discontents*, where he claims that civilization is founded on the sacrifice or expulsion of pre-oedipal polymorphous pleasures and 'impure' incestual attachments to parental love objects. What is new about Kristeva's position is her claim that what must be expelled from the subject's corporeal functioning can never be fully obliterated but hovers at the border of the subject's identity, threatening apparent unities and stabilities with disruption and possible dissolution. Her point is that it is impossible to exclude the threatening or anti-social elements with any finality. They recur and threaten the subject not only in those events Freud described as the 'return of the repressed' – that is, in psychical symptoms – they are also a necessary accompaniment of sublimated and socially validated activities, such as the production of art, literature and knowledges, as well as socially unacceptable forms of sexual drives. Even in the most sacrosanct, purified and socially sanctioned of activities, the unclean and the improper must be harnessed. The subject's recognition of this impossibility provokes the sensation and attitude that she calls 'abjection'. [. . .]

The objects generating abjection – food, faeces, urine, vomit, tears, spit – inscribe the body in those surfaces, hollows, crevices, orifices, which will later become erotogenic zones – mouth, eyes, anus, ears, genitals. All sexual organs and erotogenic zones, Lacan claims, are structured in the form of the rim, which is the space between two corporeal surfaces, an interface between the inside and the outside of the body. These corporeal sites provide a boundary or threshold between what is inside the body, and thus part of the subject, and what is outside the body, and thus an object for the subject. This boundary must be traversed by the incorporation and/or expulsion of erotic objects. Objects are, in this sense, neither fully contained within the subject's body nor ever entirely expelled from it. [. . .]

Abjection is the underside of the symbolic. It is what the symbolic must reject, cover over and contain. The symbolic requires that a border separate or protect the subject from this abyss which beckons and haunts it: the abject entices and attracts the subject ever closer to its edge. It is an insistence on the subject's necessary relation to death, to animality and to materiality, being the subject's recognition and refusal of its corporeality. The abject demonstrates the impossibility of clear-cut borders, lines of demarcation, divisions between the clean and the unclean, the proper and the improper, order and disorder. [. . .]

Kristeva distinguishes three broad categories of abjects, against which various social and individual taboos are erected: food, waste and the signs of sexual difference (roughly corresponding to oral, anal and genital erotogenic drives). The subject's reaction to these abjects is visceral: it is usually expressed in retching, vomiting, spasms, choking – in brief, in disgust. These reactions signal bodily functions which a 'rational consciousness' cannot accept; yet the subject cannot adequately deny them either. They represent a body in revolt, a body disavowed by consciousness which it is yet unable to ignore.

Although it is highly culturally variable, it seems that all cultures have some corporeal processes which are abjected. Abjection is a by-product of the social and psychical investment in and privileging of certain bodily zones and sensations at the expense of others. It results from those corporeal functions which cannot be readily classified and thus remain ambiguous. The abject is undecidably inside and outside the body (like the skin of milk), dead and alive (like the corpse), autonomous and engulfing (like infection and pollution). It is what disturbs identity, system and order, disrupting the social boundaries demanded by the symbolic. It respects no definite positions, or rules, boundaries or socially imposed limits.

Abjection is the body's acknowledgement that the boundaries and limits imposed on it are really social projections – effects of desire, not nature. It testifies to the precarious grasp of the subject on its own identity, an assertion that the subject may slide back into the impure chaos out of which it was formed. It is, in other words, an avowal of the death drive, a movement of undoing identity.

Notes

1   J. Lacan (1953) 'Some Reflections on the Ego', *International Journal of Psychoanalysis* 34: 13.
2   R. Caillois (1984) 'Mimickry and Legendary Psychaesthenia', trans. John Shepley, *October* 31; P. Schilder (1978) *The Image and Appearance of the Human Body* (New York: International Universities Press).
3   J. Lacan (1977) 'The Mirror Stage as Formative of the Function of the I as Revealed in Psychoanalytic Experience', in *Écrits: A Selection,* trans. Alan Sheridan (London: Tavistock/Routledge & Kegan Paul), p. 3.
4   *Ibid.,* p. 13.
5   J. Kristeva (1982) *Powers of Horror: An Essay in Abjection,* trans. Leon S. Roudiez (New York: Columbia University Press).

EXERCISE: Choose three public acts or performances which fore-ground the body's physicality, one which is transgressive, one which is not and one whose status is uncertain, borderline or a matter of individual opinion: consider sexual 'entertainments', contact sports, body modification, life drawing classes, funeral practices, 'daredevil stunts', etc. Discuss what prohibitions surrounding the body each illus-trates. If an act entails scanty dress or no dress, how is it usually regarded, and what taboos governing the revealing of bodies does this demonstrate? Do different taboos operate in different contexts? Consider abject materials and acts, threats to the body's boundary or integrity, and so on. Try to relate the prohibitions you find to taboos in ordinary social life, considering how the abject is ordinarily contained. You are seeking the signs and meanings circumscribing the 'clean and proper body' in your culture.

Now consider the work of a live artist such as Karen Finlay, Ron Athey, Annie Sprinkle, Gina Pane, Franco B. or Orlan, whose performances can provoke revulsion and outcry. (If you cannot see a live performance, view a video or amass written and pictorial infor-mation.) Begin by analysing your own response to the work. If you feel revulsion, outrage or physical or emotional discomfort, precisely what assumptions about the 'proper' body are prompting those feel-ings – what is threatened in such acts? Do they resist symbolization, insisting on the body's materiality? If so, how, and what effect does that have on the 'fictional' status of the performance?

5.4 The body adorned

Elizabeth Wilson, from *Adorned in Dreams: Fashion and Modernity*, London: Virago, 1985

[Whereas others have conceived of dress variously as a semiotic system, a set of cultural 'rules', a tool of gender oppression and a badge of group identity, for cultural analyst Wilson it is instead the arena in which these and other meanings and functions converge. Occupying an ambiguous posi-tion at the interface of nature and culture, clothing and bodily adornment are, in the modern world, the points at which personal expression and public codes and mores meet. It is this capacity for semic pluralism, Wilson argues, which enables dress today to function as a means of asserting identity, a canvas on which the fragmented modern subject can represent and symbolically resolve the contradictory forces bearing on its sense of self. In recognizing the multiple dimensions to bodily adornment, she provides a tool for analysing the potential diversity of meanings that may be mobilized in stage costume.]

What is the source of this uneasiness and ambiguity, this sense that clothes have a life of their own? Clothes without a wearer, whether on a second-hand stall, in a glass case, or merely a lover's garments strewn on the floor, can affect us unpleasantly, as if a snake had shed its skin. Similarly, a pregnant woman described how the little frock hanging up in readiness for her as yet unborn child seemed like 'a ghost in reverse'.

A part of this strangeness of dress is that it links the biological body to the social being, and public to private. This makes it uneasy territory, since it forces us to recognize that the human body is more than a biological entity. It is an organism in culture, a cultural artefact even, and its own boundaries are unclear:

> Can we really assume that the limits and boundaries of the human body itself are obvious? Does 'the body' end with the skin or should we include hair, nails? . . . What of bodily waste materials? . . . Surely the decorative body arts such as tattooing, scarification, cranial modification and body painting should also be considered . . . [and] it has been shown that it is insignificant (if not inaccurate) to sharply differentiate between bodily decoration and adornment on the one hand and the clothing of the body on the other hand.[1]

No wonder we feel uneasy as we gaze at the crinolines in the costume court.

Clothing marks an unclear boundary ambiguously, and unclear boundaries disturb us. Symbolic systems and rituals have been created in many different cultures in order to strengthen and reinforce boundaries, since these safeguard purity. It is at the margins between one thing and another that pollution may leak out. Many social rituals are attempts at containment and separation, devised to prevent the defilement that occurs when matter spills from one place – or category – into another.[2]

If the body with its open orifices is itself dangerously ambiguous, then dress, which is an extension of the body yet not quite part of it, not only links that body to the social world, but also more clearly separates the two. Dress is the frontier between the self and the not-self.

In all societies the body is 'dressed', and everywhere dress and adornment play symbolic, communicative and aesthetic roles. Dress is always 'unspeakably meaningful'.[3] The earliest forms of 'clothing' seem to have been adornments such as body painting, ornaments, scarifications (scarring), tattooing, masks and often constricting neck and waist bands. Many of these deformed, reformed or otherwise modified the body. The bodies of men and of children, not just those of women, were altered – there seems to be a widespread human desire to transcend the body's limitations.

Dress in general seems then to fulfil a number of social, aesthetic and psychological functions; indeed it knots them together, and can express all simultaneously. This is true of modern as of ancient dress. What is added to dress as we ourselves know it in the West is *fashion*. The growth of the European city in the early stages of what is known as mercantile capitalism at the end of the Middle Ages saw the birth of fashionable dress, that is of something qualitatively new and different.

Fashion is dress in which the key feature is rapid and continual changing of styles. Fashion, in a sense, *is* change, and in modern Western societies no clothes are outside fashion; fashion sets the terms of all sartorial behaviour – even uniforms have been designed by Paris dressmakers; even nuns have shortened their skirts; even the poor seldom go in rags – they wear cheap versions of the fashions that went out a few years ago and are therefore to be found in second-hand shops and jumble sales. Dress still differs in detail from one community to another – middle-aged women in the English 'provinces' or in the American Midwest, or in Southern Italy or in Finland don't look exactly like one another, and they look still less like the fashion freaks of Paris or Tokyo. Nevertheless they are less different than they probably feel, for their way of dressing is inevitably determined by fashion. At 'punk' second-hand fashion stalls in the small market towns of the south of France it is possible to see both trendy young holiday makers and elderly peasants buying print 'granny frocks' from the 1940s; to the young they represent 'retro-chic', to the older women what still seems to them a suitable style. But the granny frocks themselves are dim replicas, or sometimes caricatures, of frocks originally designed by Chanel or Lucien Lelong in the late 1930s. They began life as fashion garments and not as some form of traditional peasant dress.

Even the determinedly *un*fashionable wear clothes that manifestly represent a reaction against what *is* in fashion. To be unfashionable is not to escape the whole discourse, or to get outside the parameters. Indeed the most dowdy clothes may at any moment suddenly get taken up and become, perversely, all the rage. Harold Macmillan, Prime Minister of Britain in the late 1950s and early 1960s, used to wear a shapeless, knitted cardigan – it was part of his country gentleman's persona of 'unflappability'. This (which was also and perhaps even more influentially worn by Rex Harrison as Professor Higgins in the film *My Fair Lady*) became for a season the smart item that every young woman 'had' to have. Since Macmillan himself possibly used the garment semi-deliberately as one of the stage props for his public self, its transformation into a fashion was a kind of double parody.

This is one example of the contradictory nature of fashion, with its ever swinging pendulum of styles. Changes in fashion styles not only represent reaction against what went before; they may be self-contradictory too. A nineteenth-century belle might wear military frogging on her jacket as if to undercut the femininity of her gown; in the 1960s young women bared their thighs to the crotch, yet veiled their faces with curtains of hair parted in the middle like a Victorian maiden's. Often the contradictions appear senseless. Constantly changing, fashion produces only conformity, as the outrage of the never-before-seen modulates into the good manners of the faultlessly and self-effacingly correct. To dress fashionably is both to stand out and to merge with the crowd, to lay claim to the exclusive and to follow the herd. Looked at in historical perspective its styles display a crazy relativism. At one period the breasts are bared, at another even a V-neck is daring. At one time the rich wear cloth of gold embroidered with pearls, at another beige cashmere and grey suiting. In one epoch men parade in ringlets, high heels and rouge, at another to do so is to court outcast status and physical abuse.

Yet despite its apparent irrationality, fashion cements social solidarity and imposes group norms, while deviations in dress are usually experienced as shocking and disturbing. [. . .]

The sense of unease when we are 'improperly' dressed or of disapproval when we feel that others have similarly offended, is no doubt related to the intimate dialogue between our clothes and our body. We use the phrase 'her slip was showing' (although now that slips are ceasing to be worn, by younger women at least, the phrase itself is falling into disuse) to indicate something more than slight sartorial sloppiness, to suggest the exposure of something much more profoundly ambiguous and disturbing; it reminds us that the naked body underneath the clothes and paint is somehow unfinished, vulnerable and leaky at the margins.

Yet at the same time the limits of conventional dress act as a barrier we attempt constantly to breach, a boundary we dare to cross. It is both defence and attack, both shield and sword.

In the twentieth century the morality of dress has become to a large extent disassociated from the rigid behavioural codes that once sustained it. This means that although it remains an emotive subject, it cannot be quite so normative as once it was. Its stylistic changes do retain a compulsive and seemingly irrational quality but at the same time fashion is freed to become both an aesthetic vehicle for experiments in taste and a political means of expression for dissidence, rebellion and social reform. This is possible, also, because in the twentieth century fashion, without losing its obsession with the new and the different, with change and exclusivity, has been mass-produced.

The mass production of fashionable styles – itself highly contradictory – links the politics of fashion to fashion as art. It is connected both to the evolution of styles that circulate in 'high' and avant-garde art; and to popular culture and taste.

Those fashion commentators, therefore, who still feel able to discuss fashion in terms largely of social psychology – as primarily a form of *behaviour* – miss its significance for the twentieth century. An investigator of the psychology of clothes might interview individuals to discover their feelings about their clothes and might observe the sartorial behaviour of various social groupings. This could be developed into an anthropological or ethnographic perspective towards Western fashion as though this were no more than simply a particular kind of 'sartorial behaviour' similar to the sartorial behaviour of 'traditional' or 'ancient' societies. This is often done, but misses the crucial historical dimension of fashion – as though we were to discuss the films of Antonioni in terms of the conventions of ancient Greek tragedy, as if both expressed some eternal 'human spirit'. To reduce fashion to psychology also excludes, or at best minimizes, the vital *aesthetic* element of fashion. Fashion's changing styles owe far less to psychological quirks than to the evolution of aesthetic styles generally.

It is not that the behavioural aspect of dress is without interest, but this book is intended to some extent as a corrective to that approach, which inevitably overplays the unintentional, irrational and seemingly absurd aspects of dress, and particularly of fashionable exaggeration. Of course dress does 'speak' status, it does betray the unconscious of both the individual and the group, it does have a moral dimension. *Adorned in Dreams*, however, explores it as a cultural phenomenon, as an aesthetic medium for the expression of ideas, desires and beliefs circulating in society. Fashion is, after all, 'a form of visual art, a creation of images with the visible self as its medium'.[4] Like any other aesthetic enterprise fashion may then be understood as ideological, its function to resolve formally, at the imaginary level, social contradictions that cannot be resolved.[5] [. . .]

How then can we explain so double-edged a phenomenon as fashion? It may well be true that fashion is like all

> cultural phenomena, especially of a symbolic and mythic kind, [which] are curiously resistant to being imprisoned in one . . . 'meaning'. They constantly escape from the boxes into which rational analysis tries to pack them: they have a Protean quality which seems to evade definitive translation into non-symbolic – that is, cold unresonant, totally explicit, once-for-all-accurate – terms.[6]

This suggests that we need a variety of 'takes' on fashion if the reductive and normative moralism of the single sociological explanation is to be avoided while we yet seek to go beyond the pure description of the art historian. The attempt to view fashion through several different pairs of spectacles simultaneously – of aesthetics, of social theory, of politics – may result in an obliquity of view, even of astigmatism or blurred vision, but it seems that we must attempt it.

It would be possible to leave fashion as something that simply appears in a variety of distinct and separate 'discourses', or to say that it is itself merely one among the constellation of discourses of postmodernist culture. Such a pluralist position would be typical of postmodernist or post-structuralist theoretical discourse (today the dominant trend among the avant-garde and formerly 'left' intelligentsia): a position that repudiates all 'over arching theories' and 'depth models' replacing these with a multiplicity of 'practices, discourses and textual play . . . or by multiple surfaces'.[7] Such a view is 'populist' and 'democratic' in the sense that no one practice or activity is valued above any other; moral and aesthetic judgements are replaced by hedonistic enjoyment of each molecular and disconnected artefact, performance or experience. Such extreme alienation 'derealizes' modern life, draining from it all notion of meaning. Everything then becomes play; nothing is serious. And fashion does appear to express such a fragmented sensibility particularly well – its obsession with surface, novelty and style for style's sake highly congruent with this sort of postmodernist aesthetic.

Yet fashion clearly does also tap the unconscious source of deep emotion, and at any rate is about more than surface. Fashion, in fact, is not unlike Freud's vision of the unconscious mind. This could contain mutually exclusive ideas with serenity; in it time was abolished, raging emotions were transformed into concrete images, and conflicts magically resolved by being metamorphosed into symbolic form.

From within a psychoanalytic perspective, moreover, we may view the fashionable dress of the Western world as one means whereby an always fragmentary self is glued together into the semblance of a unified identity. Identity becomes a special kind of problem in 'modernity'. Fashion speaks a tension between the crowd and the individual at every stage in the development of the nineteenth- and twentieth-century metropolis. The industrial period is often, inaccurately, called the age of 'mass man'. Modernity creates fragmentation, dislocation. It creates the vision of 'totalitarian' societies peopled by identical zombies in uniform. The fear of depersonalization haunts our culture. 'Chic', from this perspective, is then merely the uniform of the rich, chilling, anti-human and rigid. Yet modernity has also created the individual in a new way – another paradox that fashion well expresses. Modern individualism is an exaggerated yet fragile sense of self – a raw, painful condition.

Our modern sense of our individuality as a kind of wound is also, paradoxically, what makes us all so fearful of not sustaining the autonomy of the self; this fear transforms the idea of 'mass man' into a threat of self-annihilation. The way in which we dress may assuage that fear by stabilizing our individual identity. It may bridge the loneliness of 'mass man' by connecting us with our social group. Fashion, then, is essential to the world of modernity, the world of spectacle and mass-communication. It is a kind of connective tissue of our cultural organism. And, although many individuals experience fashion as a form of bondage, as a punitive, compulsory way of falsely expressing an individuality that by its very gesture (in copying others) cancels itself out, the final twist to the contradiction that is fashion is that it often does successfully express the individual.

Notes

1   T. Polhemus (ed.) (1978) *Social Aspects of the Human Body* (Harmondsworth: Penguin), p. 28.
2   M. Douglas (1966) *Purity and Danger: An Analysis of Concepts of Pollution and Taboo* (Harmondsworth: Penguin).
3   T. Carlyle (1831) *Sartor Resartus* (London: Curwen Press).
4   A. Hollander (1975) *Seeing Through Clothes* (New York: Avon Books).
5   F. Jameson (1981) *The Political Unconscious: Narrative as Socially Symbolic Act* (London: Methuen), p. 79.
6   B. Martin (1981) *A Sociology of Contemporary Cultural Change* (Oxford: Basil Blackwell), p. 28.
7   F. Jameson (1984) 'Postmodernism, or the Cultural Logic of Late Capitalism', *New Left Review* 146 (July/August).

EXERCISE: Choose a production of a play you know and assemble pictures of its characters' costumes. Selecting three contrasting examples, analyse each in detail for their multiple levels of significance. View them as self-expression, revealing the characters' inner personalities, fantasies and desires; as socially coded, signifying class, gender, social hierarchies, group membership; as symbolic, attributing to individuals abstract qualities; as the bearers of 'moral' injunction, upholding or contravening rules of decency: distinguish as many different dimensions of meaning as you can. Only when you have exhausted each costume analytically should you consider its varied meanings together, noting which appear complementary, which antagonistic, etc. You are seeking that diversity of meanings symbolically resolved in dress, by which costume design signifies each character's 'identity'.

Now analyse the relationship between all the different costumes, noting when the qualities they suggest complement, parallel or oppose each other, to discern the overall pattern of vestimentary meaning. How does that pattern inflect the play? Does it align the characters in predictable or unpredictable ways; does it reflect the play's themes as written, or supplement, challenge or alter them? If this proves difficult, try mentally transposing some costumes, noting how your conception of the production alters. You are seeking the way costume design *interprets* the written text.

Part six

The space of
performance

Space is a continuum, no more than the name we give to the combination of three dimensions, and most of the divisions within it which we acknowledge are of human manufacture. As a consequence such divisions tend to have a significance which is beyond the merely functional. If walls and perimeters have a concrete existence and a practical purpose, they also divide space symbolically, partitioning the world according to criteria which are cultural. This has particular importance for performance, founded as it is on specific perceptions of space. When in orthodox theatre we see the actor as King Lear, we are performing an essentially interpretative act, translating real bodies, words and movements into the objects of another, hypothetical world; and we do so at least partly on the understanding that everything within the defined spatial compass of the stage is to be read differently from the objects seen elsewhere. This containment of our reading activities, a conceptual 'framing', is often signalled as appropriate by a physical 'key' (see **Goffman**). The literal frame surrounding a painting, the plinths on which statues are displayed, arches overhanging the playing areas of traditional theatres and stages raised above the level of the audience – all these act as the material equivalents of conceptual borders, separating readable space from the

155

ordinary space surrounding it to shape the viewer's response. This is not to say that all performed events are framed in the same manner, for festivals, ballet, stand-up comedy and circus all establish their own kinds of inter-pretative space. Indeed, the history of theatre in the twentieth century provides numerous examples of practitioners who rejected orthodox spatial arrange-ments, seeking to have their stages understood in new ways. Such experiments are not without their political dimension, for, as **Brecht**, **Mulvey**, **Diamond** and **Gilbert** demonstrate, to control symbolic space is effectively to control the audience's reading of the event, and hence the meanings that may be discerned there.

The following pieces examine the symbolic loading of space from quite different directions. Yi-Fu Tuan (b. 1930) meditates on how performers and spectators establish, empower and experience space. The distinction Robert Weimann draws between two general kinds of dramatic space offers a way of understanding the spatial arrangements of modern performance. Marvin Carlson (b. 1935) looks at the existing symbolic resonance of the space in which performances are situated.

(In this volume, see also **Bristol**, **Bakhtin**, **Goffman**, **Turner**.)

Further reading: useful theoretical approaches to space are given by Jameson 1991, Lefebvre 1991, Massey and Allen (eds) 1984 and Soja 1989; Hall 1959, 1966 and Watson 1970 deal with proxemics in ways useful for exploring stage space, although a good, short introduction to this can be found in Whitmore 1994: the theatrical juxtaposition of fictional and non-fictional space is central to the **Brecht**, **Diamond** and **Gilbert** pieces in this volume; for analyses of modern urban space see Pile 1996 and Watson and Gibson (eds) 1995.

6.1 Enacting space

Yi-Fu Tuan, from 'Space and Context', in *By Means of Performance: Intercultural Studies of Theatre and Ritual*, eds Richard Schechner and Willa Appel, Cambridge: Cambridge University Press, 1990

[Fundamentally interdisciplinary, geographer Tuan's work combines perspec-tives drawn from such diverse fields as anthropology, philosophy and sociology. Basic to his position in the following piece is the understanding that performance space is a product of its perceptual context. He uses the term 'performance' in the broadest sense, to include all human acts carried out with a real or notional spectator in mind, and so with an awareness that they are expressive. A feature of human consciousness *per se*, this self-awareness is nevertheless mobilized in different ways within different cultural situations, each performative event providing a unique spectator-performance relationship and framing of its acts. It is via the dynamics of these relationships or frames that performance space is defined; as that area which is judged symbolically charged, and hence 'readable'. Space in this sense is less a physically demarcated domain than the perceived product of interpretative conventions, formed in a complex relationship between viewer and viewed and the cultural expectations they share.]

Unrehearsed acts

Infants do not perform. Their self-consciousness and consciousness of others are minimally developed. The space they occupy is small; likewise the world they perceive. As they grow older they gain greater mobility, acquire more control over space, and become more aware of the expectation and critical appraisal of others. They have fallen from innocence into culture – into a life of performance. Older children and adults are subject to attacks of shyness and even stage fright. On important occasions people rehearse the gestures and words that they may be called upon to present. Even in casual talk among friends, there are those moments when the voices of others are tuned out as an individual prepares the words that s/he hopes to contribute, words with accompanying gestures that will raise her in the esteem of others. The shyness and self-consciousness come out of the premonition that the rehearsal may be inadequate, or that it may not produce the desired result. Worse is the feeling that one's posture, motions and words may transmit messages that are not part of one's intention: this is the actor's fear of inducing laughter at the wrong places. Normally, social exchange is not so dire. Friends appear to be paying attention. When this happens, space expands and resonates as in a music hall with perfect acoustics. Friends, however, can look distracted and yet say, unconvincingly, 'Go on, we are listening.' Space then turns cold and dead; one's voice begins to sound tinselly and disembodied.[1]

Under what conditions do we adults shed our status as cultural beings? I was going to say, 'while we perform our natural functions in the privacy of the bathroom'. Perform? The word sounds right. We remain actors. After all, as toddlers we perform on the pot to the applause of our parents. Perhaps we are truly natural beings at the moment before

157

we fall asleep. The status of the sleeping body is curious. On the one hand, it seems a mere object vulnerable to the predatory gaze of others. It is an object that occupies space but does not command it. On the other hand, a sleeping body can emanate a sense of power. People may gaze but not too close. Any time the eyes may open and in a flash destroy a relationship of inferiority and superiority. An aura of drama can surround a sleeping body – the drama of its imminent repossession of a world.

Someone has a heart attack and collapses on the floor. Such a sudden and dramatic movement is yet not a performance. Witnesses become frantic and calm down only after they have straightened the body, placed the arms in repose across the breast, and pulled a sheet over the face. The contorted body, even though it is known to be dead, cannot be left in the natural – that is, unlearned and undeliberated – posture of collapse. An onlooker instinctively feels that the contorted posture cannot be maintained. The corpse may spring back to life in protest. An electric tension fills the space surrounding the body until it is laid out like an effigy over a tomb and the eyelids are closed.[2]

The following story comes out of the death camp at Treblinka. A dancer stands naked in line waiting for her turn to enter the gas chamber. We see a human being with its natural power to command space reduced to a body taking up space, passively submitting to the prospect of death. A guard tells her to step out of line and dance. She does, and carried away by her authoritative action and by her repossession of a self and a world she dances up to the guard – now within the compass of *her* space – takes his gun and shoots him. What a surprise to the guard that a zombie-like creature can spring back to life by means of performance![3]

The desperately sick and the dying in a hospital have withdrawn from the field of action. They submit to nature. Yet how strong is the call upon them to perform – to die with dignity or peacefully, and perhaps with a gesture or words that reassure the living. The hospital, unless one is inured to its ambience, is a dramatic place. To people who work there, it can seem a life-enhancing place where babies are born, and the sick and the old die. Birth, pain and death give focus to life. Someone like Walt Whitman, who volunteered service in a hospital, would have appreciated the quickening of the senses in a world where the senses are *in extremis*.[4]

The hospital as theater? That would seem to be a frivolous idea. Yet the operating room is often called the theater. Space there is charged with tension and high drama. Who are the spectators and who the actors? In a teaching hospital, the medical students are the spectators; they are seated on rising tiers of benches that overlook the operating table in center stage. The doctors and nurses are the actors, but also spectators when they are not actively engaged. What about the anesthetized patient? All he has to do is to lie still and breathe. Yet his is the cynosure of attention. Isn't this an actor's ideal – to sway multitudes without seeming to act at all?

Anthropologists like Erving Goffman have familiarized us with the idea that in almost any social setting we not only act but put on an act whether we know it or not (Goffman 1974). But from the viewpoint of the participants this 'not knowing' makes a crucial difference. It is what makes life seem normal and sane albeit also somewhat boring. After prolonged submersion in this normal life, we wish an opportunity to put on an act, to dramatize ourselves and our world; we wish for a quickened sense of life, which can also be got vicariously by watching a performance – sports, plays and even a car accident. Normal, ordinary routines are themselves not worth watching. Yet this is not quite correct. The sort of things that people do every day *are* worth watching, provided we can look without being looked at. Hence the popularity of sidewalk cafés where one can sit and watch the street scene. Hence also the peculiar fascination of catching glimpses of ordinary life behind the illuminated windows of tenement houses which may happen when, in the early hours of the evening, we ride on an elevated train back to our suburban home. We see a family having supper and then, through another window, a man scratching his armpit or watching TV. Because they cannot see us, we who can see them feel like the gods; and what lie open to our gaze are the unguarded and unrehearsed – hence vulnerable and genuine – moments in people's lives.[5]

Conscious performance

In ordinary activities, we are conscious of space and time and make calculations concerning them out of practical needs. We are not, however, usually aware of how our bodies form patterns and rhythms, or of how our bodies command space. In ritual and theater, people are of course far more conscious of their relations. A choreographer or (for that matter) a football coach may well think of human bodies as merely devices for defining space and time. The different ways that people can be aware of space or try to create spectral realms and spatial sculptures by means of bodily movements and gestures are almost infinite. Here are a few

A human figures sits on the ground, legs crossed Buddha-fashion. Calm space surrounds it. The figure stands. It stays still and yet projects

159

a sense of imminent action, charging the space ahead with tense potency. As the figure moves, space takes on a fluid and dynamic character. To the individual in action, space is primarily a kinesthetic feeling – a feeling that reaches well beyond the body. To the spectator, space is kinesthetic feeling to the extent that he is able to identify with the performer. But to the spectator, space is also a visual pattern 'out there' – a pattern woven by the performing figure. Where several figures appear, their positions and motions define space. Again, compared with performers, spectators are more fully conscious of the overall visual pattern of space: the space of spectators – even while it visibly changes before their eyes – is less packed with tingling energy than the space experienced by performers.

Although space and time can be separated for purposes of analytical efficiency, in most of life's activities and in performance they cannot. A still figure is as much an image of time as of space. A figure that moves swiftly and fluidly across the stage represents quite a different image of time from one that moves slowly or jerkily. When we look at the face of a clock we see 'time' rather than 'space'. When we watch performing figures, do we say to ourselves, 'spatial patterns' or 'temporal rhythms'? The answer may be neither, because in experience space and time are inseparable.

Consider a procession. A 4 July parade may begin at the fire station and end at the post office. These points have no particular significance. The movement is linear and directional, but it is pseudo-directional because the goal does not matter. What counts is the movement itself. Questions of 'where to' and 'what for' are barely raised. By contrast, a religious procession has a goal which is the sacred circuit or center. Space-time, aptly represented by an arrow, is directional. This sense of linearity and direction weakens, however, if many pauses occur along the way. It also weakens if processioners depart freely from the moving stream to mix with the spectators. When this happens, the distinction between route and place, procession and *in situ* festival becomes fuzzy. [. . .]

The space of a traditional festival is hard to describe because it is heterogeneous, multilocal and shifting. Neither space nor time is likely to be sharply defined. A festival may last several days. It begins when people start to drift in, a few performers set up their stalls and try out an act or two, and it ends as loosely and informally as it starts. The space of the festival is the space of these movements and activities. There are a few physical markers: the market square itself, a tent here and there, some benches and stage props. But these physical markers do not by any means define and exhaust the experience of space and place. The events are heterogeneous and may occur simultaneously. Performers are also spectators and vice versa. People may pay little attention to the formal events. They go there to gawk, eat, drink, chat and flirt. They go to immerse themselves in *life* – that is, a confusion of sounds, colors, and movements that nevertheless are undergirded by a sense of order and common purpose. No one can have or would want to have a bird's-eye view of the festival as a whole. To do so would require the sort of distancing that is antithetical to the celebration of life.

Theater, in so far as it grew out of religious festivals and performances, is necessarily a mixed genre. A theatrical occasion may last many hours, filled with heterogeneous events. Again people may go in and out, eat and drink, talk with each other and with performers. Performing space may be fluid, hard to separate at times from spectator space. How many of us are old enough to remember the afternoon matinée at the neighborhood movie house? A show there still retains a bit of the air of a festival. Children run in and out to buy ice cream and soda pop. They shout their encouragement to the hero crushed by a falling skyscraper at the end of a serial. The show itself is a mixed genre of newsreel, cartoon, serial, supporting feature and main feature. Nowadays, when we go to an arts cinema, we are likely to be confronted by *Wild Strawberries* with no dressing or sweeteners whatsoever. A critical distinction between 'traditional' and 'modern' theater is that whereas the former is a celebration of life, the latter is a criticism – a deconstruction? – of life and a cold look at death

Participation and space

Performance presupposes the spectator. Even when we perform alone, a part of the self stands aside, appreciating and evaluating what we do. Or the lone performer is conscious of the eye of God. In ordinary social life, we are performers one moment and spectators the next. A similar fluidity of roles exists in a festival: having done one's act as juggler one may stand aside and watch someone else's show. Festivals celebrate life. Hence everyone wants to participate, to join actively in the happy motions of celebrations. Space is kaleidoscopic, rarely well defined – a reflection of the surging, shifting, inchoate character of life. Popular theater exhibits some of the traits of a village festival. Chinese opera, for instance, has never become a solemn High Art for the elite: people who attend it drink tea, crack watermelon seeds, shout approval at their favorite arias, walk about and visit with friends as they see fit. Comedies, in general, have this informal festive character. The audience laughs and laughter is active participation: what barrier may exist between performing space and spectator space is thus breached. Nothing truly threatening or awesome occurs in a social comedy. The audience does not feel the need to maintain a protective or deferential distance.

Ritual is different. Officiants at a ritual transform rather than perform. A priest by his gestures and incantations acts on reality as an architect-builder may be said to act on it. Is Pope John Paul II acting? Note how ambiguous that word is – and disturbing to those who want their sacerdotal figures to act but not to put on an act. Ritual places people in contact with reality – with divine potency. Hence the moments of danger from which only the consecrated and those who know precisely what to do are protected. Ordinary people do well to maintain a distance. But they are not there merely to look. They kneel, stand or join in prayers. They participate as members of a congregation, whose lives will be affected by how the ritual is conducted. In so far as ritual celebrates a success – important birth or harvest – it has some of the informal attributes of a festival. But to the degree that it claims to uphold a world, a certain seriousness and compulsion for precision prevails.

In a festival, everyone is involved, plunged in the midst of a world of exciting color, sound and movement. In sharp contrast is the bystander in a glassed-in world of his own. But what does 'involvement' mean? Surely it means more than just physical contact – touching and being touched. An anthropologist who coolly observes a festival from the sidelines is, we rightly say, minimally involved. But what about Lucretius, or a modern bystander who watches a car accident? He enjoys the safety of physical and emotional distance, and yet he is enthralled, riveted in place. A part of the spectator is engaged – a part that we call curiosity, and there is something reprehensible in being merely or idly curious, in not making a move when some action seems clearly called for.

How would we characterize the space of each type of involvement? In a festival, we may speak perhaps of interpenetrating spaces – a reflection of the heterogeneity of the events, of the people who attend (from young children to the aged and all social classes), and the absence of any sharp distinction between performers and spectators. In a football stadium, playing field and spectator area are clearly demarcated. Nevertheless, the boundary between them is easily transgressed. Excited fans may rush across it at the end of the game and even in the middle of the game when emotion runs uncontainably high. The ball sometimes flies out of the field into the spectators' seats, and spectators often try to breach their designated space with shouts and waving arms. In a physical-emotional way, spectators participate as much as they can. They are intensely – though not, perhaps, deeply – involved. At the other extreme, consider what transpires in a symphony hall or in a proscenium-stage theater. The sharpness of the separation between performance and audience space is emphasized by the use of foot- and ceiling lights and by the darkening of the hall. During a performance, take a glance at the sea of silent faces submerged in semidarkness. They look blank as though the souls behind them had departed to mingle with the music or with the stage drama. When the music stops or when the curtain falls there is a moment of silence during which the spectators wait for their souls to return. Separated physically from the object of attention, audience involvement can nevertheless be total, which should encourage us to re-evaluate the insight that separation is a pre-condition for becoming deeply absorbed.

Notes

1   Roland Barthes (1978) *A Lover's Discourse* (New York: Hill & Wang), p. 167.
2   André Maurois (1960) *Illusions* (New York: Columbia University Press), p. 76.
3   Philip P. Hallie (1969) *The Paradox of Cruelty* (Middletown: Wesleyan University Press), p. 46.
4   Lewis Hyde (1983) *The Gift: Imagination and the Erotic Life of Property* (New York: Random House), p. 206.
5   Ludwig Wittgenstein (1980) *Culture and Value* (Chicago: University of Chicago Press), pp. 4–5.

EXERCISE: Consider three performances: an activity performed for onlookers as part of everyday life (a market trader calling his wares, say, or a bartender mixing cocktails); a piece of 'environmental' theatre performed in an ordinary social location; a ritual or ceremony enacted in a special venue set aside for it. First, list the distinct spaces each carves out of general space (including any not directly visible to the audience) and the means by which it does so, noting the 'keys', in Goffman's sense, which mark their boundaries. Then discuss the role these spatial arrangements play in the audiences' reading of the events. What induces those watching to address the bartender's actions as more than merely functional? If onlookers initially view an environmental theatre piece with puzzlement, what signals might cause them to change their view and how would their perception of what occurs be altered as a consequence? Compare the ways spectators would read the three 'performance spaces'. You are seeking the different kinds of symbolical significance that space may be granted in situations of performance.

Now select a specific kind of contemporary performance venue (i.e. a proscenium-arch theatre, a stadium, a theatre in the round). Begin by briefly listing all its spatial divisions – those that define the playing area, certainly, but also any separating the visible from the hidden, the venue from the ordinary social world, and so on. Then consider how that spatial formula might shape an audience's perception of different kinds of performance. Would the divisions you noted function differently for a modern dance piece, a realist drama and a show by a popular singer? How would their significance alter in a Christian evangelist's meeting?

6.2 *Locus* and *Platea*

Robert Weimann, from *Shakespeare and the Popular Tradition: Studies in the Social Dimension of Dramatic Form and Function*, ed. Robert Schwartz, Baltimore: Johns Hopkins University Press, 1978

[Although the work of literary critic Weimann is firmly historicist, its perspective is often more developmental than contextual, concerned to chart the lineage of performance techniques, forms and aesthetics through time. In the book excerpted here he plots the origins of the popular theatre of Shakespeare's England, tracing the development of its performance strategies from roots in medieval culture and beyond. The following fragment focuses on antecedents to that theatre's use of space. The two forms of theatrical space he finds in use in late medieval drama, the *platea* and the *locus*, comprise more than literal areas; instead, they represent contrasting ways in which space was used by performers, and read by audiences. In offering this fundamental distinction between the spaces of the telling and the told, his formulation addresses issues similar to those explored by modern theorists of radical political performance (see **Brecht, Diamond, Gilbert**), providing a way of viewing the formations of space characteristic of drama today.]

Platea and *locus*: flexible dramaturgy

Actually, the difference between the pageant stage and the circular theater may not have been as great as has been assumed. As Richard Hosley has shown, the various kinds of medieval theater used either a 'focused' or a 'dispersed' mode of production.[1] [. . .] In both, the distinction between a 'place' or platform-like acting area (the *platea*), and a scaffold, be it a *domus*, *sedes* or throne (the *locus*), is the one factor that is of key importance. Functionally, the *locus* corresponded to the scaffold in the circular theater and to the throne or hut on the pageant stage. In each case fixed, symbolic locations near and on the larger unlocalized acting area tend to define a more particular kind of action. [. . .]

At the start of the *Passion Play II*, for example, the following direction is given:

> *What tyme that processyon is enteryd in to the place and the herowdys takyn his schaffalde · and pylat and annas and cayphas here schaffaldys Also than come ther An exposytour in doctorys wede thus seyng* (XXIX, I)

The 'processyon', here probably the entrance of the actors, moves into the *place* surrounded by the audience. After Herod has mounted his *schaffalde*, and Pilate, Ananias and Caiphas have also mounted theirs (the plural *schaffaldys* is quite clear), an *exposytour*, standing on the *place*, or perhaps striding back and forth on it, addresses himself directly to the audience. He reminds them that the play now beginning is a continuation of the story shown there last year (the *Passion Play I*). Herod then reveals himself (possibly from behind a curtain, in accordance with the direction *here the herowndys xal shewe hymselfe and speke*) and begins to threaten from his high seat: 'Now sees of your talkyng . . . Not o word I charge you that ben here present . . .' The characteristic demand for silence introduces a longer monologue and a shorter dialogue, which are followed by Herod's withdrawal, again into his scaffold pavilion, after he has explained:

> Thanne of these materys serys take hede
> Ffor A whyle I wele me rest
> Appetyde requyryth me so in dede
> And ffesyk tellyth me it is the best.
>
> (66–9)

[. . .] A somewhat unmotivated reference to 'ffesyk' serves to explain Herod's withdrawal. Thus, a representational (in fact, even a psychological) motive is supplied to justify a non-representational convention: illusion and interpretation first begin to assert themselves in a *locus*. Yet the passage remains a mere verbal gesture that is not integrated into the dramatic process itself, even when it does suggest the more strictly localized character of the fixed or 'focused' mode in the handling of the scaffold (as *sedes*). Associated with the scaffold is a rudimentary element of verisimilitude that has not really come to terms with the more episodic and dispersed nature of *platea* production; for in the latter, the play world continues to be frankly treated as a theatrical dimension of the real world. The tension that Herod's withdrawal creates between the illusion of a representational action and the theatrical convention of a non-representational dramaturgy seems very clumsy and naive. And yet, the unity that contains a contradiction between 'realism' and 'convention' – which T. S. Eliot considered to be 'impure art'[2] in Shakespeare – is remarkable in spite of its awkwardness. (It was to be the interplay between 'realism' and 'convention' that brought *locus* and *platea* together in the maturing Elizabethan drama.) Herod's 'need' to 'rest' is itself, for example, a representational indication that his physical presence on the scaffold is to be ignored in the action that follows: for he is not supposed to hear the news that Christ has been taken prisoner, which is brought by the messenger who subsequently enters the 'place'. [. . .]

In addition to these symbolic scaffolds there is an acting area that was called the 'place' thirteen times in the *Ludus Coventriae*. This is where the procession of actors makes its appearance, where the messenger moves, and where Jesus is led until 'they reach the hall'. This 'hall', already referred to as the 'mothalle' (the court and meeting-place), serves as a scenic unit in midplace, where Christ is brought to judgement and where Pilate, Caiphas and Ananias meet. This is obviously a focal point of dramatic action, and it corresponds to the 'cownsel hous' mentioned in scene thirty-one (635–6) and described in more detail in scene twenty-six:

> *here the buschopys with here clerkys and the Pharaseus mett and the myd place and ther xal be a lytil oratory with stolys and cusshonys clenly be-seyn lych as it were a cownsel hous ...*

(124–5)

The 'hall' is not only an important locality, it is also centrally situated. The stools and cushions to which the direction refers obviously serve to create some impression of verisimilitude, but the phrase 'lych as it were

a cownsel hous' makes it clear that a real house, which would have inter-
fered with the audience's view, did not stand there. Even without the
physical 'house', though, this locality would have assumed the function
of a central *locus*, which – like some of the scaffolds or frame structures
– created a heightened level of mimetic representation and, perhaps, rudimentary elements of the illusion of actuality.

Such a technical relationship between scaffold and 'place' allowed,
and indeed presupposed, a highly flexible mode of production through
which the representation of biblical myth and the expression of self can
be seen as integral parts of the 'doubleness' and the 'strangely comprehensive two-ways facingness' of the late medieval dramatic vision. The
dual values of scaffold and 'place' do not, of course, provide a causal or
mechanical explanation of this doubleness. Neither are the functions
of scaffold and 'place' always so clearly distinguishable that they can be
reduced to a simple formula. Nevertheless, in the *Ludus Coventriae*, as
in the related conventions of the pageant wagon, there is an important
functional difference between *platea* and *locus*. As a rule, it was the more
highly ranked persons who sat on the scaffolds, God the father, the 'King'
in *The Pride of Life*, Decius (enthroned as in the Fouquet miniature).
Significantly, while some high-born members of the audience were also
seated on these scaffolds, or at any rate on neighboring scaffolds, the
ordinary public stood crowded below in the *champ*. This was the case in
The Castle of Perseverance: the noble 'syrys semly' sat at the sides of the
scaffolds while the simple 'wytis' were in the 'pleyn place', that is, in the
middle of the green or field. It was among these simple folk, or in front
of them, that soldiers and serfs, the shouting messenger of 'N-town', and
of course the devil, grimacing 'in the most orryble wyse' (465–6), played
their parts.

Such functional differences between *platea* and *locus* can perhaps
best be discussed in terms of the French theater. In the early Norman
Adam play *diabolus* and the demons repeatedly appeared *per plateus*
amongst the audience. This arrangement recurs in the later French miracle
plays and probably achieves the greatest degree of dramatic consistency
in *Saint Didier*, *Saint Christophe* and *Saint Bernard de Menthon*, in which
a fool repeatedly appears to speak dialect and nonsense, allude to contemporary events and parody the saint. This fool quite clearly occupies the
platea; he speaks to the soldiers, servants and beggars, and to the audience, while the serious or high-born persons in the play seem unaware of
his existence despite his lengthy comments on their actions and deport-
ment. Contemporaneous with the audience, the fool here dissociates himself
from the world and time of the *locus* as he glosses the symbolic action

for the audience: 'This must have happened long, long ago', he tells them directly.

Such a clearly defined and far-reaching differentiation between the dramatic conventions of the high- and low-born characters is hardly to be found in the English miracle and mystery plays. The scenic position of the French fool does, however, correspond somewhat to that of the burlesque doctor's servant Colle in *The Play of the Sacrament*, who is expressly directed to come out 'into the place' (444–5). The clowning boy Hawkyn in *Mary Magdalene* probably acted close to the audience in a similar way: his grotesque nonsense prayer (1185–201) ends with an execration, but the *presbyter* and *rex* take no notice of it. In the interlude of the Tudor period it was still customary for the lower characters to move about in a neutral area rubbing shoulders with the plebeian audience: 'the comic and disreputable characters (those who call for "room") . . . speak mainly to by-standers adjoining the "place" – the least dignified members of the audience'.[3]

Such spatial differentiation allowed for complex and sometimes quite rich and suggestive drama. Christ, for instance, moved about the 'place' in the *Ludus Coventriae*, quashing spatial and social distinctions, reasserting his common humanity, and giving the *sermo humilis* a new dignity and function. From the point of view of staging, Christ's position corresponded to that of *Humanum Genus*, the central human figure who moved about in the middle of the 'place' in *The Castle of Perseverance*, and was led or enticed to the various scaffolds. There it was not the judges and priests who were enthroned, but God, Lucifer and a host of allegorical figures.

The relationship between *locus* and *platea* was, to be sure, complex and variable; and this rather formal association of figures does not do full justice to that rich variability. But as a rule the English scaffold corresponds to the continental *domus*, *tentus* or *sedes* which delimit a more or less fixed and focused scenic unit. On the pageant wagon this might be a shepherd's hut or the stable at Bethlehem; in the mystery plays of Valenciennes these *loca* were set up side-by-side – hall, temple, palace, hell, etc. In Lucerne they were called *tenti*, and in Mons there was a *maisonette*. Scaffolds such as these gradually became the small, temporary, curtained pavilions or porchlike booths that, among other things, answered the need for an 'inner stage' or 'upper chamber' in the Elizabethan drama.

Unlike these *loca*, which could assume an illusionary character, the *platea* provided an entirely non-representational and unlocalized setting; it was the broad and general acting area in which the communal festivities were conducted. Here the audience could – as in the performance of

The Castle of Perseverance – share the setting with both the actors and the 'stytelerys' who acted as stewards or supervisors. The Latin word *platea* (Gr. πλατεῖα, Ital. *piazza*) originally indicated the open space between houses – a street or a public place at ground level. As Italian usage suggests, the *platea* developed into the ground floor of an auditorium. But, before the separation of actors and audience was taken for granted, the *platea* or 'place' corresponded to the 'plain' in the Cornish Round or 'the green' in Lindsay's *Satire of the Three Estates*.

The changing theatrical functions of this area are extremely important to an understanding of the pre-Shakespearean popular theater. And although Richard Southern originally saw no connection between the *platea* and the Elizabethan platform stage,[4] it may be reasonable to assume that while the main acting area in Shakespeare's theater did not perhaps develop directly out of the *platea* it did take on and expand some of the *platea*'s basic functions. The scaffold, once its platform had become the main acting area, was likely to be increasingly dissociated from the earlier representational assumptions of the *loca*; the 'place', however, retained the unlocalized quality that remained so important on the later platform stage. In the medieval drama it is the symbolic function of the various *loca* that tended to distance them from the audience. Herod, sitting atop his scaffold, physically objectified his high rank and manner by means of a spatial distance that also facilitated the kind of representational mimesis implicit in the drawing of the curtain because of the illusionary need for 'rest'. Appropriately, this Herod exploited almost none of the comic features normally associated with his audience contact; it is only when the actor, by threatening or raging, upset a sense of distance from within the *platea* or a *platea*-like position that the representational quality of the role disappeared, to be replaced by an anachronistic form of semi-ritual burlesque and self-expression.

[. . .] One of the most interesting material and practical prerequisites for this relationship is the juxtaposition of the symbolic, representational dimension of the scaffold stage against the actual *platea* in the form of a street, a village green or a marketplace surrounded by spectators. What is involved, though, is not the *confrontation* of the world and time of the play with that of the audience, or any serious *opposition* between representational and non-representational standards of acting, but the most intense interplay of both. Such an interplay makes it ultimately impossible to assign to *platea* and *locus* any consistent and exclusive mode of acting. At the same time, this interplay allows (and, indeed, calls for) the mixture of the comic and the serious or the absence of a structural division between monologue and dialogue. In short, both *platea* and *locus* are related to specific locations and types of action and acting, but each is meaningless without the functioning assumptions of the other.

Notes

1   R. Hosley (1971) 'Three Kinds of Outdoor Theatre Before Shakespeare', *Theatre Survey* 12: 1–33, p. 26.
2   T. S. Eliot (1932) *Selected Essays 1917–1932* (London: Faber & Faber), pp. 114–16.
3   T. W. Craik (1958) *The Tudor Interlude: Stage, Costume, Acting* (Leicester: Hopethorn Press), p. 23.
4   See R. Southern (1958) *The Medieval Theatre in the Round* (London: Faber), and (1973) *The Staging of Plays Before Shakespeare* (London: Faber).

EXERCISE: Choose a twentieth-century play in which the distinction between fictional and non-fictional space is problematized (e.g. Peter Shaffer's *Equus*, Thornton Wilder's *Our Town*, Bertolt Brecht's *The Caucasian Chalk Circle*, Jean Genet's *The Blacks*, Tom Stoppard's *Rosencrantz and Guildenstern are Dead*). Begin by breaking the text down into those sections, threads or elements which require a *locus* and those which suggest a *platea*, and discuss the differences in the ways these spaces demand to be 'read'. How do your own interpretative assumptions and activities change when your gaze shifts from a *locus* to a *platea*? Then consider the author's purpose in juxtaposing those spaces. How do they relate to the work's themes? Are there parallels between the events represented and the audience's own experience of interpreting them?

6.3 Environmental space

Marvin Carlson, from *Places of Performance: The Semiotics of Theatre Architecture*, Ithaca and London: Cornell University Press, 1989

[Carlson's wide-ranging work has been instrumental in the modern development of Performance Studies as a discipline, addressing such fundamental areas as theatre semiotics, the history of theatrical theory and the analysis of live art. The perspective he adopts in the following piece is broadly that of 'Urban Semiotics'; the term, however, does not do justice to the historical scholarship he brings to the task of reading the built environment. The specificity and detail of this analysis is crucial, for it is the precise symbolic resonance of areas and structures, rather than any general significance to space, which inflects theatregoers' experience of a performance. By priming audiences to seek in a work meanings consonant with those of its environs, the piece suggests, the urban space informs the act of interpretation, working to frame the event before it has begun.]

The city as theatre

The late Middle Ages and early Renaissance constitute the major historical period when theatre existed as an important part of urban life without any specific architectural element being devoted to its exclusive use. The absence of a specifically theatrical structure from the medieval city's repertory of architectural objects by no means indicates that the physical situation of theatre performance within the city was devoid of symbolic significance. On the contrary, a situation allowing those producing a performance to place it in whatever locale seemed most suitable meant that theatre could use to its own advantage the already existing connotations of other spaces both in themselves and in their placement within the city, and this was in fact consistently done. Such a dynamic was particularly congenial to the medieval world view, which delighted in the discovery of correspondences and in building rich symbolic structures by relating various systems of signs to each other.

The symbolic center of the medieval town was the cathedral, and nowhere else in the city was so rich a trove of symbolic referents concentrated. A famous passage in Hugo's *Notre Dame de Paris* considers the cathedral as the central repository of signs for its culture. Legend, allegory, doctrine, the whole sum of medieval knowledge of the world, divine and human, was here represented in painting, sculpture, stained glass and space. At the same time this fabric of symbols, rich as it was, also served as a setting, a container for the even more central symbolic systems of the performed rituals of the church, by which the citizens of the city were led to a direct participation in the divine mysteries.

The liturgical drama that grew up within the cathedral occupied a position somewhere between religious ritual and the rich cadre of architecture, sculpture and stained glass which enclosed that ritual, and drew upon the symbolic potential of each. Carol Heinz has documented the close connection between the massive west fronts that appeared during the Carolingian period and the architectural and iconographic symbols of death and resurrection of the time. As the common theme of portals in the western façade, the last judgement also came to be associated with this area, as did baptism (the symbolic death and resurrection of the penitent sinner).[1] An altar to the Savior was often placed here in relation to these events. It is in this part of the cathedral, already rich with appropriate associations, that Heinz suggests the first liturgical Easter plays were presented. The more traditional view has placed these performances near the high altar, with the crypt beneath serving as an icon for the tomb. Whichever view is correct, historians agree that the new dramatic presentation built upon the connotations already present in a space created for non-dramatic purposes.

Gradually liturgical performances came to utilize other parts of the cathedral, and the same dynamic continued. The cathedral itself was architecturally oriented with the presumed world axes, the main line running east and west, with a lesser north–south crossing. To the east lay Jerusalem and the presumed site of the lost Eden, and the celebrant entering the cathedral moved in this direction to reach the high altar. The path of church processions, east toward the high altar or west toward the altar of the Savior, already evocative of world or cosmic journeys, were in turn echoed by movements along these same axes in the liturgical dramas – the journey to Emmaus, the race of the disciples to the tomb, the journey of the Magi.

The tripartite division of the cathedral east–center–west into choir, nave and narthex provided a supplementary spatial orientation. Between the altar of the Savior, with its evocation of the passion, the resurrection and the last judgement, and the eastern altar of the Virgin, suggesting the nativity and the church itself, the middle of the nave or the crossing of the transepts provided a less heavily charged religious space, the space not only of processions toward one end of the church or the other, but of more 'earthly' locations required by the liturgical dramas. [. . .]

Early-twentieth-century scholars considered the mystery plays presented outside the church to be direct descendants of these liturgical dramas, but more recent research has challenged this theory, citing as evidence not only the historical overlap of the forms, but their many important differences in organization, themes and social function.[2] Nevertheless in the matters of spatial and urban signification, liturgical and mystery performances had important similarities. The general east–west symbolism predated the construction of the great cathedrals and was by no means restricted to them. A similar symbolic system was to be found in almost every outdoor organization of medieval drama where the physical configuration would allow it. At Frankfurt (c. 1350), Lucerne (1583) and Donaueschingen (c. 1600), to take only three famous examples, there was a platform representing Heaven to the east, like the high altar in a cathedral, an infernal Hell-Mouth at the opposite western end, and earthly locations scattered between. Frankfurt and Lucerne both used a temple as an element to define this central area, and all three placed the crucifixion midway between the earthly center and paradise.

Cities offered a variety of richly significant locations for the performance of religious drama. In many of them the space immediately adjacent to the cathedral was apparently employed, as for the famous medieval play, the *Jeu d'Adam*, with the cathedral as a whole serving as the abode of God and probably of the angelic choir.[3] Like the cathedral crypt, cemeteries and burial grounds served as defining locales for passion and resurrection plays, for example, in Rouen and Vienna. Often a particularly favored locale was the marketplace, which like the encompassing city could be seen as a symbol of the stage upon which Everyman played his earthly role. The connotations of the market space made it especially suitable for this function. Usually contiguous to the town hall, surrounded by the dwellings and places of business of the city's mercantile leaders, itself the center for trade, recreation and social intercourse, it was in fact the stage on which the new urban bourgeois class played out their lives, the secular if not the geographical heart of the city, as the cathedral was the spiritual heart (though these two orientations were not as clearly separated as they later became, business organizations such as the medieval guilds still having an important religious component). The mystery plays, written in the vernacular and stressing the similarity between the physical world of their biblical subjects and that of their audience, were extremely well served by a space redolent of those vernacular and contemporary concerns, just as the more abstract and ritualistic liturgical drama was well served by the surrounding iconography of the cathedral.

On a grander scale, the city as a whole could also be utilized as a theatrical space. Indeed Lewis Mumford sees that as one of its central functions: 'Whatever the practical needs of the Medieval town, it was above all things, in its busy turbulent life, a stage for the ceremonies of the Church. Therein lay its drama and its ideal consummation.' The key to the medieval city Mumford finds in the moving pageant or procession,

> above all in the great religious procession that winds about the streets and places before it finally debouches into the church or

the cathedral for the great ceremony itself. These great processions united, as did the ceremonies of the church, spectators, communicants, and participants. Even the tortuous windings of the Medieval streets contributed to this effect, by affording those in the procession glimpses of other participants so that they became spectators as well, as they can never be in a formal parade on a straight street.[4]

These great processions and the dramatic pageants that, like them, moved through the medieval city, by claiming that entire city as their setting, also made a claim for the involvement of every citizen that went even beyond that of the great spectacles in the marketplace. But though the dramatic performances may not have directly involved the same large numbers of citizens as the great processions, they still encouraged active participation by regularly erasing any possible barrier between performance and public space. The Viennese passion of the fifteenth century that began in the marketplace doubtless assumed the secular and social connotations of that area, but when the actor portraying Christ subsequently bore his cross through the winding streets of the city to the distant cemetery where the crucifixion was to be represented, the spectators along his path were drawn even more directly into the symbolic world of the play, becoming active participants in the cosmic drama of sacrifice and redemption in a city that during this performance took on the connotations of the universal city, Jerusalem.

In the later Middle Ages the religious and dramatic processions shared the urban stage with another sort of procession, outwardly similar but with a radically different set of connotations, the royal entry. Many religious processions proceeded from one of the city gates to the cathedral, a trajectory symbolizing the approach to the spiritual center of the community, though other trajectories – even the totally opposite one from city center to edge – were possible, as the Viennese passion demonstrates. Such flexibility was impossible for the entry, which, representing the welcome to the city of an important guest, necessarily had to move from the gates (a major symbolic location for this sort of ceremony) to the center, represented usually by the cathedral or the palace that was to house the privileged visitor. The early royal entries were essentially little more than such welcomes, but as the sovereign power increased and the autonomy of the city declined, the connotations of these ceremonies reflected the change. The opening of the city gates or the presentation of the keys to them came to symbolize submission and acknowledgement of superior power, and the procession to the city's heart became an act of possession and a demonstration of authority.

No longer was the princely visitor greeted along this pathway by symbols of the city's wealth, power and prosperity; he was met instead by monuments and allegorical paintings and tableaux reflecting his own significance. The city was still used as a theatre space, but one appropriated from its inhabitants by the prince. Once this usurpation was completed, the city was no longer available as stage primarily for the separate scenes of the citizens' dramas – marriage and funeral processions or civic-religious pageantry – but became rather the scene for the display of princely power, at which citizens were present by sufferance – as spectators only.

The physical arrangement of the medieval city was in many ways unsuitable for these displays of princely power. Whatever the allegorical symbols of dominance and authority gathered on the tableaux vivants that were placed along the prince's route, the message conveyed by the urban space itself was very different. The narrow and tortuous medieval streets, with overhanging structures and capricious widenings and narrowings, suggested no connotations of subservience or even tractability, but rather those of a stubborn individuality. The path the prince followed to the heart of the city was not an easy one, and it suggested in terms of spatial dynamics less a triumphant procession than the rather uneasy threading of a potentially menacing labyrinth.

Notes

1   C. Heinz (1963) *Recherches sur les rapports entre l'architecture et la liturgie à l'époque carolingienne* (Paris: Éditions du Seuil).
2   See O. B. Hardison (1965) *Christian Rite and Christian Drama in the Middle Ages* (Baltimore: Johns Hopkins Press).
3   See G. Frank (1944) 'Genesis and Staging of the *Jeu d'Adam*', *PMLA* 39: 7–17.
4   L. Mumford (1961) *The City in History: Its Origins, its Transformations, and its Prospects* (London: Secker & Warburg), p. 277.

EXERCISE: Choose a performance venue you have attended and discuss the symbolic resonances provided by its environs. Consider the character of the area (is it known for business, commercial entertainment, budget housing?), any landmarks or monuments in close proximity, the type of building (modernist or 'traditional', dilapidated or grand) surrounding it, the architecture (external and internal) of the theatre itself, and so on. How did these shape your expectations – indeed, your *experience* – of the event?

Now widen your perspective: take a map of your town or city and divide it into areas according to the associations that gather to them, drawing in the borders. Choosing (1) a popular entertainment form, (2) a political or experimental work and (3) a Greek classic or a play by Shakespeare, discuss how different locations and venues would mediate audience responses. How would you view differently performances of Shakespeare's *Othello* staged in a commercial zone, an area known for art galleries and the community hall of the town's poorest borough? How would those same locations shape your expectations and perceptions of a show by a popular comedian? What would be the effect of staging a political play outside the headquarters of a major business concern or at the foot of a public monument; or a live art performance in a church? Do not ask which space would be most appropriate; rather, consider how each would mediate or supplement the meanings of the performance itself.

Part seven

Spectator and audience

As heirs to the artistic realism of the nineteenth century, we are perhaps still inclined to think of artworks as windows on to the 'real world', and of ourselves as the neutral, passive recipients of their meaning. But meaning does not exist in the material world, it is a human product, a product of *culture*, and the interpretation of plays and paintings, novels and films requires a reader who is culturally competent. Such competence comprises broadly two qualities. First, the spectator must possess particular social knowledges. The relationship between the material signifier and the conceptual signified is, in **Saussure**'s terms, 'arbitrary'; that is, the meaning of an image, action or word, spoken or written, is not inherent to it but is conventional, the result of an unspoken agreement between individuals of the same interpretative community. To understand the material artwork in given ways, then, is to position it perceptually within culturally specific orders of meaning. Second, the spectator must be active in the process of decoding, employing not only the necessary knowledges but the required interpretative strategies. As part of this, the reader him/herself is in a sense 'produced'. To undertake the appropriate reading activities is essentially to perform a given role, if only momentarily; to decode the text in ways which are ultimately determined by it. The relationship between viewer

audience
& various areas

and viewed is thus a symbiotic one, the viewer performing interpretative acts predicted by the viewed, while the viewed itself – the object as it is *perceived* – is in turn constructed, endowed with meaning, in the gaze of the viewer. This complex and shifting relationship between the producers and consumers of objects, the cultural context in which they operate, and the knowledges which shape their operations, has political consequences, for, as **Althusser** asserts, it is by such means that individuals are 'interpellated'. In Film Studies, where the exploration of this issue is arguably most advanced, the ways in which the reading practices demanded by films themselves provide a position and 'identity' for their reader has long been at the centre of debate. What is ultimately at stake in such questions is the ideological positioning of the individual as subject, and the possible means of that subjectivity's subversion.

depends on their culture

Most of the pieces included in this volume implicitly assume the activities of a perceiving subject: a viewer or reader who, for such as **Lévi-Strauss**, **Geertz** and **Goffman**, is adept with the knowledges and interpretative practices specific to his or her culture; one already politically interpellated in the cases of **Althusser**, **Cixous** and **Bristol**; whereas **Brecht**, **Grosz** and **Lyotard** each in their different ways posit a spectator who is capable of change, of rejecting received views to adopt new, interrogative positions. What differentiates the following excerpts is that the perceiving subject is their *central* concern. They are arranged in order of increasing 'magnitude'. Starting from the subjective, largely acultural philosophy of Phenomenology, aesthetician Wolfgang Iser (b. 1926) describes the individual reader's active role in the creation of textual meaning. Laura Mulvey (b. 1941) expands the perspective to encompass the social and political, exploring the psychic processes undertaken by spectators of film and the way these are gender-coded. Raymond Williams (1921–88) examines the necessarily historically and culturally specific relationship between artwork and audience.

Further reading: Berger 1972 is an introductory text on spectatorship in art, an interesting read designed to challenge preconceptions, while Bryson 1983, Foster (ed.) 1988 and Silverman 1983, although still accessible, are more advanced studies, dealing with spectatorship and subjectivity from different directions; the theatre audience specifically is addressed in Bennett 1983, Blau 1990 and Pavis 1982, and the audience for dance in Foster 1986; the gendered spectator of performance is examined in Rapi and Chowdhry (eds) 1998 and Senelick 1992; for radical spectatorship see **Brecht**, **Gilbert**, **Diamond** and **hooks** in this volume; for cinema and the gendered spectator see de Lauretis 1984 and Penley (ed.) 1988; Metz 1975 and Baudry 1974/5 provided what are probably the dominant models of the ungendered cinematic spectator, although these are difficult pieces which require some work.

7.1 The interactive spectator

Wolfgang Iser, from 'Interaction between Text and Reader', in Susan Suleiman and Inge Crosman (eds), *The Reader in the Text: Essays on Audience and Interpretation*, Princeton: Princeton University Press, 1980

[Iser is a key theorist of the German school of *Rezeptionsästhetik*, and the greatest influence on his work is that of the founder of Phenomenology, philosopher Edmund Husserl (1859–1938). Husserl argued that consciousness is always consciousness *of* something, as it is on our perception of objects, rather than on the objects *per se*, that our conception of ourselves and our world is founded. Thus for Husserl's pupil, the aesthetician Roman Ingarden (1893–1970), artworks achieve full existence only in someone's reading of them, for the 'work' is more than the material thing, it comprises the meanings and experiences generated by our interpretation of that thing. Iser similarly argues that the literary work is virtual, produced in the interaction of text and reader. This interaction is provoked and governed by what he terms 'blanks', missing connections between the text's diverse components, segments and viewpoints. It is in creatively filling such gaps, finding a position from which the text's parts unite into a cohesive whole, that the reader comes to articulate imaginatively the work's overall vision of reality. Although Iser deals with the reading of novels, his theories may be adapted to explore the spectator's interpretation of performance, his or her active, creative engagement with the fictional world it conjures.]

Central to the reading of every literary work is the interaction between its structure and its recipient. This is why the phenomenological theory of art has emphatically drawn attention to the fact that the study of a literary work should concern not only the actual text but also, and in equal measure, the actions involved in responding to that text. The text itself simply offers 'schematized aspects'[1] through which the aesthetic object of the work can be produced.

From this we may conclude that the literary work has two poles, which we might call the artistic and the aesthetic: the artistic pole is the author's text, and the aesthetic is the realization accomplished by the reader. In view of this polarity, it is clear that the work itself cannot be identical with the text or with its actualization but must be situated somewhere between the two. It must inevitably be virtual in character, as it cannot be reduced to the reality of the text or to the subjectivity of the reader, and it is from this virtuality that it derives its dynamism. As the reader passes through the various perspectives offered by the text, and relates the different views and patterns to one another, he sets the work in motion, and so sets himself in motion, too. [. . .]

In assessing interpersonal relationships R. D. Laing writes: 'I may not actually be able to see myself as others see me, but I am constantly supposing them to be seeing me in particular ways, and I am constantly acting in the light of the actual or supposed attitudes, opinions, needs, and so on the other has in respect of me.'[2] Now, the views that others have of me cannot be called 'pure' perception; they are the result of interpretation. And this need for interpretation arises from the structure of interpersonal experience. We have experience of one another in so far as we know one another's conduct; but we have no experience of how others experience us.

In his book *The Politics of Experience*, Laing pursues this line of thought by saying: '*your experience of me is invisible to me and my experience of you is invisible to you*. I cannot experience your experience. You cannot experience my experience. We are both invisible men. All men are invisible to one another. Experience is man's invisibility to man.'[3] It is this invisibility, however, that forms the basis of interpersonal relations – a basis which Laing calls 'no-thing'. 'That which is really "between" cannot be named by any things that come between. The between is itself no-thing.'[4] In all our interpersonal relations we build upon this 'no-thing', for we react as if we knew how our partners experienced us; we continually form views of their views, and then act as if our views of their views were realities. Contact therefore depends upon our continually filling in a central gap in our experience. Thus, dyadic and dynamic interaction comes about only because we are unable to experience how we experience one another, which in turn proves to be a propellant to interaction. Out of this fact arises the basic need for interpretation, which regulates the whole process of interaction. As we cannot perceive without preconception, each percept, in turn, makes sense to us only if it is processed, for pure perception is quite impossible. Hence dyadic interaction is not given by nature but arises out of an interpretative activity, which will contain a view of others and, unavoidably, an image of ourselves.

An obvious and major difference between reading and all forms of social interaction is the fact that with reading there is no *face-to-face-situation*.[5] A text cannot adapt itself to each reader it comes into contact with. The partners in dyadic interaction can ask each other questions in order to ascertain how far their images have bridged the gap of the inexperienceability of one another's experiences. The reader, however, can never learn from the text how accurate or inaccurate are his views of it. Furthermore, dyadic interaction serves specific purposes, so that the interaction always has a regulative context, which often serves as a *tertium comparationis*. There is no such frame of reference governing the text–reader relationship; on the contrary, the codes which might regulate this interaction are fragmented in the text, and must first be reassembled or, in most cases, restructured before any frame of reference can be established. Here, then, in conditions and intention, we find two basic differences between the text–reader relationship and the dyadic interaction between social partners.

Now, it is the very lack of ascertainability and defined intention that brings about the text–reader interaction, and here there is a vital link with dyadic interaction. Social communication, as we have seen, arises out of the fact that people cannot experience how others experience them, and not out of the common situation or out of the conventions that join both partners together. The situations and conventions regulate the manner in which gaps are filled, but the gaps in turn arise out of the inexperienceability and, consequently, function as a basic inducement to communication. Similarly, it is the gaps, the fundamental asymmetry between text and reader, that give rise to communication in the reading process; the lack of a common situation and a common frame of reference corresponds to the 'no-thing', which brings about the interaction between persons. Asymmetry and the 'no-thing' are all different forms of an indeterminate, constitutive blank, which underlies all processes of interaction. With dyadic interaction, the imbalance is removed by the establishment of pragmatic connections resulting in an action, which is why the preconditions are always clearly defined in relation to situations and common frames of reference. The imbalance between text and reader, however, is undefined, and it is this very indeterminacy that increases the variety of communication possible.

Now, if communication between text and reader is to be successful, clearly the reader's activity must also be controlled in some way by the text. The control cannot be as specific as in a *face to face situation*, equally it cannot be as determinate as a social code, which regulates social interaction. However, the guiding devices operative in the reading process have

181

to initiate communication and to control it. This control cannot be understood as a tangible entity occurring independently of the process of communication. Although exercised *by* the text, it is not *in* the text. This is well illustrated by a comment Virginia Woolf made on the novels of Jane Austen:

> Jane Austen is thus a mistress of much deeper emotion than appears upon the surface. She stimulates us to supply what is not there. What she offers is, apparently, a trifle, yet is composed of something that expands in the reader's mind and endows with the most enduring form of life scenes which are outwardly trivial. Always the stress is laid upon character ... The turns and twists of the dialogue keep us on the tenterhooks of suspense. Our attention is half upon the present moment, half upon the future ... Here, indeed, in this unfinished and in the main inferior story, are all the elements of Jane Austen's greatness.[6]

What is missing from the apparently trivial scenes, the gaps arising out of the dialogue – this is what stimulates the reader into filling the blanks with projections. He is drawn into the events and made to supply what is meant from what is said. What is said only appears to take on significance as a reference to what is not said; it is the implications and not the statements that give shape and weight to the meaning. But as the unsaid comes to life in the reader's imagination, so the said 'expands' to take on greater significance than might have been supposed: even trivial scenes can seem surprisingly profound. The 'enduring form of life' which Virginia Woolf speaks of is not manifested on the printed page; it is a product arising out of the interaction between the text and reader.

Communication in literature, then, is a process set in motion and regulated, not by a given code, but by a mutually restrictive and magnifying interaction between the explicit and the implicit, between revelation and concealment. What is concealed spurs the reader into action, but this action is also controlled by what is revealed; the explicit in its turn is transformed when the implicit has been brought to light. Whenever the reader bridges the gaps, communication begins. The gaps function as a kind of pivot on which the whole text–reader relationship revolves. Hence, the structured blanks of the text stimulate the process of ideation to be performed by the reader on terms set by the text. [...]

In order to spotlight the communication process we shall confine our consideration to how the blanks trigger off and simultaneously control the reader's activity. Blanks indicate that the different segments and patterns of the text are to be connected even though the text itself does not say so. They are the unseen joints in the text, and as they mark off schemata and textual perspectives from one another, they simultaneously prompt acts of ideation on the reader's part. Consequently when the schemata and perspectives have been linked together, the blanks 'disappear'.

If we are to grasp the unseen structure that regulates but does not formulate the connection or even the meaning, we must bear in mind the various forms on which the textual segments are presented to the reader's viewpoint in the reading process. Their most elementary form is to be seen on the level of the story. The threads of the plot are suddenly broken off, or continued in unexpected directions. One narrative section centers on a particular character and is then continued by the abrupt introduction of new characters. These sudden changes are often denoted by new chapters and so are clearly distinguished; the object of this distinction, however, is not separation so much as a tacit invitation to find the missing link. Furthermore, in each articulated moment, only segments of textual perspectives are present to the reader's wandering viewpoint.

In order to become fully aware of the implication, we must bear in mind that a narrative text, for instance, is composed of a variety of perspectives which outline the author's view and also provide access to what the reader is meant to visualize. [...] Although these may differ in order of importance, none of them on its own is identical to the meaning of the text, which is to be brought about by their constant intertwining through the reader in the reading process. An increase in the number of blanks is bound to occur through the frequent subdivisions of each of the textual perspectives; thus the narrator's perspective is often split into that of the implied author's set against that of the author as narrator. The hero's perspective may be set against that of the minor characters. The fictitious reader's perspective may be divided between the explicit position ascribed to him and the implicit attitude he must adopt to that position.

As the reader's wandering viewpoint travels between all these segments, its constant switching during the time flow of reading intertwines them, thus bringing forth a network of perspectives, within which each perspective opens a view not only of others but also of the intended imaginary object. Hence no single textual perspective can be equated with this imaginary object, of which it forms only one aspect. The object itself is a product of interconnection, the structuring of which is to a great extent regulated and controlled by blanks. [...]

Now we are in a position to qualify more precisely what is actually meant by reader participation in the text. If the blank is largely responsible for the activities described, then participation means that the reader is not simply called upon to 'internalize' the positions given in the text, but he is induced to make them act upon and so transform each other, as a result of which the aesthetic object begins to emerge. The structure of the blank organizes this participation, revealing simultaneously the intimate connection between this structure and the reading subject. This interconnection completely conforms to a remark made by Piaget: 'In a word, the subject is there and alive, because the basic quality of each structure is the structuring process itself.'[7] The blank in the fictional text appears to be a paradigmatic structure; its function consists in initiating structured operations in the reader, the execution of which transmits the reciprocal interaction of textual positions into consciousness. The shifting blank is responsible for a sequence of colliding images, which condition each other in the time flow of reading. The discarded image imprints itself on its successor, even though the latter is meant to resolve the deficiencies of the former. In this respect the images hang together in a sequence, and it is by this sequence that the meaning of the text comes alive in the reader's imagination.

Notes

1   R. Ingarden (1973) *The Literary Work of Art*, trans. George G. Grabowicz (Evanston: University of Illinois), p. 267.

2   R. D. Laing, H. Phillipson and A. R. Lee (1966) *Interpersonal Reception: A Theory and a Method of Research* (New York: Springer Publishing Company), p. 4.

3   R. D. Laing (1968) *The Politics of Experience* (Harmondsworth: Penguin), p. 16. Laing's italics.

4   *Ibid.*, p. 34.

5   See also E. Goffman (1972) *Interaction Ritual: Essays on Face-to-face Behavior* (New York: Pantheon).

6   V. Woolf (1957) *The Common Reader: First Series*, ed. Andrew McNellie (London: Hogarth Press), p. 174.

7   J. Piaget (1973) *Structuralism*, trans. and ed. Chaninah Maschler (London: Routledge & Kegan Paul), p. 134.

EXERCISE: Choose a modern, non-realist drama (an expressionist or symbolist play, perhaps, or a work by Harold Pinter, W. B. Yeats, Eugene O'Neill or the older August Strindberg). Consider what the spectator must contribute to interpret it successfully, taking into account its temporal (narrative) and spatial (on/off stage) blanks, the relations between its different media – words, actions, images, etc. – and the unspoken logic underpinning its events. In explaining its 'distortion' of the real world, must the spectator translate its images and events metaphorically, or assume a 'distorting' consciousness as viewer, or posit specific forces (psychological, economic, divine) as the cause of what occurs? What do you have to 'fill in' to link one scene or piece of action with the next, or one viewpoint with another? What must you assume about offstage action(s) – what is the relationship between the events shown and the wider fictional world? If you are dealing with a performance, examine also the relationship between dialogue, set, acting, lighting, and so on. You are seeking the knowledge a spectator must contribute, and the strategies he or she must adopt in order to weave those words, actions and images which comprise the 'drama' into a cohesive whole.

7.2 The gaze

Laura Mulvey, from 'Visual Pleasure and Narrative Cinema',
***Screen* 16/3 (autumn): 6–18, 1975**

[Although Mulvey's essay has been subject to criticism (see Modleski 1988, Wood 1989), and its conclusions reconsidered by the author herself (Mulvey 1989), it nevertheless exerted probably the greatest formative influence on modern feminist film theory of any single work. She places the issue of gender identity firmly at the centre of her discussion, like **Cixous** delineating a binary opposition between the (active) masculine and (passive) feminine. Mulvey's formulation is distinct, however, in that she sees this binary as embedded not merely in the cultural object or act to be viewed but also in the gaze of the viewer (see also Berger 1972). Adapting Sigmund Freud's psychic/visual mechanisms of scopophilia and ego identification (see also **Diamond**), she describes the two principal modes of pleasure available to the filmgoer, and the ways these variously construct the feminine. The fragment reproduced here, taken from the unrevised essay at the author's request, thus provides an analytical tool with which the psychic dimension of spectatorship, and its gender orientation, can be understood.]

Pleasure in looking/fascination with the human form

A. The cinema offers a number of possible pleasures. One is scopophilia [pleasure in looking]. There are circumstances in which looking itself is a source of pleasure, just as, in the reverse formation, there is pleasure in being looked at. Originally, in his *Three Essays on Sexuality*, Freud isolated scopophilia as one of the component instincts of sexuality which exist as drives quite independently of the erotogenic zones. At this point he associated scopophilia with taking other people as objects, subjecting them to a controlling and curious gaze. His particular examples centre on the voyeuristic activities of children, their desire to see and make sure of the private and forbidden (curiosity about other people's genital and bodily functions, about the presence or absence of the penis and, retrospectively, about the primal scene). In this analysis scopophilia is essentially active. [. . .] Although the instinct is modified by other factors, in particular the constitution of the ego, it continues to exist as the erotic basis for pleasure in looking at another person as object. At the extreme, it can become fixated into a perversion, producing obsessive voyeurs and Peeping Toms whose only sexual satisfaction can come from watching, in an active controlling sense, an objectified other.

At first glance, the cinema would seem to be remote from the undercover world of the surreptitious observation of an unknowing and unwilling victim. What is seen on the screen is so manifestly shown. But the mass of mainstream film, and the conventions within which it has consciously evolved, portray a hermetically sealed world which unwinds magically, indifferent to the presence of the audience, producing for them a sense of separation and playing on their voyeuristic fantasy. Moreover the extreme contrast between the darkness in the auditorium (which also isolates the spectators from one another) and the brilliance of the shifting patterns of light and shade on the screen helps to promote the illusion of voyeuristic separation. Although the film is really being shown, is there to be seen, conditions of screening and narrative conventions give the spectator an illusion of looking in on a private world. Among other things, the position of the spectators in the cinema is blatantly one of repression of their exhibitionism and projection of the repressed desire on to the performer.

B. The cinema satisfies a primordial wish for pleasurable looking, but it also goes further, developing scopophilia in its narcissistic aspect. The conventions of mainstream film focus attention on the human form. Scale, space, stories are all anthropomorphic. Here, curiosity and the wish to look intermingle with a fascination with likeness and recognition: the human face, the human body, the relationship between the human form and its surroundings, the visible presence of the person in the world. Jacques Lacan has described how the moment when a child recognizes its own image in the mirror is crucial for the constitution of the ego. Several aspects of this analysis are relevant here. The mirror phase occurs at a time when children's physical ambitions outstrip their motor capacity, with the result that their recognition of themselves is joyous in that they imagine their mirror image to be more complete, more perfect than they experience in their own body. Recognition is thus overlaid with misrecognition: the image recognized is conceived as the reflected body of the self, but its misrecognition as superior projects this body outside itself as an ideal ego, the alienated subject which, re-introjected as an ego ideal, gives rise to the future generation of identification with others. This mirror-moment predates language for the child. [. . .]

C. Sections A and B have set out two contradictory aspects of the plea- surable structures of looking in the conventional cinematic situation. The first, scopophilic, arises from pleasure in using another person as an object of sexual stimulation through sight. The second, developed through narcis- sism and the constitution of the ego, comes from identification with the image seen. Thus, in film terms, one implies a separation of the erotic identity of the subject from the object on the screen (active scopophilia), the other demands identification of the ego with the object on the screen through the spectator's fascination with and recognition of his like. The first is a function of the sexual instincts, the second of ego libido. This dichotomy was crucial for Freud. Although he saw the two as interacting and overlaying each other, the tension between instinctual drives and self- preservation polarizes in terms of pleasure. But both are formative structures, mechanisms not meaning. In themselves they have no signifi- cation, they have to be attached to an idealization. Both pursue aims in indifference to perceptual reality, creating the imagized, eroticized concept of the world that forms the perception of the subject and makes a mockery of empirical objectivity.

During its history, the cinema seems to have evolved a particular illusion of reality in which this contradiction between libido and ego has found a beautifully complementary fantasy world. In *reality* the fantasy world of the screen is subject to the law which produces it. Sexual instincts and identification processes have a meaning within the symbolic order which articulates desire. Desire, born with language, allows the possibility of transcending the instinctual and the imaginary, but its point of reference continually returns to the traumatic moment of its birth: the castration complex. Hence the look, pleasurable in form, can be threatening in content, and it is woman as representation/image that crystallizes this paradox.

Woman as image, man as bearer of the look

A. In a world ordered by sexual imbalance, pleasure in looking has been split between active/male and passive/female. The determining male gaze projects its fantasy on to the female figure, which is styled accordingly. In their traditional exhibitionist role women are simultaneously looked at and displayed, with their appearance coded for strong visual and erotic impact so that they can be said to connote *to-be-looked-at-ness*. Woman displayed as sexual object is the *leitmotif* of erotic spectacle: from pin-ups to strip-tease, from Ziegfeld to Busby Berkeley, she holds the look, plays to and signifies male desire. Mainstream film neatly combines spectacle and narrative. (Note, however, how in the musical song-and-dance numbers interrupt the flow of the diegesis.) The presence of woman is an indispensable element of spectacle in normal narrative film, yet her visual presence tends to work against the development of a story-line, to freeze the flow of action in moments of erotic contemplation. This alien presence then has to be integrated into cohesion with the narrative. As Budd Boetticher has put it:

> What counts is what the heroine provokes, or rather what she represents. She is the one, or rather the love or fear she inspires in the hero, or else the concern he feels for her, who makes him act the way he does. In herself the woman has not the slightest importance.

(A recent tendency in narrative film has been to dispense with this problem altogether; hence the development of what Molly Haskell has called the 'buddy movie', in which the active homosexual eroticism of the central male figures can carry the story without distraction.) Traditionally, the woman displayed has functioned on two levels: as erotic object for the characters within the screen story, and as erotic object for the spectator within the auditorium, with a shifting tension between the looks on either side of the screen. For instance, the device of the show-girl allows the two looks to be unified technically without any apparent break in the diegesis. A woman performs within the narrative, the gaze of the spectator and that of the male characters in the film are neatly combined without breaking narrative verisimilitude. For a moment the sexual impact of the performing woman takes the film into a no man's land outside its own time and space. Thus Marilyn Monroe's first appearance in *The River of No Return* and Lauren Bacall's songs in *To Have and Have Not*. Similarly, conventional close-ups of legs (Dietrich, for instance) or a face (Garbo) integrate into the narrative a different mode of eroticism. One part of a fragmented body destroys the Renaissance space, the illusion of depth demanded by the narrative; it gives flatness, the quality of a cut-out or icon, rather than verisimilitude, to the screen.

B. An active/passive heterosexual division of labour has similarly controlled narrative structure. According to the principles of the ruling ideology and the psychical structures that back it up, the male figure cannot bear the burden of sexual objectification. Man is reluctant to gaze at his exhibitionist like. Hence the split between spectacle and narrative supports the man's role as the active one of advancing the story, making things happen. The man controls the film fantasy and also emerges as the representative of power in a further sense: as the bearer of the look of the spectator, transferring it behind the screen to neutralize the extra-diegetic tendencies represented by woman as spectacle. This is made possible through the processes set in motion by structuring the film around a main controlling figure with whom the spectator can identify. As the spectator identifies with the main male protagonist, he projects his look on to that of his like, his screen surrogate, so that the power of the male protagonist as he controls events coincides with the active power of the erotic look, both giving a satisfying sense of omnipotence. [. . .] In contrast to woman as icon, the active male figure (the ego ideal of the identification process) demands a three-dimensional space corresponding to that of the mirror recognition, in which the alienated subject internalized his own representation of his imaginary existence. He is a figure in a landscape. Here the function of film is to reproduce as accurately as possible the so-called natural conditions of human perception. Camera technology (as exemplified by deep focus in particular) and camera movements (determined by the action of the protagonist), combined with invisible editing (demanded by realism), all tend to blur the limits of screen space. The male protagonist is free to command the stage, a stage of spatial illusion in which he articulates the look and creates the action.

C.1. Sections A and B have set out a tension between a mode of representation of woman in film and conventions surrounding the diegesis. Each is associated with a look: that of the spectator in direct scopophilic contact with the female form displayed for his enjoyment (connoting male fantasy) and that of the spectator fascinated with the image of his like set in an illusion of natural space, and through him gaining control and possession of the woman within the diegesis. [. . .]

But in psychoanalytic terms, the female figure poses a deeper problem. She also connotes something that the look continually circles around but disavows: her lack of a penis, implying a threat of castration and hence unpleasure. Ultimately, the meaning of woman is sexual difference, the absence of the penis is visually ascertainable, the material evidence on which is based the castration complex essential for the organization of entrance to the symbolic order and the law of the father. Thus the woman as icon, displayed for the gaze and enjoyment of men, the active controllers of the look, always threatens to evoke the anxiety it originally signified. The male unconscious has two avenues of escape from this castration anxiety: preoccupation with the re-enactment of the original trauma (investigating the woman, demystifying her mystery), counterbalanced by the devaluation, punishment or saving of the guilty object (an avenue typified by the concerns of the *film noir*); or else complete disavowal of castration by the substitution of a fetish object or turning the represented figure itself into a fetish so that it becomes reassuring rather than dangerous (hence overvaluation, the cult of the female star). This second avenue, fetishistic scopophilia, builds up the physical beauty of the object, transforming it into something satisfying in itself. The first avenue, voyeurism, on the contrary, has associations with sadism: pleasure lies in ascertaining guilt (immediately associated with castration), asserting control and subjugating the guilty person through punishment or forgiveness. This sadistic side fits in well with narrative. Sadism demands a story, depends on making something happen, forcing a change in another person, a battle of will and strength, victory/defeat, all occurring in a linear time with a beginning and an end. Fetishistic scopophilia, on the other hand, can exist outside linear time as the erotic instinct is focused on the look alone. These contradictions and ambiguities can be illustrated more simply by using works by Hitchcock and Sternberg, both of whom take the look almost as the content or subject matter of many of their films. Hitchcock is the more complex, as he uses both mechanisms. Sternberg's work, on the other hand, provides many pure examples of fetishistic scopophilia.

C.2. Sternberg once said he would welcome his films being projected upside-down so that story and character involvement would not interfere with the spectator's undiluted appreciation of the screen image. This statement is revealing but ingenuous: ingenuous in that his films do demand that the figure of the woman (Dietrich, in the cycle of films with her, as the ultimate example) should be identifiable. But revealing in that it empha- sizes the fact that for him the pictorial space enclosed by the frame is paramount, rather than narrative or identification processes. While Hitchcock goes into the investigative side of voyeurism, Sternberg produces the ultimate fetish, taking it to the point where the powerful look of the male protagonist (characteristic of traditional narrative film) is broken in favour of the image in direct erotic rapport with the spectator. The beauty of the woman as object and the screen space coalesce; she is no longer the bearer of guilt but a perfect product, whose body, stylized and frag- mented by close-ups, is the content of the film and the direct recipient of the spectator's look. Sternberg plays down the illusion of screen depth; his screen tends to be one-dimensional, as light and shade, lace, steam, foliage, net, streamers and so on reduce the visual field. There is little or no mediation of the look through the eyes of the main male protagonist. On the contrary, shadowy presences like La Bessiere in *Morocco* act as surrogates for the director, detached as they are from audience identifi- cation. Despite Sternberg's insistence that his stories are irrelevant, it is significant that they are concerned with situation, not suspense, and cyclical rather than linear time, while plot complications revolve around misun- derstanding rather than conflict. The most important absence is that of the controlling male gaze within the screen scene. The high point of emotional drama in the most typical Dietrich films, her supreme moments of erotic meaning, take place in the absence of the man she loves in the fiction. There are other witnesses, other spectators watching her on the screen, their gaze is one with, not standing in for, that of the audience. At the end of *Morocco*, Tom Brown has already disappeared into the desert when Amy Jolly kicks off her gold sandals and walks after him. At the end of *Dishonoured*, Kranau is indifferent to the fate of Magda. In both cases, the erotic impact, sanctified by death, is displayed as a spectacle for the audience. The male hero misunderstands and, above all, does not see.

In Hitchcock, by contrast, the male hero does see precisely what the audience sees. However, in the films I shall discuss here, he takes fascina- tion with an image through scopophilic eroticism as the subject of the film. Moreover, in these cases the hero portrays the contradictions and tensions experienced by the spectator. In *Vertigo* in particular, but also in *Marnie* and *Rear Window*, the look is central to the plot, oscillating between voyeurism and fetishistic fascination. [. . .] Hitchcock has never concealed his interest in voyeurism, cinematic and non-cinematic. His heroes are exemplary of the symbolic order and the law – a policeman (*Vertigo*), a dominant male possessing money and power (*Marnie*) – but their erotic drives lead them into compromised situations. The power to subject another person to the will sadistically or to the gaze voyeuristically is turned on to the woman as the object of both. Power is backed by a certainty of legal right and the established guilt of the woman (evoking castration, psycho-analytically speaking). True perversion is barely concealed under a shallow mask of ideological correctness – the man is on the right side of the law, the woman on the wrong. Hitchcock's skilful use of identification processes and liberal use of subjective camera from the point of view of the male protagonist draw the spectators deeply into his position, making them share his uneasy gaze. The spectator is absorbed into a voyeuristic situation within the screen scene and diegesis, which parodies his own in the cinema. In an analysis of *Rear Window*, Douchet takes the film as a metaphor for the cinema. Jeffries is the audience, the events in the apartment block opposite correspond to the screen. As he watches, an erotic dimension is added to his look, a central image to the drama. His girlfriend Lisa had been of little sexual interest to him, more or less a drag, so long as she remained on the spectator side. When she crosses the barrier between his room and the block opposite, their relationship is re-born erotically. He does not merely watch her through his lens, as a distant meaningful image, he also sees her as a guilty intruder exposed by a dangerous man threatening her with punishment, and thus finally [enabling him to] save her. Lisa's exhibitionism has already been established by her obsessive interest in dress and style, in being a passive image of visual perfection; Jeffries's voyeurism and activity have also been established through his work as a photo-journalist, a maker of stories and captor of images. However, his enforced inactivity, binding him to his seat as a spectator, puts him squarely in the fantasy position of the cinema audience.

EXERCISE: Choose a film in which vision or the gaze plays a central role (e.g. Dorothy Arzner's *Dance Girl Dance*, Peter Weir's *Witness*, Roger Spottiswoode's *Under Fire*) and carefully select two scenes, one which invites a scopophilic gaze and another which privileges ego identification. Explore in detail the means by which they achieve this, considering the focusing and movement (or not) of the camera, the framing of the picture, the relationship between character or action and the surrounding environment, and so on. How do these two visual modes support or mediate the film's content, its narrative and themes?

Now turn to the live performances you have already seen during your studies (videos of productions will not serve) and seek the theatrical equivalents of those gaze forms. Consider movement, lighting, the type of stage and use of stage space, the gaze *within* the play world, any direct address to the audience, and so on. Whose viewpoint did you identify with as spectator, and with what *theatrical* means was this identification promoted? What was the role of spectacle, and who was its focus? Were both gaze forms gendered in your productions; if not, were they used in the service of some other structure of power?

7.3 Structure of feeling

Raymond Williams, from *Marxism and Literature*, Oxford: Oxford University Press, 1977

[True to its roots in Marxist theory, Williams's 'cultural materialism' typically seeks to relate texts and performances to their cultural and historical contexts. Rather than view those contexts as monolithic, however, he stresses their inherent complexity and pluralism, and hence their potential for contradiction and change. Ideology, he asserts, is never unified but always takes at least three concurrent forms: current ruling ideas constitute the *dominant ideology*, those coming to prominence comprise the *emergent*, while the *residual* describes those whose formerly dominant position has waned (Williams 1977, 1981). This concern for the precise social and historical location of ideas is evident in the following piece. The rise of a new form, aesthetic or sensibility, he argues, necessarily marks a wider shift in thought, one common to both the artists who produce the work and those audiences able to appreciate it. His term for this consciousness, 'structure of feeling', describes an experience of an apparently personal order but which is nevertheless shared, and hence social. In emphasizing that cultural forms are *lived*, experienced subjectively as ways of viewing the world, representing it, and so on, he provides a means of understanding spectators' individual responses as social and historical phenomena.]

In most description and analysis, culture and society are expressed in an habitual past tense. The strongest barrier to the recognition of human cultural activity is this immediate and regular conversion of experience into finished products. What is defensible as a procedure in conscious history, where on certain assumptions many actions can be definitively taken as having ended, is habitually projected, not only into the always moving substance of the past, but into contemporary life, in which relationships, institutions and formations in which we are still actively involved are converted, by this procedural mode, into formed wholes rather than forming and formative processes. Analysis is then centred on relations between these produced institutions, formations and experiences, so that now, as in that produced past, only the fixed explicit forms exist, and living presence is always, by definition, receding.

When we begin to grasp the dominance of this procedure, to look into its centre and if possible past its edges, we can understand, in new ways, that separation of the social from the personal which is so powerful and directive a cultural mode. If the social is always past, in the sense that it is always formed, we have indeed to find other terms for the undeniable experience of the present: not only the temporal present, the realization of this and this instant, but the specificity of present being, the inalienably physical, within which we may indeed discern and acknowledge institutions, formations, positions, but not always as fixed products, defining products. And then if the social is the fixed and explicit – the known relationships, institutions, formations, positions – all that is present and moving, all that escapes or seems to escape from the fixed and the explicit and the known, is grasped and defined as the personal: this, here, now, alive, active, 'subjective'. [. . .]

Yet it is the reduction of the social to fixed forms that remains the basic error. Marx often said this, and some Marxists quote him, in fixed ways, before returning to fixed forms. The mistake, as so often, is in taking terms of analysis as terms of substance. Thus we speak of a world view or of a prevailing ideology or of a class outlook, often with adequate evidence, but in this regular slide towards a past tense and a fixed form suppose, or even do not know that we have to suppose, that these exist and are lived specifically and definitively, in singular and developing forms. Perhaps the dead can be reduced to fixed forms, though their surviving records are against it. But the living will not be reduced, at least in the first person; living third persons may be different. All the known complexities, the experienced tensions, shifts and uncertainties, the intricate forms of unevenness and confusion, are against the terms of the reduction and soon, by extension, against social analysis itself. Social forms are then often admitted for generalities but debarred, contemptuously, from any possible relevance to this immediate and actual significance of being. And from the abstractions formed in their turn by this act of debarring – the 'human imagination', the 'human psyche', the 'unconscious', with their 'functions' in art and in myth and in dream – new and displaced forms of social analysis and categorization, overriding all specific social conditions, are then more or less rapidly developed.

Social forms are evidently more recognizable when they are articulate and explicit. We have seen this in the range from institutions to formations and traditions. We can see it again in the range from dominant systems of belief and education to influential systems of explanation and argument. All these have effective presence. Many are formed and deliberate, and some are quite fixed. But when they have all been identified they are not a whole inventory even of social consciousness in its simplest sense. For they become social consciousness only when they are lived, actively, in real relationships, and moreover in relationships which are more than systematic exchanges between fixed units. Indeed just because all consciousness is social, its processes occur not only between but within the relationship and the related. And this practical consciousness is always more than a handling of fixed forms and units. [. . .] Practical consciousness is almost always different from official consciousness, and this is not only a matter of relative freedom or control. For practical consciousness is what is actually being lived, and not only what it is thought is being lived. Yet the actual alternative to the received and produced fixed forms is not silence: not the absence, the unconscious, which bourgeois culture has mythicized. It is a kind of feeling and thinking which is indeed social and material, but each in an embryonic phase before it can become fully articulate and defined exchange. Its relations with the already articulate and defined are then exceptionally complex.

This process can be directly observed in the history of a language. In spite of substantial and at some levels decisive continuities in grammar and vocabulary, no generation speaks quite the same language as its predecessors. The difference can be defined in terms of additions, deletions and modifications, but these do not exhaust it. What really changes is something quite general, over a wide range, and the description that often fits the change best is the literary term 'style'. It is a general change, rather than a set of deliberate choices, yet choices can be deduced from it, as well as effects. Similar kinds of change can be observed in manners, dress, building and other similar forms of social life. It is an open question – that is to say, a set of specific historical questions – whether in any of these changes this or that group has been dominant or influential, or whether they are the result of much more general interaction. For what we are defining is a particular quality of social experience and relationship, historically distinct from other particular qualities, which gives the sense of a generation or of a period. The relations between this quality and the other specifying historical marks of changing institutions, formations and beliefs, and beyond these the changing social and economic relations between and within classes, are again an open question: that is to say, a set of specific historical questions. The methodological consequence of such a definition, however, is that the specific qualitative changes are not *assumed* to be epiphenomena of changed institutions, formations and beliefs, or merely secondary evidence of changed social and economic relations between and within classes. At the same time they are from the beginning taken as social experience, rather than as 'personal' experience or as the merely superficial or incidental 'small change' of society. They are social in two ways that distinguish them from reduced senses of the social as the institutional and the formal: first, in that they are *changes of presence* (while they are being lived this is obvious; when they have been lived it is still their substantial characteristic); second, in that although they are emergent or pre-emergent, they do not have to await definition, classification or rationalization before they exert palpable pressures and set effective limits on experience and on action.

Such changes can be defined as changes in *structures of feeling*. The term is difficult, but 'feeling' is chosen to emphasize a distinction from more formal concepts of 'world view' or 'ideology'. It is not only that we must go beyond formally held and systematic beliefs, though of course we have always to include them. It is that we are concerned with meanings and values as they are actively lived and felt, and the relations between these and formal or systematic beliefs are in practice variable (including historically variable), over a range from formal assent with private dissent to the more nuanced interaction between selected and interpreted beliefs and acted and justified experiences. An alternative definition would be structures of experience: in one sense the better and wider word, but with the difficulty that one of its senses has that past tense which is the most important obstacle to recognition of the area of social experience which is being defined. We are talking about characteristic elements of impulse, restraint and tone; specifically affective elements of consciousness and relationships: not feeling against thought, but thought as felt and feeling as thought: practical consciousness of a present kind, in a living and interrelating continuity. We are then defining these elements as a 'structure': as a set, with specific internal relations, at once interlocking and in tension. Yet we are also defining a social experience which is still *in process*, often indeed not yet recognized as social but taken to be private, idiosyncratic and even isolating, but which in analysis (though rarely otherwise) has its emergent, connecting and dominant characteristics, indeed its specific hierarchies. These are often more recognizable at a later stage, when they have been (as often happens) formalized, classified and in many cases built into institutions and formations. By that time the case is different; a new structure of feeling will usually already have begun to form, in the true social present.

Methodologically, then, a 'structure of feeling' is a cultural hypothesis, actually derived from attempts to understand such elements and their connections in a generation or period, and needing always to be returned, interactively, to such evidence. It is initially less simple than more formally structured hypotheses of the social, but it is more adequate to the actual range of cultural evidence: historically certainly, but even more (where it matters more) in our present cultural process. The hypothesis has a special relevance to art and literature, where the true social content is in a significant number of cases of this present and affective kind, which cannot without loss be reduced to belief-systems, institutions or explicit general relationships, though it may include all these as lived and experienced, with or without tension, as it also evidently includes elements of social and material (physical or natural) experience which may lie beyond, or be uncovered or imperfectly covered by, the elsewhere recognizable systematic elements. The unmistakable presence of certain elements in art which are not covered by (though in one mode they may be reduced to) other formal systems is the true source of the specializing categories of 'the aesthetic', 'the arts' and 'imaginative literature'. We need, on the one hand, to acknowledge (and welcome) the specificity of these elements – specific feelings, specific rhythms – and yet to find ways of recognizing their specific kinds of sociality, thus preventing that extraction from social experience which is conceivable only when social experience itself has been categorically (and at root historically) reduced. We are then not only concerned with the restoration of social content in its full sense, that of a generative immediacy. The idea of a structure of feeling can be specifically related to the evidence of forms and conventions – semantic figures – which, in art and literature, are often among the very first indications that such a new structure is forming. These relations will be discussed in more detail in subsequent chapters, but as a matter of cultural theory this is a way of defining forms and conventions in art and literature as inalienable elements of a social material process: not by derivation from other social forms and pre-forms, but as social formation of a specific kind which may in turn be seen as the articulation (often the only fully available articulation) of structures of feeling which as living processes are much more widely experienced.

For structures of feeling can be defined as social experiences in solution, as distinct from other social semantic formations which have been precipitated and are more evidently and more immediately available. Not all art, by any means, relates to a contemporary structure of feeling. The effective formations of most actual art relate to already manifest social formations, dominant or residual, and it is primarily to emergent formations (though often in the form of modification or disturbance in older forms) that the structure of feeling, as solution, relates. Yet this specific solution is never mere flux. It is a structured formation which, because it is at the very edge of semantic availability, has many of the characteristics of a preformation, until specific articulations – new semantic figures – are discovered in material practice: often, as it happens, in relatively isolated ways, which are only later seen to compose a significant (often in fact minority) generation; this often, in turn, the generation that substantially connects to its successors. It is thus a specific structure of particular linkages, particular emphases and suppressions, and, in what are often its most recognizable forms, particular deep starting-points and conclusions. Early Victorian ideology, for example, specified the exposure caused by poverty or by debt or by illegitimacy as social failure or deviation; the contemporary structure of feeling, meanwhile, in the new semantic figures of Dickens, of Emily Brontë, and others, specified exposure and isolation as a general condition, and poverty, debt or illegitimacy as its connecting instances. An alternative ideology, relating such exposure to the nature of the social order, was only later generally formed: offering explanations but now at a reduced tension: the social explanation fully admitted, the intensity of experienced fear and shame now dispersed and generalized.

EXERCISE: Choose a play of a form or genre which emerged at a definable point in history and list its distinctive features. If you are uncertain how to find these, compare the piece to a play of a kind already in existence when it emerged, mentally transplanting features of your chosen drama into it; note those which prove alien to the older aesthetic, at home only in the new. Then consider what the audience must feel, know or assume in order to appreciate each feature. What conception of human beings must spectators recognize in order to understand the characters? On what value or belief systems does the play's judgement of them rest? If your drama is a kind of tragedy, what forces bring about the protagonist's downfall; if a comedy, what does it assume to be laughable? You are seeking the ideas or feelings underlying the drama's defining characteristics.

Now start to locate the play in its wider historical landscape: research the period in your library, each person choosing and copying a range of texts or artefacts from that time and culture (e.g. paintings or pieces of music, short passages of philosophy or theology or aesthetics, dress fashions, poems, leisure pursuits, political manifestos, examples of new architecture). Pooling your selections, search them for those qualities you found in the emergent play, or their equivalents. Is abstraction, symbolism or a refusal of illusion common to a range of pieces, or is a shared mood of irony, naivety or idealism evident? If the events of the play are driven by magic or morality or heightened emotion, can you find its equivalent in a form of architecture? If its characters conform to a Christian or Darwinian or psychoanalytic view of the human subject, does a painting presume the same subject as viewer? Be prepared to think abstractly and, if necessary, to rethink your knowledges or feelings to make connections between different art forms. When you have plotted the connections, consider what picture of the spectator they collectively offer – what kind of audience the drama *assumes*. You are seeking those ideas and feelings, shared by author and audience, which made the play meaningful.

Part eight

At the borders
of performance

'Performance' is not an unproblematic concept, for as the writings of such diverse theorists as **Goffman**, **Althusser**, **Foucault** and **Butler** variously demonstrate, any bald distinction between performative and 'real', functional behaviour is in practice a difficult one to maintain. As part of everyday life we not only enact given social roles – doctor, woman, American, football fan – using conventional behavioural signatures, we also shape our actions to accord with conceptions of ourselves which may be cultural and ideological, as well as psychological, in origin. As **Tuan** notes, even when alone we frequently posit a notional viewer as spectator to our activities, implicitly judging them to be expressive although there is no one present to whom they might express. Most of our acts, then, are 'framed' in Goffman's sense: as self-conscious beings we reflect upon our actions as expressions of self; as social animals we constantly produce behaviours to be read by others. But if such framing is evident in individual actions, it is particularly significant for those we undertake as communities. Culture is not communicated solely via static artefacts such as books and paintings, it is also enacted, given a concrete, 'readable' form in rites and ceremonies, sporting contests, festivals, and so on. Writing in 1959 on the means by which traditions and values are communicated in modern

India, Milton Singer termed such events 'cultural performances' to distinguish them from the 'artistic performances' of dance, theatre, and so on (see Singer 1959 and1972). As Joseph Roach (1996) notes, as social activities the former constitute a kind of cultural 'memory', a means of recording, transmitting and, when necessary, forgetting, by which communities reproduce and recreate themselves.

The pieces in this section both represent varied disciplinary perspectives and deal with different kinds of cultural performance. Anthropologist Victor Turner (1920–83) sets the stage by positioning performances within a broad socio-historical frame, arguing for a basic distinction between those that predate and postdate industrialization. Literary critic Michael Bristol (b. 1940) analyses the way in which official performances reproduce ideological conceptions of society. The opposite focus is chosen by philosopher and literary theorist Mikhail Bakhtin (1895–1975), who describes a form of event which opposes hegemonic cultural systems. Anthropologist Clifford Geertz (b. 1923) explores how sport, ostensibly a pure entertainment genre, actually functions symbolically to generate 'textual' meaning.

(In this volume, see also **Foucault, Tuan, Carlson**.)

Further reading: Read freely among Geertz 1973 and 1983 (complete volumes), Macaloon (ed.) 1984, Moore and Myerhoff (eds) 1977, Roach 1996 and Turner 1969, 1974, 1987 for an introduction to the broad field of cultural performance; Bell 1992, van Gennep 1960 and Hughes-Freeland (ed.) 1997 each approach the topic of ritual in a different way, but all in an accessible form; Bergeron 1971, Cannadine and Price (eds) 1987 and Kertzer 1988 are readable studies of state and political ceremony; Bristol 1985, Fuoss 1997 and Cohen-Cruz (ed.) 1998 offer readings of actual radical political performances; for critical readings of sport see Barthes 1972b, James 1963 and Whiting and Masterson (eds) 1974.

8.1 Liminal and liminoid

Victor Turner, from 'Liminal to Liminoid, in Play, Flow, and Ritual: An Essay in Comparative Symbology', in *From Ritual to Theatre: The Human Seriousness of Play*, New York: Performing Arts Journal, 1982

[Addressing topics ranging from ritual to contemporary drama, anthropologist Turner consistently explored the social character of performance, and perhaps the most enduring influences on this work were those of sociologist Émile Durkheim and anthropologist Arnold van Gennep. It is van Gennep's analysis of the time/space of ritual (1960), and the distinction Durkheim draws between the 'mechanical solidarity' of agrarian societies and the 'organic solidarity' of the modern (1995), which inform his discussion of *limina* in the following extract. Limina (as in *limen* or 'threshold') are symbolic activities – rituals, festivals, entertainments, etc. – which punctuate socio-economic production, comprising the cultural life of the community. In pre-industrial societies such events are indeed part of the communal round, and function in support of the prevailing socio-cultural order. But from industrialization's reorganization of time emerged new forms of cultural activity, critical of the status quo. Turner's division of limina into 'liminal' and 'liminoid' forms thus marks not only their emergence from different social formations but also their contrasting positions within those formations, their capacity to support or subvert the ruling order.]

Now let us consider the clear division between *work* and *leisure* which modern industry has produced, and how this has affected all symbolic genres, from ritual to games and literature. [. . .] Dumazedier dismisses the view that leisure has existed in all societies at all times. In archaic and tribal societies, he maintains, 'work and play alike formed part of the ritual by which men sought communion with the ancestral spirits. Religious festivals embodied both work and play.'[1] Yet religious specialists such as shamans and medicine-men did not constitute a 'leisure class' in Thorstein Veblen's sense,[2] since they performed religious or magical functions for the whole community (and, as we have seen, shamanism is a 'diligent and laborious' profession). Similarly, in the agricultural societies of recorded history,

> the working year followed a timetable written in the very passage of the days and seasons: in good weather work was hard, in bad weather it slackened off. Work of this kind had a natural rhythm to it, punctuated by rests, songs, games, and ceremonies; it was synonymous with the daily round, and in some regions began at sunrise, to finish only at sunset ... the cycle of the year was also marked by a whole series of sabbaths and feast days. The sabbath belonged to religion; feast days, however, were often occasions for a great investment of energy (not to mention food) and constituted the obverse or opposite of everyday life [often characterized by symbolic inversion and status reversal]. But the ceremonial [or ritual]

aspect of these celebrations could not be disregarded; they stemmed from religion [defined as sacred *work*], not leisure [as we think of it today] . . . They were imposed by religious requirements . . . [and] the major European civilizations knew more than 150 workless days a year.[3]

Sebastian de Grazia has argued that the origins of leisure can be traced to the way of life enjoyed by certain aristocratic classes in the course of Western civilization.[4] Dumazedier disagrees, pointing out the idle state of Greek philosophers and sixteenth-century gentry cannot be defined *in relation to* work, but rather *replaces work altogether*. Work is done by slaves, peasants or servants. True leisure only exists when it complements or rewards work. This is not to say that many of the refinements of human culture did not come from this aristocratic idleness. Dumazedier thinks that it is significant that the Greek word for having nothing to do (*schole*) also means 'school'. 'The courtiers of Europe, after the end of the Middle Ages, both invented and extolled the ideal of the humanist and gentleman.'[5]

'Leisure', then, presupposes 'work': it is a non-work, even an anti-work phase in the life of a person who also works. If we were to indulge in terminological neophily, we might call it *anergic* as against *ergic*. Leisure arises, says Dumazedier, under two conditions. First, society ceases to govern its activities by means of common ritual obligations: some activities, including work and leisure, become, at least in theory, *subject to individual choice*. Second, the work by which a person earns his or her living is 'set apart from his other activities: its limits are no longer "natural" but arbitrary – indeed, it is organized in so definite a fashion that it can easily be separated, both in theory and in practice, from his free time'. It is only in the social life of industrial and post-industrial civilizations that we find these necessary conditions. Other social theorists, both radical and conservative, have pointed out that leisure is the product of industrialized, rationalized, bureaucratized, large-scale socio-economic systems with arbitrary rather than natural delimitation of 'work' from 'free time' or 'time out'. Work is now organized by industry so as to be separated from 'free time', which includes, in addition to leisure, attendance to such personal needs as eating, sleeping and caring for one's health and appearance, as well as familial, social, civic, political and religious obligations (which would have fallen within the domain of the work–play continuum in tribal society). Leisure is predominantly an urban phenomenon, so that when the concept of leisure begins to penetrate rural societies, it is because agricultural labor is tending towards an industrial, 'rationalized' mode of organization, and because rural life is becoming permeated by the urban values of industrialization – this holds good for the 'Third World' today as well as for the rural hinterlands of long-established industrial societies. [. . .]

Technological development, political and industrial organization by workers, action by liberal employers, revolutions in many parts of the world, have had the cumulative effect of bringing more leisure into the 'free-time' of industrial cultures. In this leisure, symbolic genres, both of the entertainment and instructive sorts, have proliferated. In my book *The Ritual Process*,[6] I have spoken of some of these as 'liminal' phenomena. In view of what I have just said, is liminality an adequate label for this set of symbolic activities and forms? Clearly, there are some respects in which these 'anergic' genres share characteristics with the 'ludergic' rituals and myths (if we contrast the Hindu and Judaic ritual style) of archaic, tribal and early agrarian cultures. Leisure can be conceived of as a betwixt-and-between, a neither-this-nor-that domain between two spells of work or between occupational and familial and civic activity. [. . .] Just as when tribesmen make masks, disguise themselves as monsters, heap up disparate ritual symbols, invert or parody profane reality in myths and folk-tales, so do the genres of industrial leisure, the theatre, poetry, novel, ballet, film, sport, rock music, classical music, art, 'pop art, etc., *play* with the factors of culture, sometimes assembling them in random, grotesque, improbable, surprising, shocking, usually experimental combinations. But they do this in a much more complicated way than in the liminality of tribal initiations, multiplying specialized genres of artistic and popular entertainments, mass culture, pop culture, folk culture, high culture, counterculture, underground culture, etc., as against the relatively limited symbolic genres of 'tribal' society, and within each allowing lavish scope to authors, poets, dramatists, painters, sculptors, composers, musicians, actors, comedians, folksingers, rock musicians, 'makers' generally, to generate not only weird forms but also, and not infrequently, models, direct and parabolic or aesopian, that are highly critical of the status quo as a whole or in part. [. . .] The liminal phases of tribal society invert but do not usually subvert the status quo, the structural form, of society; reversal underlines to the members of a community that chaos is the alternative to cosmos, so they'd better stick to cosmos, i.e., the traditional order of culture, though they can for a brief while have a whale of a good time being chaotic, in some saturnalian or lupercalian revelry, some charivari, or institutionalized orgy. But supposedly 'entertainment' genres of industrial society are often *subversive*, satirizing, lampooning, burlesquing or subtly putting down the central values of the basic, work-sphere society, or at least of selected sectors of that society. The word 'entertain', incidentally, is derived from Old French *entretenir*, to 'hold apart', that is, to create a liminal or liminoid space in which performances may take place. Some of these entertainment genres, such as the 'legitimate' or 'classical' theatre, are historically continuous with ritual, as in the cases of Greek tragedy or Japanese Noh theatre, and possess something of the sacred seriousness, even the *rites de passage* structure of their antecedents. Nevertheless, crucial differences separate the structure, function, style, scope and symbology of the *liminal* in tribal and agrarian ritual and myth from what we may perhaps call the 'liminoid', or leisure genres, of symbolic forms and action in complex, industrial societies. [. . .]

I have used the term 'anti-structure', mainly with reference to tribal and agrarian societies, to describe both liminality and what I have called 'communitas'. I meant by it not a structural reversal, a mirror-imaging of 'profane' workaday socio-economic structure, or a fantasy-rejection of structural 'necessities', but the liberation of human capacities of cognition, affect, volition, creativity, etc., from the normative constraints incumbent upon occupying a sequence of social statuses, enacting a multiplicity of social roles and being acutely conscious of membership in some corporate group such as a family, lineage, clan, tribe, nation, etc., or of affiliation with some pervasive social category such as a class, caste, sex or age-division. Socio-cultural systems drive so steadily towards consistency that human individuals get off these normative hooks only in rare situations in small-scale societies, and not too frequently in large-scale ones. Nevertheless, the exigencies of structuration itself, the process of containing new growth in orderly patterns or schemata, has an Achilles' heel. This is the fact that when persons, groups, sets of ideas, etc., move from one level or style of organization or regulation of the interdependence of their parts or elements to another level, there has to be an interfacial region or, to change the metaphor, an interval, however brief, of *margin* or *limen*, when the past is momentarily negated, suspended or abrogated, and the future has not yet begun, an instant of pure potentiality when everything, as it were, trembles in the balance. (Like the trembling quarterback with all the 'options' but with the very solid future moving menacingly towards him!) In tribal societies, owing to the general overriding homogeneity of values, behavior and social structural rules, this instant can be fairly easily contained or dominated by social structure, held in check from innovative excess, 'hedged about', as anthropologists delight to say, by 'taboos', 'checks and balances', etc. Thus, the tribal liminal, however exotic in appearance, can never be much more than a subversive flicker. It is put into the service of normativeness almost as soon as it appears. Yet I see it as a kind of institutional capsule or pocket which contains the germ of future social developments, of societal change, in a way that the central tendencies of a social system can never quite succeed in being, the spheres where law and custom, and the modes of social control ancillary to these, prevail. Innovation can take place in such spheres, but most frequently it occurs in interfaces and limina, then becomes *legislated* in central sectors. For me, such relatively 'late' social processes, historically speaking, as 'revolution', 'insurrection' and even 'romanticism' in art, characterized by freedom in form and spirit, emphasis on feeling and originality, represent an inversion of the relation between the normative and the liminal in 'tribal' and other essentially conservative societies. For in these modern processes and movements, the seeds of cultural transformation, discontent with the way things are culturally, and social criticism, always implicit in the pre-industrial liminal, have become situationally central, no longer a matter of the interface between 'fixed structures' but a matter of the holistically developmental. Thus revolutions, whether successful or not, become the *limina*, with all their initiatory overtones, between major distinctive structural forms or orderings of society. It may be that this is to use 'liminal' in a metaphorical, not in the 'primary' or 'literal' sense advocated by van Gennep,[7] but this usage may help us to think about global human society, to which all specific historical social formations may well be converging. Revolutions, whether violent or non-violent, may be the totalizing liminal phases for which the limina of tribal *rites de passage* were merely foreshadowings or premonitions. [. . .]

When we compare liminal with liminoid processes and phenomena, then, we find crucial differences as well as similarities. Let me try to set some of these out. In a crude, preliminary way they provide some delimitation of the field of comparative symbology.

(1) *Liminal phenomena* tend to predominate in tribal and early agrarian societies possessing what Durkheim has called 'mechanical solidarity',[8] and dominated by what Henry Maine has called 'status'. *Liminoid phenomena* flourish in societies with 'organic solidarity', bonded reciprocally by 'contractual' relations, and generated by and following the industrial revolution, though they perhaps begin to appear on the scene in city-states on their way to becoming empires (of the Graeco-Roman type) and in feudal societies. [. . .]

(2) *Liminal phenomena* tend to be collective, concerned with calendrical, biological, social-structural rhythms or with crises in social processes whether these result from internal adjustments or external adaptations or remedial measures. Thus they appear at what may be called 'natural

breaks', natural disjunctions in the flow of natural and social processes. They are thus enforced by socio-cultural 'necessity', but they contain *in nuce* 'freedom' and the potentiality for the formation of new ideas, symbols, models, beliefs. *Liminoid phenomena* may be collective (and when they are so, are often directly derived from liminal antecedents) but are more characteristically individual products though they often have collective or 'mass' effects. They are not cyclical, but continuously generated, though in the times and places apart from work settings assigned to 'leisure' activities.

(3) *Liminal phenomena* are centrally integrated into the total social process, forming with all its other aspects a complete whole, and representing its necessary negativity and subjunctivity. *Liminoid phenomena* develop apart from the central economic and political processes, along the margins, in the interfaces and interstices of central and servicing institutions – they are fragmentary, and experimental in character.

(4) *Liminal phenomena* tend to confront investigators rather after the manner of Durkheim's 'collective representations',[9] symbols having a common intellectual and emotional meaning for all the members of the group. They reflect, on probing, the history of the group, i.e., its collective experience, over time. They differ from preliminal or postliminal collective representation in that they are often reversals, inversions, disguises, negations, antitheses of quotidian, 'positive' or 'profane' collective representations. But they share their mass, collective character.

Liminoid phenomena tend to be more idiosyncratic, quirky, to be generated by specific named individuals and particular groups – 'schools', circles, and coteries – they have to compete with one another for general recognition and are thought of at first as ludic offerings placed for sale on the 'free' market – this is at least true of liminoid phenomena in nascent capitalistic and democratic-liberal societies. Their symbols are closer to the personal-psychological than to the 'objective-social' typological pole.

(5) *Liminal phenomena* tend to be ultimately eufunctional even when seemingly 'inversive' for the working of the social structure, ways of making it work without too much friction. Liminoid phenomena, on the other hand, are often parts of social critiques or even revolutionary manifestos – books, plays, paintings, films, etc., exposing the injustices, inefficiencies and immoralities of the mainstream economic and political structures and organizations.

In complex, modern societies both types coexist in a sort of cultural pluralism. But the liminal – found in the activities of churches, sects and movements, in the initiation rites of clubs, fraternities, masonic orders and other secret societies, etc. – is no longer world wide. Nor are the liminoid phenomena which tend to be the leisure genres of art, sport, pastimes, games, etc., practised by and for particular groups, categories, segments and sectors of large-scale industrial societies of all types. But for most people the liminoid is still felt to be freer than the liminal, a matter of choice, not obligation. The *liminoid* is more like a commodity – indeed, often *is* a commodity, which one selects and pays for – than the liminal, which elicits loyalty and is bound up with one's membership or desired membership in some highly corporate group. One *works* at the liminal, one *plays* with the liminoid.

Notes

1   J. Dumazedier (1968) 'Leisure', in David Sills (ed.), *Encyclopedia of the Social Sciences* (New York: Macmillan and Free Press), p. 248.
2   T. Veblen (1957) *The Theory of the Leisure Class* (London: Allen & Unwin). First published 1899.
3   *Ibid.*, p. 249.
4   S. de Grazia (1962) *Of Time, Work, and Leisure* (New York: Twentieth Century Fund).
5   Dumazedier, 'Leisure', p. 249.
6   V. Turner (1969) *The Ritual Process* (Chicago: Aldine).
7   A. van Gennep (1960) *The Rites of Passage*, trans. Monika B. Vizedom and Gabrielle L. Caffee (London: Routledge & Kegan Paul). First published 1909.
8   É. Durkheim (1995) *The Elementary Forms of Religious Life* (Book III), trans. Karen E. Fields (New York: The Free Press). First published 1912.
9   *Ibid.*

EXERCISE: Select three cultural performances (from your own society) which may be considered liminal, and three which are liminoid. Aim to make your choices as diverse as possible: think about local festivals and national ceremonies, group pastimes, sporting occasions, public entertainments, rites of passage such as initiation ceremonies, weddings and funerals, and holiday celebrations such as Christmas and Thanksgiving. First, analyse the symbology of each event – not only its literal symbols but also the symbolic roles its participants perform, the social structures or relationships they enact, and so on. To what alternative vision of the world does each give concrete form? If it offers opportunities for playfulness or creativity, what is created and/or played with? You are seeking to view the performance in terms of the time/space of anti-structure.

Now consider the effect or function of your events, what they do for, to or within a social whole. If liminal forms enact communality, can you generalize about the kinds of social grouping which typically employ them? What wider social structures or rules are such events ultimately supportive of, and how? What is the basis of the communality presumed by the liminoid – what do participants share? In what ways are your liminoid performances *critical* of the socio-cultural order? What characteristics of each form make it appropriate to the supportive or subversive ends to which it is used?

8.2 The pageant

Michael Bristol, from *Carnival and Theatre: Plebeian Culture and the Structure of Authority in Renaissance England*, New York and London: Methuen, 1985

[Bristol's book addresses early modern carnival (see **Bakhtin**) as a popular, often oppositional cultural form, and in the following extract he considers the kind of official performative practice against which it was posed. His description of state-sanctioned pageantry as 'allegory' captures its quality of *readability*, its capacity to shape momentarily the physical environment in accordance with a hypothetical metaphysical order, thereby appearing to validate ideological conceptions of society. But the term also encapsulates the way such performances demand a mode of reading which, by requiring the spectator to translate the material world into signs of the immaterial, itself supports the notion of a 'higher', 'natural' order. In describing this specific historical instance of a more general performance aesthetic, Bristol provides a tool for analysing ideologically expressive cultural performances today.]

Although common people in early modern England did not participate in elections, respond to opinion polls or read newspapers, they were nevertheless actively engaged in public life. This engagement was by no means limited to parochial interests but extended to the politics of the wider world, and to the deployment of power and authority on a national and even an international scale. Communication between the centers of power and the people as a whole was accomplished in a number of ways, but spectacle, pageantry and public gatherings in the streets and village squares were of primary importance because they were capable of affecting large numbers of people in a reasonably short time, and because they could leave a memorable impression on their audiences. [. . .]

Travesty and social order

Official pageantry, which includes the royal progress, religious processions and much civic pageantry, is a display of ranks and categories of the social structure, idealized in mythological, historical or biblical images. Social structure is made visible by allegorical representation. For some observers, a public procession is a central and privileged objectification of what is real and essential in the social order, for it is in this act of public pedagogy that the various ranks and functions of society are fully enumerated, their order of ethical precedence given as an order of deployment in a public space. The court, members of the aristocracy and representatives of the lower orders perform as themselves and as the figural anticipation of more perfect forms to be fulfilled in a providential unfolding of history. Official pageantry makes the ideals of the social order objectively present in the here and now. The prince appears in person, either as a performer or as a uniquely privileged spectator. The procession itself expresses governing concepts of degree and difference, hierarchical plenitude, and social and political harmony.

> And upon the same Saturday, the Queen came forth from the Tower towards Westminster, in goodly array; as hereafter followeth.
>
> She passed the streets first, with certain strangers, their horses trapped with blue silk; and themselves in blue velvet with white feathers, accompanied two and two. Likewise Squires, Knights, Barons, and Baronets, Knights of the Bath clothed in violet garments, edged with ermine like Judges. Then following: The Judges of the Law, and Abbots . . .
>
> And then followed Bishops, two and two; and the Archbishops of York and Canterbury; the Ambassadors of France and Venice, the Lord Mayor with a mace; Master Garter the King of Heralds, and the King's coat armour upon him, with the Officers of Arms, appointing every state in their degree . . .
>
> Then the Master of the Guard, with the guard on both sides of the streets in good array; and all the constables well beseen in

> velvet and damask coats with white staves in their hand; setting every man in his array and order in the streets.[1]

The project of 'appointing every estate in their degree' and 'setting every man in array and order' is based on the conviction that there is an invisible but nevertheless real and absolute order that exists independently of human artifice. The ideal system is part of a larger, cosmic hierarchy of orderly differentiation, superiority and inferiority, in which every element has a determinate place. The procession, objectively and hierarchically organized in space, is a natural and ideally appropriate image of society. The city streets become a stage, the royal personality occupies the center of a theatrical performance. But this stage is not a locus of transitory illusions: it is a space where the politics of love and reciprocity are fully revealed.

> in all her passage she did not only shew her most gracious love towards the people in general; but also privately, if the baser personages had either offered Her grace any flowers or such like, as a signification of their good will; or moved her to any suit, she most gently (to the common rejoicings of all lookers on, and private comfort of the party) stayed her chariot, and heard their requests. So that, if a man should say well, he could not better term the City of London that time, than a Stage wherein was shewed the wonderful Spectacle of a noble hearted Princess towards her most loving people; and the people's exceeding comfort in beholding so worthy a Sovereign, and hearing so prince-like a voice.[2]

Events of this kind are motivated to some degree by partisan or dynastic interest and political expediency. The Tudor kings and queens used the royal entry partly as a political technique to confirm their questionable legitimacy. Behind this pragmatic use of public spectacle is the undoubtedly sincere belief, not only that degree and precedence are essential to social well-being but also that the display of rank and difference in a magnificent style is a necessary link between ideals and their here-and-now implementation.

Allegory is considerably more than a mere technique or instrument of representation in official pageantry: the nature of the allegorical symbol is an essential part of the truth about nature and society. The social structure is itself a kind of allegory, in that its order is also a sign of other, larger orders that form a chain of significance leading to that which does not signify – the divine Logos. The majesty of the prince, his or her appearance in ceremonial procession, discloses a hidden co-ordination and sympathy between the temporal order maintained by constituted authority and the providentially ordered domains of nature and history. In spectacles of authority there is 'a kind of mimetic magic, as if, by the sheer force of poetry and spectacle, incipient war and dissolution could be metamorphosed into harmony and peace'.[3] The magic symbols of official spectacle and pageantry ought to be an efficacious technique for promoting social cohesion and social discipline, although in practice never so efficacious as temporal authority might wish. Nevertheless, principles of similitude and hierarchical enumeration supply a cognitive basis for interpreting social conflict and its relation to the idealizations of the social structure.

The image of authority in official pageantry is a political instrument through which the power of a vertically organized social structure may be employed in order to dispel social dissonance and conflict. The forces of disorder, it is assumed, are transitory delusions, forms of error and spiritual darkness that vanish in the light radiated by the revealed source and agent of order. In the dialectic of official pageantry, princely splendor and magnanimity pursue and defeat discord, because discord has no ontological status. Conflict and social dissonance arise from marginal or subordinated levels of creation that refuse to remain in naturally prescribed positions, but the pretense can never be sustained, because it is a manifestation of that which is excluded and powerless.

De jure power and authority do not openly advocate substantive social change. Instead, authority presents itself as the traditionally sanctioned and therefore naturally elevated agency of changeless, already perfected and complete, reality. The figure of authority is at once distanced from the here and now by self-identification with a mythological and legendary past, and at the same time fulfills and completes the here and now by revealing the underlying harmony of a continuous and durable social structure. In Elizabethan times, the ideology of the monarchy and its clientele, as well as the ideology of its opponents among the elite and privileged community, combines imagery from classical and epic literature, and native legend, with nostalgic imagery of a chivalric past, to create a language in which particular questions of continuity, change, political legitimacy and the allocation of power may he argued. In official pageantry this symbolic language remains at a distance from ordinary citizens, who view these matters of state as deferential and wondering spectators.

The epically distanced and idealized structure of official pageantry represents peace and abundance maintained by a collective acknowledge-

ment of order in the magnanimity of the prince and the respectful obedience of his subjects. The actual processes of material production happen
behind the scenes: spiritual and physical well-being are the consequence
of a providentially ordained structure. The achievement of prosperity and
abundance is not the result of progress, social reform or even the deliberate implementation of ameliorative policy. Instead, abundance is the
natural consequence of some higher, more ideal, process of justice
embodied in the principle of social hierarchy. The prince, in this context,
is represented as the rebirth or return of an earlier and more nearly perfect
principle of equity, an idea used in the ideology of power since antiquity
and revived with great frequency both in the literature and ceremonial
pageantry of the court, and also in the streets of Renaissance cities and
towns.

Allegory is a way of representing a coherent order operating through
the complexity and apparent disorder of social experience. As a strategy
for the interpretation of social reality, allegory is the desire to secure
valued meaning from contamination by contingent speech. However, the
specific instances of allegory in royal processions and civic pageantry do
not all value the same meanings, nor do they represent the unified
consciousness of a monolithic ruling elite. The 'official culture' is not a
single 'ruling class' but a mobile, shifting pattern of more or less durable
alliances and coalitions. The civic pageants often dramatize and draw
attention to specific political or economic debts and obligations, or express
the intention of consolidating an old alliance or creating a new one. This
contingent and instrumental use of allegorical symbols is made possible
by a tremendously complex elaboration of alternative allegorical meanings, but the public display of such alternative meanings frustrates and
confuses the desire to protect valued symbols from both inadvertent and
wilful misinterpretation.[4] The proliferation of iconographic and emblem-
atic codes makes allegory self-consciously problematic, self-reflexive and
therefore no longer allegorical. As an element of a signifying chain refer-
ring ultimately to the Logos, an allegorical symbol is incompatible with
mimesis. To display such a symbol in the public square is to invite quotation, and therefore misquotation and abusive mimicry. Despite their
elaborate and magnificent splendor, the allegorical displays of official
pageantry often reveal the pathos of historical anxiety.

> Any person, any object, any relationship can mean absolutely
> anything else. With this possibility a destructive, but just verdict is
> passed on the profane world; it is characterized as a world in which
> the detail is of no great importance ... all of the things which are

used to signify derive, from the very fact of their pointing to something else, a power which makes them appear no longer commensurable with profane things, which raises them onto a higher plane, and which can, indeed, sanctify them. Considered in allegorical terms, then, the profane world is both elevated and devalued.[5]

The pathos of allegorical representation derives from the fertility of allegory, its power to generate surplus meanings. But because it is so susceptible to 'demonic' misappropriation, allegorical literature becomes gradually saturated by the melancholy sternness of secular coercion and enforcement.

Notes

1   J. Nicholls (1823) *The Progresses and Public Processions of Queen Elizabeth*, 3 vols (London: John Nicholls & Son), vol. II, p. 46.
2   Nicholls, *Progresses*, vol. III, p. 220.
3   S. Orgel (1971) 'The Poetics of Spectacle', *New Literary History* 2: 367.
4   R. Tuve (1966) *Allegorical Imagery*, ed. Thomas P. Roche (Princeton: Princeton University Press), pp. 57–143 and passim.
5   W. Benjamin (1977) *The Origins of German Tragic Drama*, trans. John Osborne (London: NLB), p. 175.

EXERCISE: Choose an official ceremony (e.g. a royal investiture, a military parade, a High Church rite) and, addressing all its elements as allegorical symbols, discuss what abstract concepts or principles they represent. Work in detail, taking into account its use and organization of space (horizontal and vertical, kinetic and static); symbolic objects, including costume or clothing; the kinds of posture, gesture, movement and general comportment demanded of participants and viewers; any adornment of the built or natural environment; the significance of venue; music or other sounds, or their absence. Reading the event as a unified whole, consider what vision of the world's underlying order it expresses. What is signified when a priest lifts sacred objects, or soldiers march in perfect formation? How does the ceremonial crowning of a king ideologically validate the associated form of government? You are seeking to read the event metaphorically, to discern the way it shapes the real world to express a particular view *of* that world.

8.3 Carnival

Mikhail Bakhtin, from *Rabelais and His World*, trans. Hélène Iswolsky, Cambridge, Mass.: MIT Press, 1968 [originally published 1965]

[It is perhaps not insignificant that, coming to adulthood in a Russia over-shadowed by Stalin's dictatorship, Bakhtin should focus on cultural forms which resist totalized, monolithic meaning. Writing on the novel, he champions what he terms the 'dialogic' form, whose polyphony of competing voices stands in implicit critique of the unitary discourse of the 'monologic' work (Bakhtin 1982). He finds a similar resistance to sanctioned authority in Carnival. If official celebration reproduces the ideology of the ruling order (see **Bristol**), Bakhtin's carnival does the reverse, inverting and mocking its rules and symbols, and denying its hierarchies – even refusing its separa-tion of performer from spectator: 'degrading' all that is exalted and metaphysical to the level of the merely material to create a space free of official order. This anti-authoritarian logic is inherent to the event, for rather than expressing an abstract political theory which might itself become hege-monic, its libertarian ethos is born of a general, popular recognition that *all* socio-political systems are man-made, and hence ephemeral. In as much as all political regimes invest in symbols, hierarchies and codes of 'proper' conduct, Bakhtin's theory is still relevant today, so that, in describing a species of event from the historical past, he also provides a model for radical cultural performance in the present.]

Carnival festivities and the comic spectacles and ritual connected with them had an important place in the life of medieval man. Besides carni-vals proper, with their long and complex pageants and processions, there was the 'feast of fools' (*testa stultorum*) and the 'feast of the ass'; there was a special free 'Easter laughter' (*risus paschalis*), consecrated by tradi-tion. Moreover, nearly every Church feast had its comic folk aspect, which was also traditionally recognized. Such, for instance, were the parish feasts, usually marked by fairs and varied open-air amusements, with the partic-ipation of giants, dwarfs, monsters and trained animals. A carnival atmosphere reigned on days when mysteries and *soties* were produced. This atmosphere also pervaded such agricultural feasts as the harvesting of grapes (*vendange*) which was celebrated also in the city. Civil and social ceremonies and rituals took on a comic aspect as clowns and fools, constant participants in these festivals, mimicked serious rituals such as the tribute rendered to the victors at tournaments, the transfer of feudal rights or the initiation of a knight. Minor occasions were also marked by comic protocol, as for instance the election of a king and queen to preside at a banquet 'for laughter's sake' (*roi pour rire*). [. . .]

Because of their obvious sensuous character and their strong element of play, carnival images closely resemble certain artistic forms, namely the spectacle. In turn, medieval spectacles often tended toward carnival folk culture, the culture of the marketplace, and to a certain extent became one of its components. But the basic carnival nucleus of this culture is by no means a purely artistic form nor a spectacle and does not, generally speaking, belong to the sphere of art. It belongs to the borderline between art and life. In reality, it is life itself, but shaped according to a certain pattern of play.

In fact, carnival does not know footlights, in the sense that it does not acknowledge any distinction between actors and spectators. Footlights would destroy a carnival, as the absence of footlights would destroy a theatrical performance. Carnival is not a spectacle seen by the people; they live in it, and everyone participates because its very idea embraces all the people. While carnival lasts, there is no other life outside it. During carnival time life is subject only to its laws, that is, the laws of its own freedom. It has a universal spirit; it is a special condition of the entire world, of the world's revival and renewal, in which all take part. Such is the essence of carnival, vividly felt by all its participants. It was most clearly expressed and experienced in the Roman Saturnalias, perceived as a true and full, though temporary, return of Saturn's golden age upon earth. The tradition of the Saturnalias remained unbroken and alive in the medieval carnival, which expressed this universal renewal and was vividly felt as an escape from the usual official way of life.

Clowns and fools, which often figure in Rabelais's novel, are characteristic of the medieval culture of humor. They were the constant, accredited representatives of the carnival spirit in everyday life out of carnival season. Like Triboulet[1] at the time of Francis I, they were not actors playing their parts on a stage, as did the comic actors of a later period, impersonating Harlequin, Hanswurst, etc., but remained fools and clowns always and wherever they made their appearance. As such they represented a certain form of life, which was real and ideal at the same time. They stood on the borderline between life and art, in a peculiar mid-zone, as it were; they were neither eccentrics nor dolts, neither were they comic actors. [. . .]

In the framework of class and feudal political structure this specific character [to festive life] could be realized without distortion only in the carnival and in similar marketplace festivals. They were the second life of the people, who for a time entered the utopian realm of community, freedom, equality and abundance.

On the other hand, the official feasts of the Middle Ages, whether ecclesiastic, feudal or sponsored by the state, did not lead the people out of the existing world order and created no second life. On the contrary, they sanctioned the existing pattern of things and reinforced it. The link with time became formal; changes and moments of crisis were relegated to the past. Actually, the official feast looked back to the past and used the past to consecrate the present. Unlike the earlier and purer feast, the official feast asserted that all was stable, unchanging, perennial: the existing hierarchy, the existing religious, political and moral values, norms and prohibitions. It was the triumph of a truth already established, the predominant truth that was put forward as eternal and indisputable. This is why the tone of the official feast was monolithically serious and why the element of laughter was alien to it. The true nature of human festivity was betrayed and distorted. But this true festive character was indestructible; it had to be tolerated and even legalized outside the official sphere and had to be turned over to the popular sphere of the marketplace.

As opposed to the official feast, one might say that carnival celebrated temporary liberation from the prevailing truth and from the established order; it marked the suspension of all hierarchical rank, privileges, norms and prohibitions. Carnival was the true feast of time, the feast of becoming, change and renewal. It was hostile to all that was immortalized and completed.

The suspension of all hierarchical precedence during carnival time was of particular significance. Rank was especially evident during official feasts; everyone was expected to appear in the full regalia of his calling, rank and merits and to take the place corresponding to his position. It was a consecration of inequality. On the contrary, all were considered equal during carnival. Here, in the town square, a special form of free and familiar contact reigned among people who were usually divided by the barriers of caste, property, profession and age. The hierarchical background and the extreme corporative and caste divisions of the medieval social order were exceptionally strong. Therefore such free, familiar contacts were deeply felt and formed an essential element of the carnival spirit. People were, so to speak, reborn for new, purely human relations. These truly human relations were not only a fruit of imagination or abstract thought; they were experienced. The utopian ideal and the realistic merged in this carnival experience, unique of its kind.

This temporary suspension, both ideal and real, of hierarchical rank created during carnival time a special type of communication impossible in everyday life. This led to the creation of special forms of marketplace speech and gesture, frank and free, permitting no distance between those who came in contact with each other and liberating from norms of etiquette and decency imposed at other times. A special carnivalesque, marketplace style of expression was formed which we find abundantly represented in Rabelais's novel.

During the century-long development of the medieval carnival, prepared by thousands of years of ancient comic ritual, including the primitive Saturnalias, a special idiom of forms and symbols was evolved – an extremely rich idiom that expressed the unique yet complex carnival experience of the people. This experience, opposed to all that was ready-made and completed, to all pretense at immutability, sought a dynamic expression; it demanded ever changing, playful, undefined forms. All the symbols of the carnival idiom are filled with this pathos of change and renewal, with the sense of the gay relativity of prevailing truths and authorities. We find here a characteristic logic, the peculiar logic of the 'inside out' (à l'envers), of the 'turnabout', of a continual shifting from top to bottom, from front to rear, of numerous parodies and travesties, humiliations, profanations, comic crownings and uncrownings. A second life, a second world of folk culture is thus constructed; it is to a certain extent a parody of the extracarnival life, a 'world inside out'. We must stress, however, that the carnival is far distant from the negative and formal parody of modern times. Folk humor denies, but it revives and renews at the same time. Bare negation is completely alien to folk culture. [. . .]

Let us say a few initial words about the complex nature of carnival laughter. It is, first of all, a festive laughter. Therefore it is not an individual reaction to some isolated 'comic' event. Carnival laughter is the laughter of all the people. Second, it is universal in scope; it is directed at all and everyone, including the carnival's participants. The entire world is seen in its droll aspect, in its gay relativity. Third, this laughter is ambivalent: it is gay, triumphant and at the same time mocking, deriding. It asserts and denies, it buries and revives. Such is the laughter of carnival.

Let us enlarge upon the second important trait of the people's laughter: that it is also directed at those who laugh. The people do not exclude themselves from the wholeness of the world. They, too, are incomplete, they also die and are revived and renewed. This is one of the essential differences of the people's festive laughter from the pure satire of modern times. The satirist whose laughter is negative places himself above the object of his mockery, he is opposed to it. The wholeness of the world's comic aspect is destroyed, and that which appears comic becomes a private reaction. The people's ambivalent laughter, on the other hand, expresses the point of view of the whole world; he who is laughing also belongs to it. [. . .]

It is usually pointed out that in Rabelais's work the material bodily principle, that is, images of the human body with its food, drink, defecation and sexual life, plays a predominant role. Images of the body are offered, moreover, in an extremely exaggerated form. [. . .] Sometimes they were seen as a typical manifestation of the Renaissance bourgeois character, that is, of its material interests in 'economic man'.

Actually, the images of the material bodily principle in the work of Rabelais (and of the other writers of the Renaissance) are the heritage, only somewhat modified by the Renaissance, of the culture of folk humor. They are the heritage of that peculiar type of imagery and, more broadly speaking, of that peculiar aesthetic concept which is characteristic of this folk culture and which differs sharply from the aesthetic concept of the following ages. We shall call it conditionally the concept of grotesque realism.

The material bodily principle in grotesque realism is offered in its all-popular festive and utopian aspect. The cosmic, social and bodily elements are given here as an indivisible whole. And this whole is gay and gracious.

In grotesque realism, therefore, the bodily element is deeply positive. [. . .] The leading themes of these images of bodily life are fertility, growth and a brimming-over abundance. Manifestations of this life refer not to the isolated biological individual, not to the private, egotistic 'economic man', but to the collective ancestral body of all the people. Abundance and the all-people's element also determine the gay and festive character of all images of bodily life; they do not reflect the drabness of everyday existence. The material bodily principle is a triumphant, festive principle, it is a 'banquet for all the world'. This character is preserved to a considerable degree in Renaissance literature, and most fully, of course, in Rabelais.

The essential principle of grotesque realism is degradation, that is, the lowering of all that is high, spiritual, ideal, abstract; it is a transfer to the material level, to the sphere of earth and body in their indissoluble unity. Thus 'Cyprian's supper' and many other Latin parodies of the Middle Ages are nothing but a selection of all the degrading, earthy details taken from the Bible, the Gospels and other sacred texts. In the comic dialogues of Solomon with Morolf which were popular in the Middle Ages, Solomon's sententious pronouncements are contrasted to the flippant and debasing dictums of the clown Morolf, who brings the conversation down to a strongly emphasized bodily level of food, drink, digestion and sexual life. One of the main attributes of the medieval clown was precisely the transfer of every high ceremonial gesture or ritual to the material sphere; such was the clown's role during tournaments, the knight's initiation, and so forth. It is in this tradition of grotesque realism that we find the source of the scenes in which Don Quixote degrades chivalry and ceremonial. [. . .]

Not only parody in its narrow sense but all the other forms of grotesque realism degrade, bring down to earth, turn their subject into flesh. This is the peculiar trait of this genre which differentiates it from all the forms of medieval high art and literature. The people's laughter which characterized all the forms of grotesque realism from immemorial times was linked with the bodily lower stratum. Laughter degrades and materializes.

Note

1   Fevrial, or Le Feurial, was the court fool of Francis I and of Louis XII. He appears repeatedly in Rabelais's *Gargantua* and *Pantagruel* under the name of Triboulet.

EXERCISE: Choose the non-official communal event in your society which most precisely corresponds to Bakhtin's formula for carnival: think about genuine carnivals and *mardi gras* celebrations, certainly, but also marches, street parades, political protests and demonstrations, popular festivals, etc. Compare and contrast it to the ceremony you analysed in the **Bristol** exercise to consider the ways in which your carnival subjects the structures, strategies and images of official performance to (1) *inversion* (the 'inside out') and (2) *degradation*. If your official ceremony invested objects or images with symbolic meaning, does your carnival misuse officially sanctioned symbols, or create new, parodic symbologies? If the former gave concrete form to social distinctions or hierarchies, how does the latter treat them? Consider uses of space, representations of bodies, bodily processes and behaviours, juxtapositions of seriousness with mockery, and so on. When you have amassed sufficient detail, try to develop an overview of the carnival's relationship to the ruling socio-cultural order.

Is there a sense in which it turns the official world 'upside down'? Does it 'degrade' its meanings, reducing them to merely material words and images? Ground all your points in the concrete details of the events, trying to pair each feature of official performance with its carnival nemesis.

8.4 Deep play

Clifford Geertz, from 'Deep Play: Notes on the Balinese Cockfight', in *The Interpretation of Cultures: Selected Essays*, London: Fontana, 1973 [originally published 1972]

[The writing of Geertz, one of the most influential anthropologists working today, is firmly interpretative, concerned to elicit the meanings encoded in cultural practices. More empirical than overtly theoretical, his method of 'thick description' (1973) entails relating acts to their cultural context in far-reaching detail to discern their significance for the people of that culture. Having so described a Balinese cockfight and the circumstances surrounding it – the betting, the preparation, the local and family allegiances involved – in the following excerpt he employs Jeremy Bentham's concept of 'deep play' to explore the basis of such events' cultural resonance. His use of the term, however, involves a reversal of values; whereas for Bentham the absence of any practical, utilitarian dimension to such entertainments makes them merely pointless, this same quality is for Geertz evidence of their symbolic importance. It is on this basis that he addresses the cockfight as a dramatization of themes central to the culture of those who take part, 'a story they tell themselves about themselves'.]

Playing with fire

Bentham's concept of 'deep play' is found in his *The Theory of Legislation*.[1] By it he means play in which the stakes are so high that it is, from his utilitarian standpoint, irrational for men to engage in it at all. If a man whose fortune is a thousand pounds (or ringgits) wages five hundred of it on an even bet, the marginal utility of the pound he stands to win is clearly less than the marginal disutility of the one he stands to lose. In genuine deep play, this is the case for both parties. They are both in over their heads. Having come together in search of pleasure they have entered into a relationship which will bring the participants, considered collectively, net pain rather than net pleasure. Bentham's conclusion was, therefore, that deep play was immoral from first principles and, a typical step for him, should be prevented legally.

But more interesting than the ethical problem, at least for our concerns here, is that despite the logical force of Bentham's analysis men do engage in such play, both passionately and often, and even in the face of law's revenge. For Bentham and those who think as he does (nowadays mainly lawyers, economists and a few psychiatrists), the explanation is, as I have said, that such men are irrational – addicts, fetishists, children, fools, savages, who need only to be protected against themselves. But for the Balinese, though naturally they do not formulate it in so many words, the explanation lies in the fact that, in such play, money is less a measure of utility, had or expected, than it is a symbol of moral import, perceived or imposed.

It is, in fact, in shallow games, ones in which smaller amounts of money are involved, that increments and decrements of cash are more nearly synonyms for utility and disutility, in the ordinary, unexpanded sense – for pleasure and pain, happiness and unhappiness. In deep ones, where the amounts of money are great, much more is at stake than material gain: namely, esteem, honor, dignity, respect – in a word, though in Bali a profoundly freighted word, status. It is at stake symbolically, for (a few cases of ruined addict gamblers aside) no one's status is actually altered by the outcome of a cockfight; it is only, and that momentarily, affirmed or insulted. But for the Balinese, for whom nothing is more pleasurable than an affront obliquely delivered or more painful than one obliquely received – particularly when mutual acquaintances, undeceived by surfaces, are watching – such appraisive drama is deep indeed.

This, I must stress immediately, is not to say that the money does not matter, or that the Balinese is no more concerned about losing five hundred ringgits than fifteen. Such a conclusion would be absurd. It is because money *does*, in this hardly unmaterialistic society, matter and matter very much that the more of it one risks, the more of a lot of other things, such as one's pride, one's poise, one's dispassion, one's masculinity, one also risks, again only momentarily but again very publicly as well. In deep cockfights an owner and his collaborators, and, as we shall see, to a lesser but still quite real extent also their backers on the outside, put their money where their status is. [. . .]

Feathers, blood, crowds and money

[. . .] Like any art form – for that, finally, is what we are dealing with – the cockfight renders ordinary, everyday experience comprehensible by presenting it in terms of acts and objects which have had their practical consequences removed and been reduced (or, if you prefer, raised) to the level of sheer appearances, where their meaning can be more powerfully articulated and more exactly perceived. The cockfight is 'really real' only to the cocks – it does not kill anyone, castrate anyone, reduce anyone to animal status, alter the hierarchical relations among people, or refashion the hierarchy; it does not even redistribute income in any significant way. What it does is what, for other peoples with other temperaments and other conventions, *Lear* and *Crime and Punishment* do; it catches up these themes – death, masculinity, rage, pride, loss, beneficence, chance – and, ordering them into an encompassing structure, presents them in such a way as to throw into relief a particular view of their essential nature. It puts a construction on them, makes them, to those historically positioned to appreciate the construction, meaningful – visible, tangible, graspable – 'real', in an ideational sense. An image, fiction, a model, a metaphor, the cockfight is a means of expression; its function is neither to assuage social passions nor to heighten them (though, in its playing-with-fire way it does a bit of both), but, in a medium of feathers, blood, crowds and money, to display them.

The question of how it is that we perceive qualities in things – paintings, books, melodies, plays – that we do not feel we can assert literally to be there has come, in recent years, into the very center of aesthetic theory. Neither the sentiments of the artist, which remain his, nor those of the audience, which remain theirs, can account for the agitation of one painting or the serenity of another. We attribute grandeur, wit, despair, exuberance to strings of sounds; lightness, energy, violence, fluidity to blocks of stone. Novels are said to have strength, buildings eloquence, plays momentum, ballets repose. In this realm of eccentric predicates, to say that the cockfight, in its perfected cases at least, is 'disquietful' does not seem at all unnatural, merely, as I have just denied it practical consequence, somewhat puzzling.

The disquietfulness arises, 'somehow', out of a conjunction of three attributes of the fight: its immediate dramatic shape; its metaphoric content; and its social context. A cultural figure against a social ground, the fight is at once a convulsive surge of animal hatred, a mock war of symbolical selves, and a formal simulation of status tensions, and its aesthetic power derives from its capacity to force together these diverse realities. The reason it is disquietful is not that it has material effects (it has some, but they are minor); the reason that it is disquietful is that, joining pride to selfhood, selfhood to cocks, and cocks to destruction, it brings to imaginative realization a dimension of Balinese experience normally well obscured from view. The transfer of a sense of gravity into what is in itself a rather blank and unvarious spectacle, a commotion of beating wings and throbbing legs, is effected by interpreting it as expressive of something unsettling in the way its authors and audience live, or, even more ominously, what they are.

As a dramatic shape, the fight displays a characteristic that does not seem so remarkable, until one realizes that it does not have to be there: a radically atomistical structure. Each match is a world unto itself, a particulate burst of form. There is the matchmaking, there is the betting, there is the fight, there is the result – utter triumph and utter defeat – and there is the hurried, embarrassed passing of money. The loser is not consoled. People drift away from him, look around him, leave him to assimilate his momentary descent into non-being, reset his face and return, scarless and intact, to the fray. Nor are winners congratulated, or events rehashed; once a match is ended the crowd's attention turns totally to the next, with no looking back. A shadow of the experience no doubt remains with the principals, perhaps even with some of the witnesses of a deep fight, as it remains with us when we leave the theater after seeing a powerful play well performed; but it quite soon fades to become at most a schematic memory – a diffuse glow or an abstract shudder – and usually not even that. Any expressive form lives only in its own present – the one it itself creates. But, here, that present is severed into a string of flashes, some more bright than others, but all of them disconnected, aesthetic quanta. Whatever the cockfight says, it says in spurts.

But, as I have argued lengthily elsewhere, the Balinese live in spurts. Their life, as they arrange it and perceive it, is less a flow, a directional movement out of the past, through the present, toward the future than an on–off pulsation of meaning and vacuity, an arhythmic alternation of short periods when 'something' (that is, something significant) is happening, and equally short ones where 'nothing' (that is, nothing much) is – between what they themselves call 'full' and 'empty' times, or, in another idiom, 'junctures' and 'holes'. In focusing activity down to a burning-glass dot, the cockfight is merely being Balinese in the same way in which everything from the monadic encounters of everyday life, through the clanging pointillism of *gamelan* music, to the visiting-day-of-the-gods temple celebrations is. It is not an imitation of the punctuateness of Balinese social life, nor a depiction of it, nor even an expression of it; it is an example of it, carefully prepared.

If one dimension of the cockfight's structure, its lack of temporal directionality, makes it seem a typical segment of the general social life, however, the other, its flat-out, head-to-head (or spur-to-spur) aggressiveness, makes it seem a contradiction, a reversal, even a subversion of it. In the normal course of things, the Balinese are shy to the point of obsessiveness of open conflict. Oblique, cautious, subdued, controlled, masters of indirection and dissimulation – what they call *alus*, 'polished', 'smooth' – they rarely face what they can turn away from, rarely resist what they can evade. But here they portray themselves as wild and murderous, with manic explosions of instinctual cruelty. A powerful rendering of life as the Balinese most deeply do not want it (to adapt a phrase Frye has used of Gloucester's blinding) is set in the context of a sample of it as they do in fact have it. And, because the context suggests that the rendering, if less than a straightforward description, is none the less more than an idle fancy; it is here that the disquietfulness – the disquietfulness of the *fight*, not (or, anyway, not necessarily) its patrons, who seem in fact rather thoroughly to enjoy it – emerges. The slaughter in the cock ring is not a depiction of how things literally are among men, but, what is almost worse, of how, from a particular angle, they imaginatively are.

The angle, of course, is stratificatory. What, as we have already seen, the cockfight talks most forcibly about is status relationships, and what it says about them is that they are matters of life and death. That prestige is a profoundly serious business is apparent everywhere one looks in Bali – in the village, the family, the economy, the state. A peculiar fusion of Polynesian title ranks and Hindu castes, the hierarchy of pride is the moral backbone of the society. But only in the cockfight are the sentiments upon which that hierarchy rests revealed in their natural colors. Enveloped elsewhere in a haze of etiquette, a thick cloud of euphemism and ceremony, gesture and allusion, they are here expressed in only the thinnest disguise of an animal mask, a mask which in fact demonstrates them far more effectively than it conceals them. Jealousy is as much a part of Bali as poise, envy as grace, brutality as charm; but without the cockfight the Balinese would have a much less certain understanding of them, which is, presumably, why they value it so highly.

Any expressive form works (when it works) by disarranging semantic contexts in such a way that properties conventionally ascribed to certain things are unconventionally ascribed to others, which are then seen actually to possess them. To call the wind a cripple, as Stevens does, to fix tone and manipulate timbre, as Schoenberg does, or, closer to our case, to picture an art critic as a dissolute bear, as Hogarth does, is to cross conceptual wires; the established conjunctions between objects and their qualities are altered, and phenomena – fall weather, melodic shape or cultural journalism – are clothed in signifiers which normally point to other referents. Similarly, to connect – and connect, and connect – the collision of roosters with the divisiveness of status is to invite a transfer of perceptions from the former to the latter, a transfer which is at once a description and a judgement. (Logically, the transfer could, of course, as well go the other way; but, like most of the rest of us, the Balinese are a great deal more interested in understanding men than they are in understanding cocks.)

What sets the cockfight apart from the ordinary course of life, lifts it from the realm of everyday practical affairs, and surrounds it with an aura of enlarged importance is not, as functionalist sociology would have it, that it reinforces status discriminations (such reinforcement is hardly necessary in a society where every act proclaims them), but that it provides a metasocial commentary upon the whole matter of assorting human beings into fixed hierarchical ranks and then organizing the major part of collective existence around that assortment. Its function, if you want to call it that, is interpretive: it is a Balinese reading of Balinese experience, a story they tell themselves about themselves.

Saying something of something

To put the matter this way is to engage in a bit of metaphorical refocusing of one's own, for it shifts the analysis of cultural forms from an endeavor in general parallel to dissecting an organism, diagnosing a symptom, deciphering a code, or ordering a system – the dominant analogies in contemporary anthropology – to one in general parallel with penetrating a literary text. If one takes the cockfight, or any other collectively sustained symbolic structure, as a means of 'saying something of something' (to invoke a famous Aristotelian tag), then one is faced with a problem, not in social mechanics but social semantics. For the anthropologist, whose concern is with formulating sociological principles, not with promoting or appreciating cockfights, the question is, what does one learn about such principles from examining culture as an assemblage of texts? [. . .]

In the case at hand, to treat the cockfight as a text is to bring out a feature of it (in my opinion, the central feature of it) that treating it as a rite or a pastime, the two most obvious alternatives, would tend to obscure: its use of emotion for cognitive ends. What the cockfight says it says in a vocabulary of sentiment – the thrill of risk, the despair of loss, the pleasure of triumph. Yet what it says is not merely that risk is exciting, loss depressing or triumph gratifying, banal tautologies of affect, but that it is of these emotions, thus exampled, that society is built and individuals are put together. Attending cockfights and participating in them is, for the Balinese, a kind of sentimental education. What he learns there is what his culture's ethos and his private sensibility (or, anyway, certain aspects of them) look like when spelled out externally in a collective text; that the two are near enough alike to be articulated in the symbolics of a single such text; and – the disquieting part – that the text in which this revelation is accomplished consists of a chicken hacking another mindlessly to bits.

Note

1   The phrase is found in the Hildreth translation, International Library of Psychology, note to p. 106.

EXERCISE: Choose a sport or sporting event which provokes strong emotions and/or allegiances in your culture and discuss what principles or values it 'raises to the level of appearance'. Read symbolically its rules, organization of space (movements *through* space, division into team areas, significant loci, etc.), temporal structure (pace and patterns of action or inaction, division into 'quarters', 'overs' or 'halves', the entrance and exit of players), its modes of action or conduct, paraphernalia, etc. If the sport is a story society tells about itself *to* itself, consider what picture it paints, what it presents as your society's defining characteristics. Does it genuinely reproduce social structures, dynamics or values, or does it offer instead a vision of how things 'should' be, or how they 'really' are beneath the surface? What is metaphorically represented in the sport's collision of individuals or teams? Bear in mind that you are not necessarily seeking the genuinely defining qualities of your community; rather, you are attempting to find what your community *considers* its defining qualities to be.

Now link this to its social context. Are allegiances to teams or individuals based on real communities, or are they an attempt to *create* communities imaginatively? If the former, what kinds of social relations (regional, class, ethnic, etc.) are the basis of allegiance; if the latter, what *imaginary* terms unite supporters? You are seeking to determine what is emotionally invested, what is lost or gained, in the event's outcome.

Part nine

Analysing performance

Patrice Pavis, from 'Theatre Analysis: Some Questions and a Questionnaire', *New Theatre Quarterly* **1/2: 208–12, 1985**

[The following questionnaire was designed by French performance semiotician Patrice Pavis in 1985. Pavis has since updated it, but has asked that this, the original version, be reproduced in this volume.

The questionnaire is not a theory but a tool, and so depends for its functioning on the knowledge and skills you bring to the task of using it. It will produce the best results if you use it in certain ways. Work through the questions in their given order, as soon as possible after viewing a performance. If you can, use it in groups; two or more people will always recall more detail of a performance than one, and will probably make more connections. Give as full an answer as you are able to all the questions, even – perhaps *especially* – when the answer seems too obvious to warrant stating, for in questioning the 'obvious' you will often unearth unacknowledged assumptions (yours, a practitioner's, your culture's) which shape a performance or the meanings read into it. Try to use your own immediate responses as a starting point, asking *why* you responded in that fashion: if a stage action seemed to you 'regal',

ask which of its material objects or actions signified that; if something proves difficult to understand, seek the source of the difficulty. Do not dismiss anything as 'realistic', for stage realism, no less than expressionism or symbolism, is a dramatic form, a construction of the real rather than its unproblematic reproduction. Most of all, repeat your observations when different questions require it, and be sure to highlight the repetition in your notes. The questionnaire works by first breaking a performance down into its elements. Usually performances work *on* the spectator, providing an 'experience', and we rarely differentiate between the different means by which that experience is created. Our aim here, however, is to analyse how this is achieved, and, by requiring us to view the event's components separately, the questionnaire forces us to consider how each generates part of the overall meaning. But if you repeat observations as they reoccur you will make new connections between the work's elements – finding an idea, strategy or motif which was evident in the organization of space, perhaps, also at work in performers' movements. You will thus reassemble a whole, but one strung together with connections of an analytical order.

You should aim to use the questionnaire many times over your course of study, on different kinds of performance, each time bringing in to play the theories and perspectives you have so far studied. As you do so, try to employ their terminology; new words promote new ways of thinking. When using the questionnaire for the first time it is often a good idea to treat its questions as general; instead of asking what held the elements of *this* performance together, start by considering what holds performances together generally, then specify which of those strategies this piece used.]

1. *General discussion of performance*
(a) what holds elements of performance together?
(b) relationship between systems of staging
(c) coherence or incoherence?
(d) aesthetic principles of the production
(e) what do you find disturbing about the production; strong moments or weak, boring moments?

2. *Scenography*
(a) spatial forms: urban, architectural, scenic, gestural, etc.
(b) relationship between audience space and acting space
(c) system of colours and their connotations
(d) principles of organization of space

- relationship between off-stage and on-stage
- links between space utilized and fiction of the staged dramatic text

3. *Lighting system*

4. *Stage properties*
    type, function, relationship to space and actors' bodies

5. *Costumes*
    how they work; relationship to actors' bodies

6. *Actors' performances*
(a) individual or conventional style of acting?
(b) relation between actor and group
(c) relationship between text and body, between actor and role
(d) quality of gestures and mime
(e) quality of voices
(f) how dialogues develop

7. *Function of music and sound effects*

8. *Pace of performance*
(a) overall pace
(b) pace of certain signifying systems
(c) steady or broken pace?

9. *Interpretation of story-line in performance*
(a) what story is being told?
(b) what kind of dramaturgical choices have been made?
(c) what are ambiguities in performance and what are points of explanation?
(d) how is plot structured?
(e) how is story constructed by actors and staging?
(f) what is genre of dramatic text?

10. *Text in performance*
(a) main features of translation
(b) what role is given to dramatic text in production?
(c) relationship between text and image

11. *Audience*
(a) where does performance take place?
(b) what expectations did you have of performance?
(c) how did audience react?
(d) role of spectator in production of meaning

12. *How to notate (photograph and film) this production*
(a) how to notate performance technically
(b) which images have you retained?

13. *What cannot be put into signs*
(a) what did not make sense in your interpretation of the production?
(b) what was not reducible to signs and meaning (and why)?

14.
(a) are there any special problems that need examining?
(b) any comments, suggestions for further categories for the questionnaire and the production

Bibliography

Adair, C. (1992) *Women and Dance: Sylphs and Sirens*, London: Macmillan.

Althusser, L. (1971) 'Ideology and the Ideological State Apparatuses', in *Essays on Ideology*, London: Verso.

Arthur, K. O. (1990) 'Neither Here Nor There: Towards Nomadic Reading', *New Literatures Review* 17: 31–44.

Arvon, H. (1973) *Marxist Esthetics*, trans. Helen R. Lane, Ithaca: Cornell University Press.

Ashcroft, B., G. Griffiths and H. Tiffin (1989) *The Empire Writes Back: Theory and Practice in Post-colonial Literatures*, London: Routledge.

Ashcroft, B., G. Griffiths and H. Tiffin (eds) (1995) *The Post-colonial Studies Reader*, London and New York: Routledge.

Ashcroft, B., G. Griffiths and H. Tiffin (1998) *Key Concepts in Post-colonial Studies*, London and New York: Routledge.

Aston, E. (1995) *An Introduction to Feminism and Theatre*, London: Routledge.

Austin, G. (1990) *Feminist Theories for Dramatic Criticism*, Ann Arbor: University of Michigan Press.

Bakhtin, M. (1968) *Rabelais and His World*, trans. Hélène Iswolsky, Cambridge, Mass.: MIT Press.

Bakhtin, M. (1982) *The Dialogic Imagination*, trans. Michael Holquist and Caryl Emerson, Austin: University of Texas Press.

Barker, F., P. Hulme and M. Iversen (eds) (1994) *Colonial Discourse/PostColonial Theory*, Manchester and New York: Manchester University Press.

Barthes, R. (1967) *Système de la Mode*, Paris: Éditions du Seuil; published in English (1983) as *The Fashion System*, New York: Hill & Wang.

Barthes, R. (1972a) 'Myth Today', in *Mythologies*, trans. Annette Lavers, London: Granada.

Barthes, R. (1972b) 'The World of Wrestling', in *Mythologies*, trans. Annette Lavers, London: Granada.

Barthes, R. (1974) *S/Z*, trans. Richard Miller, New York: Hill & Wang.

Barthes, R. (1977) *Image, Music, Text*, trans. Stephen Heath, London: Fontana.

Barthes, R. (1978) *A Lover's Discourse*, New York: Hill & Wang.

Bateson, G. (1955) 'The Message "This Is Play" ', in B. Schaffner (ed.), *Group Processes*, New York: Josiah Macy, Jr Foundation Proceedings.

Baudry, J.-L. (1974/5) 'Ideological Effects of the Basic Cinematographic Apparatus', *Film Quarterly*, (winter).

Bell, C. (1992) *Ritual Theory, Ritual Practice*, Oxford and New York: Oxford University Press.

Belsey, C. (1980) *Critical Practice*, London and New York: Routledge.

Benjamin, W. (1977) *The Origins of German Tragic Drama*, trans. John Osborne, London: NLB.

Bennett, S. (1983) *Theatre Audiences: A Theory of Production and Reception*, London: Routledge.

Benveniste, É. (1966) *Problems of General Linguistics*, Miami: University of Miami Press.

Berger, J. (1972) *Ways of Seeing*, New York: Viking Press.

Bergeron, D. (1971) *English Civic Pageantry: 1558–1642*, Columbia: University of South Carolina Press.

Bhabha, H. (1985) 'Signs Taken for Wonders: Questions of Ambivalence and Authority under a Tree outside Delhi, May 1817', in F. Barker *et al.* (eds), *Europe and its Others: Proceedings of the Essex Conference on the Sociology of Literature, July 1984*, vol. 1, Colchester: University of Essex.

Bignell, J. (1997) *Media Semiotics: An Introduction*, Manchester and New York: Manchester University Press.

Blau, H. (1990) *The Audience*, Baltimore: Johns Hopkins University Press.

Blau, H. (1992) *To All Appearances: Ideology and Performance*, London and New York: Routledge.

Brecht, B. (1964) 'The Street Scene', in *Brecht on Theatre: The Development of an Aesthetic*, ed. and trans. John Willett, London: Methuen.

Bredbeck, G. (1993) 'B/O – Barthes's Text/O'Hara's Trick: The Phallus, the Anus, and the Text', *PMLA* 108/2 (March): 268–82.

Bristol, M. (1985) *Carnival and Theatre: Plebeian Culture and the Structure of Authority in Renaissance England*, New York and London: Methuen.

Brown, T. A. (1874) 'The Origin of Negro Minstrelsy', in *Fun in Black; or, Sketches of Minstrel Life*, ed. Charles H. Day, New York: De Witt.

Bryson, N. (1983) *Vision and Painting: The Logic of the Gaze*, London: Macmillan.

Burt, R. (1995) *The Male Dancer: Bodies, Spectacle, Sexuality*, London: Routledge.

Butler, J. (1990a) *Gender Trouble: Feminism and the Subversion of Identity*, London: Routledge.

Butler, J. (1990b) 'Performative Acts and Gender Constitution: An Essay in Phenomenology and Feminist Theory', in S.-E. Case (ed.), *Performing Feminisms: Feminist Critical Theory and Theatre*, Baltimore: Johns Hopkins University Press.

Byg, B. (1986) 'Brecht on the Margins: Film and Feminist Theory', paper presented at the annual convention of the Modern Language Association, New York, December.

Caillois, R. (1984) 'Mimickry and Legendary Psychaesthenia', trans. John Shepley, *October* 31.

Cannadine, D. and S. Price (eds) (1987) *Rituals of Royalty: Power and Ceremonial in Traditional Societies*, Cambridge and New York: Cambridge University Press.

Carlson, M. (1989) *Places of Performance: The Semiotics of Theatre Architecture*, Ithaca and London: Cornell University Press.

Carlson, M. (1990) *Theatre Semiotics: Signs of Life*, Ithaca: Cornell University Press.

Carlson, M. (1993) *Theories of the Theatre: A Historical and Critical Survey from the Greeks to the Present*, Ithaca: Cornell University Press.

Carlson, M. (1996) *Performance: A Critical Introduction*, London and New York: Routledge.

Carlyle, T. (1831) *Sartor Resartus*, London: Curwen Press.

Case, S.-E. (ed.) (1990) *Performing Feminisms: Feminist Critical Theory and Theatre*, Baltimore: Johns Hopkins University Press.

Case, S.-E. (1991) 'Tracking the Vampire', *Differences* 3/2: 1–20.

Chi, J. and Kuckles (1991) *Bran Nue Dae: A Musical Journey*, Sydney: Currency/ Broome: Magabala Books.

Cixous, H. (1996) 'Sorties: Out and Out: Attacks/Ways Out/Forays', in *The Newly Born Woman* (with Catherine Clément), trans. Betsy Wing, London: I. B. Tauris.

Cohen-Cruz, J. (ed.) (1998) *Radical Street Performance: An International Anthology*, London and New York: Routledge.

Counsell, C. (1996) *Signs of Performance: An Introduction to Twentieth-century Theatre*, London and New York: Routledge.

Craik, T. W. (1958) *The Tudor Interlude: Stage, Costume, Acting*, Leicester: Hopethorn Press.

Culler, J. (1981) *The Pursuit of Signs: Semiotics, Literature, Deconstruction*, London: Routledge.

Damon, S. F. (1936) *Series of Old American Songs*, Providence: Brown University Library.

De Beauvoir, S. (1953) *The Second Sex*, trans. and ed. H. M. Parshley, Harmondsworth: Penguin.

Decroux, E. (1963) *Paroles sur le mime*, Paris: Gallimard.

De Lauretis, T. (1984) *Alice Doesn't: Feminism, Semiotics, Cinema*, London: Macmillan.

De Lauretis, T. (1991) 'Queer Theory: Lesbian and Gay Sexualities/An Introduction', *Differences* 3/2: iii–xvii.

Derrida, J. (1978) *Writing and Difference*, trans. Alan Bass, London: Routledge & Kegan Paul.

Diamond, E. (1996) 'Brechtian Theory/Feminist Theory: Towards a Gestic Feminist Criticism', in C. Martin (ed.), *A Sourcebook on Feminist Theatre and Performance: On and Beyond the Stage*, London: Routledge.

Dickens, C. (1972) *American Notes* [1842], New York: Penguin.

Dollimore, J. (1991) *Sexual Dissidence: Augustine to Wilde, Freud to Foucault*, Oxford: Clarendon Press.

Dorcy, J. (undated) *J'aime la mime*, Paris: Éditions Denoel.

Douglas, M. (1966) *Purity and Danger: An Analysis of Concepts of Pollution and Taboo*, Harmondsworth: Penguin.

Dumazedier, J. (1968) 'Leisure', in D. Sills (ed.), *Encyclopedia of the Social Sciences*, New York: Macmillan and Free Press.

Durkheim, É. (1995) *The Elementary Forms of Religious Life* (Book III) [1912], trans. Karen E. Fields, New York: The Free Press.

Dyer, R. (1986) *Heavenly Bodies: Film Stars and Society*, New York: St Martin's.

Eagleton, M. (ed.) (1986) *Feminist Literary Theory: A Reader*, Oxford: Basil Blackwell.

Eagleton, T. (1983) *Literary Theory: An Introduction*, Oxford: Basil Blackwell.

Eagleton, T. (1991) *Ideology: An Introduction*, London: Verso.

Elam, K. (1980) *The Semiotics of Theatre and Drama*, London: Methuen.

Elias, N. (1978) *The Civilizing Process: The History of Manners*, trans. Edmund Jephcott, Oxford: Basil Blackwell.

Eliot, T. S. (1932) *Selected Essays 1917–1932*, London: Faber & Faber.

Fanon, F. (1968) *Black Skin: White Masks*, trans. Charles Lam Markman, London: MacGibbon & Kee.

Fortier, M. (1997) *Theory/Theatre: An Introduction*, London and New York: Routledge.

Foster, H. (ed.) (1988) *Vision and Visuality*, Seattle: Bay Press.

Foster, S. L. (1986) *Reading Dancing*, Los Angeles: University of California Press.

Foster, S. L. (ed.) (1996) *Corporealities: Dancing Knowledge, Culture and Power*, London and New York: Routledge.

Foucault, M. (1972) *The Archaeology of Knowledge*, trans. A. M. Sheridan Smith, London and New York: Tavistock.

Foucault, M. (1977a) *Discipline and Punish: The Birth of the Prison*, Harmondsworth: Penguin.

Foucault, M. (1977b) 'What Is an Author?', in D. Bouchard and S. Simon (eds), *Language, Counter-memory, Practice: Selected Essays and Interviews*, Oxford: Blackwell.

Foucault, M. (1979) *The History of Sexuality*, vol. 1, trans. Robert Hurley, Harmondsworth: Penguin.

Foucault, M. (1987) *The History of Sexuality*, vol. 2, trans. Robert Hurley, Harmondsworth: Penguin.

Foucault, M. (1988) *The History of Sexuality*, vol. 3, trans. Robert Hurley, Harmondsworth: Penguin.

Fox, G. L. (1977) '"Nice Girl": The Behavioural Legacy of a Value Construct', *Signs* 4 (summer): 805–17.

Franco, M. (1995) *Dancing Modernism/Performing Bodies*, Bloomington: Indiana University Press.

Frank, G. (1944) 'Genesis and Staging of the *Jeu d'Adam*', *PMLA* 39: 7–17.

Friedan, B. (1963) *The Feminine Mystique*, New York: W.W. Norton.

Fuoss, K. (1997) *Striking Performances/Performing Strikes*, Jackson: University Press of Mississippi.

Gates, H. L. Jr (ed.) (1984) *Black Literature and Literary Theory*, London and New York: Methuen.

Gates, H. L. Jr (1986) *'Race', Writing and Difference*, Chicago and London: University of Chicago Press.

Geertz, C. (1973) 'Deep Play: Notes on the Balinese Cockfight', in *The Interpretation of Cultures: Selected Essays*, London: Fontana.

Geertz, C. (1983) 'Blurred Genres: The Refiguration of Thought', in *Local Knowledge: Further Essays in Interpretive Anthropology*, New York: Basic Books.

Giddens, A. (1984) *The Constitution of Society: Outline of the Theory of Structuration*, Berkeley: University of California Press.

Gilbert, H. (1994) 'De-scribing Orality: Performance and the Recuperation of Voice', in C. Tiffin and A. Lawson (eds), *De-scribing Empire: Post-colonialism and Textuality*, London and New York: Routledge.

Gilbert, H. and J. Tompkins (1996) *Post-colonial Drama: Theory, Practice, Politics*, London: Routledge.

Gilroy, P. (1987) *'There Ain't No Black in the Union Jack': The Cultural Politics of Race and Nation*, London: Hutchinson.

Gilroy, P. (1993) *The Black Atlantic: Modernity and Double Consciousness*, Cambridge, Mass.: Harvard University Press.

Goffman, E. (1969) *The Presentation of Self in Everyday Life*, Harmondsworth: Penguin.

Goffman, E. (1972) *Interaction Ritual: Essays on Face-to-face Behavior*, New York: Pantheon.

Goffman, E. (1974) *Frame Analysis: An Essay on the Organization of Experience*, Harmondsworth: Penguin.

Goldie, T. (1988) 'Signifier Resignified: Aborigines in Australian Literature', *Aboriginal Culture Today*, Special Issue of *Kunapipi* 10/1–2: 59–75.

Goodman, L., J. de Gay and F. Shaw (eds) (1999) *The Routledge Reader in Gender and Performance*, London and New York: Routledge.

Goodman, L. and J. de Gay (eds) (2000) *The Routledge Reader in Politics and Performance*, London and New York: Routledge.

Gramsci, A. (1971) *Selections from Prison Notebooks*, ed. and trans. Q. Hoare and G. Nowell Smith, London: Lawrence & Wishart.

Grazia, S. de (1962) *Of Time, Work, and Leisure*, New York: Twentieth Century Fund.

Greer, G. (1970) *The Female Eunuch*, New York: Bantam Books.

Groos, K. (1896) *The Play of Animals*, trans. Elizabeth L. Baldwin, New York: Appleton & Co.

Grosz, E. (1990) 'The Body of Signification', in John Fletcher and Andrew Benjamin (eds), *Abjection, Melancholia and Love: The Works of Julia Kristeva*, London and New York: Routledge.

Grosz, E. (1995) *Space, Time and Perversion: Essays on the Politics of Bodies*, London: Routledge.

Hall, E. (1959) *The Silent Language*, New York: Doubleday.

Hall, E. (1966) *The Hidden Dimension*, New York: Doubleday.

Hall, S. (1980) 'Race, Articulation and Societies Structured on Dominance', in *Sociological Theories, Race and Colonialism*, Paris: Unesco.

Hall, S. (1996a) 'Gramsci's Relevance for the Study of Race and Ethnicity', in D. Morley and K. H. Chen (eds), *Stuart Hall, Critical Dialogues in Cultural Studies*, London and New York: Routledge.

Hall, S. (1996b) 'New Ethnicities', in D. Morley and K. H. Chen (eds), *Stuart Hall, Critical Dialogues in Cultural Studies*, London and New York: Routledge.

Hallie, P. (1969) *The Paradox of Cruelty*, Middletown: Wesleyan University Press.

Hammond, D. and A. Jablow (1970) *The Africa That Never Was: Four Centuries of British Writing About Africa*, New York: Waveland Press.

Hardison, O. B. (1965) *Christian Rite and Christian Drama in the Middle Ages*, Baltimore: Johns Hopkins Press.

Hawkes, D. (1996) *Ideology*, London and New York: Routledge.

Heinz, C. (1963) *Recherches sur les rapports entre l'architecture et la liturgie à l'époque carolingienne*, Paris: Éditions du Seuil.

Held, D. (1980) *Introduction to Critical Theory: Horkheimer to Habermas*, Cambridge: Polity Press.

Hiller, S. (ed.) (1991) *The Myth of Primitivism: Perspectives on Art*, London and New York: Routledge.

Hollander, A. (1975) *Seeing Through Clothes*, New York: Avon Books.

hooks, b. (1996) 'Teaching Resistance: The Racial Politics of Mass Media', in *Killing Rage: Ending Racism*, Harmondsworth: Penguin.

Hosley, R. (1971) 'Three Kinds of Outdoor Theatre Before Shakespeare', in *Theatre Survey* 12: 1–33.

Hughes-Freeland, F. (ed.) (1997) *Ritual, Performance, Media*, London and New York: Routledge.

Hutcheon, L. (1985) *A Theory of Parody: The Teachings of Twentieth-century Art Forms*, New York: Methuen.

Hyde, L. (1983) *The Gift: Imagination and the Erotic Life of Property*, New York: Random House.

Ingarden, R. (1973) *The Literary Work of Art*, trans. George G. Grabowicz, Evanston: University of Illinois.

Irigaray, L. (1985a) *Speculum of the Other Woman*, trans. Gillian C. Gill, Ithaca: Cornell University Press.

Irigaray, L. (1985b) 'Women on the Market', in *This Sex Which Is Not One*, trans. Catherine Porter with Carolyn Burke, Ithaca: Cornell University Press.

Iser, W. (1980) 'Interaction between Text and Reader', in Susan Suleiman and Inge Crosman (eds), *The Reader in the Text: Essays on Audience and Inter-pretation*, Princeton: Princeton University Press.

Jagose, A. (1997) *Queer Theory: An Introduction*, New York: New York University Press.

James, C. L. R. (1963) *Beyond a Boundary*, London: Serpent's Tail.

Jameson, F. (ed.) (1977) *Aesthetics and Politics: Ernst Bloch, Georg Lukács, Bertolt Brecht, Walter Benjamin, Theodor Adorno*, trans. R. Taylor, London and New York: Verso.

Jameson, F. (1981) *The Political Unconscious: Narrative as Socially Symbolic Act*, London: Methuen.

Jameson, F. (1984) 'Postmodernism, or the Cultural Logic of Late Capitalism', *New Left Review* 146, (July/August).

Jameson, F. (1991) *Postmodernism, or, the Cultural Logic of Late Capitalism*, Durham: Duke University Press.

JanMohamed, A. (1985) 'The Economy of Manichean Allegory: The Function of Racial Difference in Colonialist Literature', *Critical Inquiry* 12: 59–87.

Kemble, F. A. (1969) *Journal of a Residence on a Georgian Plantation 1838–1839* [1863], Chicago: Afro-American Press.

Kershaw, B. (1992) *The Politics of Performance*, London and New York: Routledge.

Kertzer, D. (1988) *Ritual, Politics and Power*, New Haven and London: Yale University Press.

King, T. A. (1994) 'Performing "Akimbo": Queer Pride and Epistemological Prejudice', in M. Meyer (ed.), *The Politics and Poetics of Camp*, London and New York: Routledge.

Kristeva, J. (1982) *Powers of Horror: An Essay in Abjection*, trans. Leon S. Roudiez, New York: Columbia University Press.

Lacan, J. (1953) 'Some Reflections on the Ego', *International Journal of Psycho-analysis* 34: 13.

Lacan, J. (1977) *Écrits: A Selection*, trans. Alan Sheridan, London: Tavistock/Routledge & Kegan Paul.

LaCapra, D. (ed.) (1991) *The Bounds of Race: Perspectives on Hegemony and Resistance*, Ithaca, New York and London: Cornell University Press.

Laing, R. D. (1968) *The Politics of Experience*, Harmondsworth: Penguin.

Laing, R. D., H. Phillipson and A. R. Lee (1966) *Interpersonal Reception: A Theory and a Method of Research*, New York: Springer Publishing Company.

LeBarre, W. (1947) 'The Cultural Basis of Emotions and Gestures', *Journal of Personality* 16: 49–68.

Lefebvre, H. (1991) *The Production of Space*, Oxford: Blackwell.

Lévi-Strauss, C. (1963) 'The Structural Study of Myth', in *Structural Anthropology* (vol. 1), trans. Claire Jacobson and Brooke Grundfest Schoepf, Harmondsworth: Penguin.

Lévi-Strauss, C. (1969) *The Elementary Structures of Kinship*, trans. James Harle Bell, John Richard von Sturmer and Rodney Needham, Harmondsworth: Penguin.

Loomba, A. (1998) *Colonialism/Postcolonialism*, London and New York: Routledge.

Lott, E. (1995) *Love and Theft: Blackface Minstrelsy and the American Working Class*, New York and Oxford: Oxford University Press.

Lovell, T. (1983) *Pictures of Reality: Aesthetics, Politics and Pleasure*, London: British Film Institute.

Lurie, A. (1981) *The Language of Clothes*, London: Bloomsbury.

Lyotard, J.-F. (1984) *The Postmodern Condition: A Report on Knowledge*, trans. Geoff Bennington and Brian Massumi, Manchester: Manchester University Press.

Macaloon, J. (ed.) (1984) *Rite, Drama, Festival, Spectacle: Rehearsals Towards a Theory of Cultural Performance*, Philadelphia: Institute for the Study of Human Issues.

Macherey, P. (1978) *A Theory of Literary Production*, London: Routledge & Kegan Paul.

Malik, K. (1996) *The Meaning of Race: Race, History and Culture in Modern Times*, New York: New York University Press.

Manning, S. (1993) *Ecstasy and the Demon: Feminism and Nationalism in the Dances of Mary Wigman*, Berkeley, Los Angeles and London: University of California Press.

Marceau, M. (1958) 'Le halo poétique', in Jean Dorcy (ed.), *À la recherche de la mime*, Neuilly-sur-Seine: Les Cahiers de Danse et Culture.

Martin, B. (1981) *A Sociology of Contemporary Cultural Change*, Oxford: Basil Blackwell.

Martin, C. (ed.) (1996) *A Sourcebook on Feminist Theatre and Performance: On and Beyond the Stage*, London: Routledge.

Massey, D. and J. Allen (eds) (1984) *Geography Matters!*, Cambridge: Cambridge University Press.

Maurois, A. (1960) *Illusions*, New York: Columbia University Press.

Mauss, M. (1974) 'The Techniques of the Body' [1935], *Economy and Society* 2/1 (February): 70–88.

Mercer, K. (1994) *Welcome to the Jungle: New Positions in Black Cultural Studies*, London and New York: Routledge.

Merritt, R. (1978) *The Cake Man*, Sydney: Currency.

Metz, C. (1975) 'The Imaginary Signifier', *Screen* 16/2 (summer).

Meyer, M. (ed.) (1994) *The Politics and Poetics of Camp*, London and New York: Routledge.

Miles, R. (1989) *Racism*, London: Routledge.

Millett, K. (1969) *Sexual Politics*, New York: Avon Books.

Modleski, T. (1988) *The Women Who Knew Too Much: Hitchcock and Feminist Theory*, New York: Routledge.

Moi, T. (1985) *Sexual/Textual Politics: Feminist Literary Theory*, London and New York: Routledge.

Moore, S. and B. Myerhoff (eds) (1977) *Secular Ritual*, Amsterdam: Van Gorcum.

Muecke, S. (1983) 'Discourse, History, Fiction: Language and Aboriginal History', *Australian Journal of Cultural Studies* 1/1: 71–80.

Mulvey, L. (1975) 'Visual Pleasure and Narrative Cinema', *Screen*, 16/3 (autumn): 6–18.

Mulvey, L. (1989) *Visual and Other Pleasures*, Basingstoke: Macmillan. Includes revised version of 'Visual Pleasure and Narrative Cinema'.

Mumford, L. (1961) *The City in History: Its Origins, its Transformations, and its Prospects*, London: Secker & Warburg.

Nathan, H. (1977) *Dan Emmett and the Rise of Early Negro Minstrelsy* [1962], Norman: University of Oklahoma Press.

Newton, E. (1972) *Mother Camp: Female Impersonators in America*, Chicago: University of Chicago Press.

Nicholls, J. (1823) *The Progresses and Public Processions of Queen Elizabeth* (3 vols), London: John Nicholls & Son.

Nichols, T. L. (1874) *Forty Years of American Life* [1864], 2nd edn, London: Longmans Green.

Nowra, L. (1988) *Capricornia*, Sydney: Currency.

Okpewho, I. (1979) *The Epic in Africa: Towards a Poetics of the Oral Performance*, New York: Columbia University Press.

Ong, W. J. (1982) *Orality and Literacy: The Technologizing of the Word*, London: Methuen.

Orgel, S. (1971) 'The Poetics of Spectacle', *New Literary History* 2: 367.

Parker, A. and E. Kosofsky Sedgwick (eds) (1995) *Performativity and Performance*, New York: Routledge.

Pavis, P. (1982) 'The Discourse of (the) Mime', in *Languages of the Stage: Essays in the Semiology of Theatre*, trans. Susan Melrose and Barbara Behar, New York: Performing Arts Journal.

Pavis, P. (1985) 'Theatre Analysis: Some Questions and a Questionnaire', *New Theatre Quarterly* 1/2: 208–12.

Peirce, C. S. (1964) *Collected Papers of Charles Sanders Peirce*, eds Charles Hartshorne and Paul Weiss, Cambridge, Mass.: Belknap Press.

Penley, C. (ed.) (1988) *Feminism and Film Theory*, New York and London: Routledge/BFI Publishing.

Phelan, Peggy (1993) *Unmarked: The Politics of Performance*, New York: Routledge.

Piaget, J. (1973) *Structuralism*, trans. and ed. Chaninah Maschler, London: Routledge & Kegan Paul.

Pile, S. (1996) *The Body and the City: Psychoanalysis, Space and Subjectivity*, New York: Routledge.

Polhemus, T. (ed.) (1978) *Social Aspects of the Human Body*, Harmondsworth: Penguin.

Rapi, N. and M. Chowdhry (eds) (1998) *Acts of Passion: Sexuality, Gender and Performance*, New York: Harrington Park Press.

Reinelt, J. and J. Roach (eds) (1992) *Critical Theory and Performance*, Ann Arbor: University of Michigan Press.

Roach, J. (1996) *Cities of the Dead*, New York: Columbia University Press.

Rubin, G. (1975) 'The Traffic in Women: Notes on the "Political Economy" of Sex', in R. Reiter (ed.), *Toward an Anthropology of Women*, New York and London: Monthly Review Press.

Russo, M. (1994) *The Female Grotesque: Risk, Excess and Modernity*, London: Routledge.

Said, E. W. (1978) *Orientalism*, London and New York: Routledge & Kegan Paul.

Said, E. W. (1994) *Culture and Imperialism*, New York: Vintage Books.

Saussure, F. de (1974) *Course in General Linguistics*, trans. Wade Baskin, London: Fontana.

Schaffner, B. (ed.) (1955) *Group Processes*, New York: Josiah Macy, Jr Foundation Proceedings.

Schilder, P. (1978) *The Image and Appearance of the Human Body*, New York: International Universities Press.

Schneider, R. (1997) *The Explicit Body in Performance*, London: Routledge.

Senelick, L. (1992) *Gender in Performance: The Presentation of Difference in the Performing Arts*, Hanover: University Press of New England.

Showalter, E. (ed.) (1985) *The New Feminist Criticism: Essays on Women, Literature and Theory*, New York: Pantheon Books.

Silverman, K. (1983) *The Subject of Semiotics*, Oxford and New York: Oxford University Press.

Sinfield, A. (1994) *Cultural Politics – Queer Reading*, London and Philadelphia: Routledge and University of Pennsylvania Press.

Singer, M. (1959) *Traditional India: Structure and Change*, Philadelphia: American Folklore Society.

Singer, M. (ed.) (1972) *When a Great Tradition Modernizes*, New York: Praeger.

Slaughter, C. (1980) *Marxism, Ideology and Literature*, London: Macmillan.

Soja, E. (1989) *Postmodern Geographies: The Reassertion of Space in Critical Social Theory*, London: Verso.

Sontag, S. (1983) 'Notes on Camp', in *A Susan Sontag Reader*, New York: Vintage Books.

Southern, E. (1975) 'Black Musicians and Early Ethiopian Minstrelsy', *The Black Perspective in Music* 3/1: 77–83.

Southern, R. (1958) *The Medieval Theatre in the Round*, London: Faber.

Southern, R. (1973) *The Staging of Plays Before Shakespeare*, London: Faber.

Thorpe, W. H. (1966) 'Ritualization in Ontogeny: I. Animal Play', in *Philosophical Transactions of the Royal Society of London*, London: Royal Society.

Todd, J. (1988) *Feminist Literary Theory*, New York: Routledge.

Tuan, Y.-F. (1990) 'Space and Context', in R. Schechner and W. Appel (eds), *By Means of Performance: Intercultural Studies of Theatre and Ritual*, Cambridge: Cambridge University Press.

Turner, B. (1996) *The Body in Society: Explanations in Social Theory*, 2nd edn, London: Sage.

Turner, V. (1969) *The Ritual Process*, Chicago: Aldine.

Turner, V. (1974) *Dramas, Fields and Metaphors: Symbolic Action in Human Society*, Ithaca: Cornell University Press.

Turner, V. (1982) 'Liminal to Liminoid, in Play, Flow, and Ritual: An Essay in Comparative Symbology', in *From Ritual to Theatre: The Human Seriousness of Play*, New York: Performing Arts Journal.

Turner, V. (1987) *The Anthropology of Performance*, New York: Performing Arts Journal.

Tuve, R. (1966) *Allegorical Imagery*, ed. Thomas P. Roche, Princeton: Princeton University Press.

van Gennep, A. (1960) *The Rites of Passage* [1909], trans. Monika B. Vizedom and Gabrielle L. Caffee, London: Routledge & Kegan Paul.

Veblen, T. (1957) *The Theory of the Leisure Class* [1899], London: Allen & Unwin.

Walum, L. (1974) 'The Changing Door Ceremony', *Urban Life and Culture* 2/4 (January): 506–15.

Warner, M. (1985) *Monuments and Maidens: The Allegory of the Female Form*, New York: Atheneum.

Watney, S. (1991) 'Troubleshooters: Simon Watney on Outing', *Artforum* 30/3: 16–18.

Watson, O. (1970) *Proxemic Behaviour: A Cross-cultural Study*, The Hague: Mouton.

Watson, S. and K. Gibson (eds) (1995) *Postmodern Cities and Spaces*, Oxford: Blackwell.

Weeks, J. (1985) *Sexuality and its Discontents: Meaning, Myth and Modern Sexualities*, London: Routledge.

Weeks, J. (1989) *Sexuality*, London: Routledge.

Weeks, J. (1991) *Against Nature: Essays on History, Sexuality and Identity*, London: Rivers Oram.

Weimann, R. (1978) *Shakespeare and the Popular Tradition: Studies in the Social Dimension of Dramatic Form and Function*, ed. Robert Schwartz, Baltimore: Johns Hopkins University Press.

Whiting, H. and D. Masterson (eds) (1974) *Readings in the Aesthetics of Sport*, London: Lepus Books.

Whitmore, J. (1994) *Directing Postmodern Theatre: Shaping Signification in Performance*, Ann Arbor: University of Michigan Press.

Wiles, T. (1980) *The Theatre Event: Modern Theories of Performance*, Chicago: University of Chicago Press.

Williams, P. and L. Chrisman (eds) (1994) *Colonial Discourse and Post-colonial Theory: A Reader*, New York: Columbia University Press.

Williams, R. (1977) *Marxism and Literature*, Oxford: Oxford University Press.

Williams, R. (1981) *Culture*, London: Fontana.

Williamson, J. (1978) *Decoding Advertisements: Ideology and Meaning in Advertising*, London and New York: Marion Boyars.

Wilson, E. (1985) *Adorned in Dreams: Fashion and Modernity*, London: Virago.

Winter, M. H. (1948) 'Juba and American Minstrelsy', in *Chronicles of the American Dance*, ed. Paul Magriel, New York: Henry Holt.

Wittgenstein, L. (1980) *Culture and Value*, Chicago: University of Chicago Press.

Wood, R. (1989) *Hitchcock's Films Revisited*, London: Faber & Faber.

Woolf, V. (1957) *The Common Reader: First Series*, ed. Andrew McNellie, London: Hogarth Press.

Index